Henrietta Louisa (Farrer) Lear

S. Francis de Sales, bishop and prince of Geneva

Henrietta Louisa (Farrer) Lear

S. Francis de Sales, bishop and prince of Geneva

ISBN/EAN: 9783742829047

Manufactured in Europe, USA, Canada, Australia, Japa

Cover: Foto ©ninafisch / pixelio.de

Manufactured and distributed by brebook publishing software (www.brebook.com)

Henrietta Louisa (Farrer) Lear

S. Francis de Sales, bishop and prince of Geneva

S. FRANCIS DE SALES

RIVINGTONS

London .... *Waterloo Place*
Oxford .... *High Street*
Cambridge... .... *Trinity Street*

(All rights reserved.)

S. FRANCIS DE SALES

BISHOP AND PRINCE OF GENEVA

BY THE AUTHOR OF

"A Dominican Artist," "Life of Madame Louise de France,"

ETC., ETC.

"*Je veux peu de choses, ce que je veux, je veux fort peu.*"

RIVINGTONS

London, Oxford, and Cambridge

1871

PREFACE

IN writing this Life of S. Francis de Sales, the object aimed at has been less historical or ecclesiastical investigation, than a vivid and natural setting forth, so far as may be, of the holy Bishop's inner mind and life, as it can be traced in his own writings and in those of his most intimate and loving friends. For this reason, the trifling details of his life and conversation have been dwelt upon, rather than those more specially concerning his mission in Chablais, his controversial labours among Swiss and French Protestants, or his exertions on behalf of his people at the Courts of France and Savoy. These have been already written about at length, and are therefore but lightly touched here. Neither is his work as a guide of souls more than briefly sketched in this volume, and that because nothing can set it so clearly before us as his own letters; accordingly, it is proposed that this Life be speedily followed by a translation of the Spiritual Letters of S. Francis de Sales, as also of Bishop Belley's "Esprit de S. François de Sales" and the "Traité de l'Amour de Dieu." From the time the latter work and the "Vie Dévote" were published, they have been the delight of countless pious souls in all parts of the Church. Our own Archbishop

Leighton (who is thought by some greatly to resemble S. Francis de Sales) specially delighted in his writings, which he frequently made use of in his own commentary and sermons, quoting the Bishop of Geneva by name in the exposition of the Lord's Prayer (Vol. V. p. 294), and making frequent allusions to his writings elsewhere; while in familiar conversation he continually referred to some quaint saying or habit of the Saint. Who but must wander on in thought to the meeting in paradise of such and other blessed ones, who in their lives had but one aim; the service and glory of their Dear Lord and Master, and who now, safely gathered "in Patria," know, "even as they are known?" God grant to all who strive to follow in their steps the like gathering in, in His good time.

Various French Lives of S. Francis have been consulted in gathering this little volume together, but the "Esprit" is always quoted from the original. Reference to that is not generally made, for several editions having been used, the divisions are different, although the text is alike. The letters, &c., are chiefly quoted from Blaise's edition of the "Œuvres Complètes de S. François de Sales," in seventeen volumes. The letters in this edition were gathered together by Louis de Sales, a nephew of the Saint, and dedicated to his brother, Bishop Jean François de Sales, and to the Religious of the Visitation.

CONTENTS.

CHAPTER I.
Birth and Education. 1567 to 1592 .... **PAGE** 1

CHAPTER II.
Francis appointed Provost of Geneva—Ordination—First Sermon — Preaching — Celebration — Confessor and Grand Penitentiary 29

CHAPTER III.
Chablais Mission. 1594 54

CHAPTER IV.
Francis De Sales appointed Coadjutor of Geneva.— Journey to Rome. 1599. — Examination by Pope Clement VIII.—Death of Francis' Father. 1601.— Journey to Paris. 1602.—Death of Bishop De Granier. —Francis succeeds to the Diocese of Geneva. 1603.— Rule of the Episcopal Household 83

CHAPTER V.
Diocesan Work.—Intercourse with his Clergy.—Dealings with Souls.—Visit to Dijon................................ 129

CHAPTER VI.

Madame de Chantal. Death of Jeanne de Sales.—Vie Dévote. Death of the Bishop's Mother 152

CHAPTER VII.

Bishop of Belley.—Order of the Visitation.—Traité de L'Amour de Dieu.—Death of Bernard de Sales and his Wife.. 181

CHAPTER VIII.

Francis de Sales at Paris.—His Brother appointed his Coadjutor.—Visit to Avignon and Lyons.—His Death. 226

LIFE OF
S. FRANCIS DE SALES.

CHAPTER I.

BIRTH AND EDUCATION. 1567 TO 1592.

SINCE the early days of Christianity,—those fruitful times which gave an Ignatius, an Ambrose, a Chrysostom, an Augustine to the Church, there have been few men more eminently endowed with those characteristics which give the special stamp of saintliness, few men whose very name is more a household word in Christendom, suggesting all that is holiest, purest, and most loving, than the subject of this sketch, S. François de Sales. There is a beauty, a symmetry, an exquisite grace of holiness in all that concerns the venerable Bishop of Geneva, which fascinates the imagination and fills the heart, somewhat after the manner of a Holy Family of Perugino, or a Mass of Haydn. Beauty, harmony, refinement, simplicity, utter unselfconsciousness, love of God and man welling up and bursting forth as a clear fountain that never can be stayed or staunched. Such are the images and thoughts that fill the mind as we dwell upon his memory. There are some among God's servants whose mental and spiritual gifts make us unmindful of what may be lacking to them in external qualities, but S. Francis added to those higher graces the charm of singular personal attractions. A commanding stature, a peculiar though unstudied dignity of manner (we are told that he habitually moved somewhat slowly, as though to check the natural impetuosity of a vigorous, healthy frame), regular, though marked features, to which a singularly sweet smile, large blue eyes, and pencilled eyebrows gave great beauty, a complexion of almost feminine delicacy in spite of ceaseless exposure to all weathers, form a picture which seems to justify the description given by one who knew him, that "S. Francis was in appearance so gracious, at once so bright and so serious, that it was impossible to conceive a more imposing presence." His voice was deep and rich in tone, his utterance somewhat slow, and his choice of language, whether in ordinary conversation or more weighty occasions, remarkable for its gracefulness and simplicity; the same gift of happy expression which is found in his writings marking all he said, and combined with those mental qualities which we may not presume to catalogue, but would rather trace during the course of his life, producing one of the most attractive men who ever left their stamp upon the Church and the world.

Beauty, fertility, graciousness, are indeed inseparable from all that is associated with the memory of S. Francis. Who that has visited his native country of Savoy, but will linger with affectionate remembrance on those picturesque mountains, here blue and purple in their soft, clear distance, there raising in far off dignity their snowy summits against the sky ? Who does not delight to recall those blue lakes, with their richly wooded shores, the gracious abundance of vines and corn, the streams and mills, each more charming to the artist's eye than the rest ? Who can wander beside the Venetian-like canals of Annecy, or the lovely sites of Menthon, Talloires, and Doingt, or cross the winding roads by which S. Francis must so often have travelled to Chambéry, Grenoble, and Belley on the one side, to Thonon and Geneva on the other, and not indulge in many a speculation as to the impress made upon his mind by the scenery amid which he lived, and in which he so greatly delighted ; many a fancy as to the origin of those quaint similitudes between the spiritual and natural world which so often are found in his pages ?

It was in the midst of such scenery that Francis de Sales was born, and his first impressions were those of beauty and grandeur. The Chateau de Sales (now a ruin, all save the room where the saint was born, which was converted by his brother Louis into a chapel), was but a few miles from Annecy, and situated amid scenery of the same character as that which surrounds the little town. The family possessing it displayed an imposing pedigree, and Francis Seigneur de Nouvelles, father of the future Bishop of Geneva, was worthy of his ancestral honours, and had done service to his country both as a soldier and diplomatist. He married the only child and heiress of Melchior de Sionnaz, Seigneur de Vallières, de la Thuile, and de Boisy, one of the noblest families of Savoy, and in consequence took the latter name, by which he was generally known. Both husband and wife were religious people, and seem to have lived a useful, happy life amid the duties of their position, with but one drawback,—that for the first six years of their married life they were childless. When at last the blessing of offspring seemed likely to be granted her, Madame de Boisy accepted the welcome hope in the spirit of a Hannah or an Elizabeth; and continually was to be found before God's altar, offering up her unborn child to His service, anticipating the graceful cry of a countrywoman of her own,

"Je ne veux point d'enfants, si ce ne sont des saints!"[1]

---

[1] Marie Jena.

At that time Chambéry possessed a precious relic in the "Saint Suaire," or holy winding-sheet of Our Lord, said to have been handed on by Nicodemus to Gamaliel, thence to S. James, and so from one to another until Guy de Lusignan carried it to the Isle of Cyprus, whence it was brought by the Princess Margaret, widow of the last of the Lusignan race, to Chambéry. This relic was later moved to Turin; but the Sainte Chapelle, never finished since a conflagration destroyed great part, remains at Chambéry in a striking position, commanding the town. On the occasion of the Duc de Nemours' marriage with Anne d' Este, widow of the Duc de Guise, the Saint Suaire was taken to Annecy at the Duchess's request. Madame de Boisy visited the church where it rested with the deepest devotion, pouring out her soul before God with an intensity of desire that the child to whom she was about to give birth might be His for ever, imploring her loving Lord to accept him and endow him with heavenly grace, above all with a deep love for the Passion and Death of Christ; while on her part she pledged herself solemnly to look upon her child as lent to her by the Lord, to Whom he should wholly belong. Before leaving the church, Madame de Boisy felt such a loving, restful joy overflowing her soul, that she was convinced her prayers were heard, and when shortly afterwards all around were alarmed at her being taken prematurely ill, and despaired at least of her child's life, she alone remained calm and confident in her belief that all would be well. Her hope was fulfilled, and between nine and ten o'clock on the 21st August, 1567, a seven months' child was born in a room known in the family as S. Francis's room, from a painting on the wall of the great Saint of Assisi. Next day the little heir was baptized in his parish church of Thorens, receiving the names of François Bonaventure.

It does not, unfortunately, always follow that the devout aspirations of a mother's heart find their visible fulfilment, but Madame de Boisy had no cause to complain. Her little son was doubtless given every possible training in pious ways, but his natural disposition co-operated with it, and his first indications of character were stamped with loving generosity. His nurse used to take out fruit or something of the kind for him to give to the little children they met in their walks, and before he could speak he had learnt to clasp his hands in the attitude of prayer, when taken by her into church. Nursery tradition loved to tell how the first connected words Francis uttered were, "God and mama love me." Madame de Boisy had anxiously sought that of all names, the Holy Name of Jesus should first be familiar to his lips, and as soon as he was capable of learning, Francis was instructed in the Catechism and the first principles of the Faith by the Abbé Déage, an intimate friend of his parents, who remained faithfully attached to him through a long life. After one of these lessons his pleasure was to go into the village with a little bell, the sound of which drew the children of his father's tenants around him, and then Francis used to repeat to them the instruction he had received, with much emphasis and gesticulation. Pure-minded, sweet-tempered, and obedient, his natural tendencies to all that was rather supernatural than ordinary diligently cultivated by those around,—one is quite thankful yet to find him a real child, and that he could sometimes be naughty ! Thus, being strictly forbidden to approach the kitchen, Francis was once irresistibly drawn there by the sight and smell of some incomparable patties which were being taken out of the oven. The temptation was too strong, and he asked for one. The cook, possibly intending to give Francis a practical lesson, put a burning hot patty into his hand, and it was a struggle between pain and greediness, in which, however, the latter was triumphant, and the patty was speedily devoured ! A more serious misdemeanour is on record, when some workman, employed in the Chateau de Sales, having left his coat on the ground, the boy espied a silk aiguillette of brilliant colours fastened to the button-hole, and appropriated it. Francis, however, paid the due penalty of this misdeed, for when the owner missed his property and vainly sought it among the servants, M. de Boisy questioned his son as well as other people concerning the theft. Thereupon Francis confessed that he was the thief before the assembled household, and his father, resolved that this first fault should leave a lasting impression on the child's mind, administered a whipping then and there, which was never forgotten by the future saint, who counted it among the blessings of his early training.

Nevertheless, M. de Boisy looked upon his son as "more a child of grace than of nature," and he and his wife often discussed Francis's probable future, with the firm belief that God had great things in store for him. One incident is recorded which recalls S. Athanasius' childhood : Francis was found conducting a group of playfellows in procession to the parish church, where, kneeling together round the font, he taught them to kiss its base, and sing the Gloria Patri. A mind so tending to the supernatural might easily incur the danger of being over-sensitive and timid. Many years after S. Francis wrote of himself, " In my childhood I was afraid of the spirit world, and in order to cure myself of this weakness I used to arm my heart with confidence in God, and then force myself to go alone to the places which frightened me ; so that in time I grew so strong as to take delight in the silence and darkness of night, which is full of God's Presence, and amid which His angels surround us as a guardian host. Hidden beneath His wings, as a hen gathers her chickens, what can we fear?"[1]

When six years old, Francis was still innocent of book-learning, but his desire to read was urgent, so that he bribed his nurse to persuade his parents to let him learn, by the promise that "when he was big, he would give her a beautiful red gown every year." M. de Boisy considered the wish laudable, and resolved, somewhat to his wife's dismay—for a host of physical and moral dangers presented themselves to her imagination—to send Francis to a school recently established at La Roche, a little town not far from the Chateau de Sales. In spite of Madame de Boisy's alarms, Francis was sent thither, his father's good sense foreseeing that the boy's strength of character might suffer from the excessive tenderness of his devoted mother. A good tutor, M. Pierre Batailleur, accompanied Francis, and every week M. de Boisy himself visited la Roche, in order to be satisfied that his child was doing well. After a time his family arrangements causing him to leave the Chateau de Sales for that of Brens in Chablais, M. de Boisy moved Francis to the principal school of Annecy, where some of his cousins were already. These school days seem

[1] *Letter to a Religious*, Sept. 9, 1619.

to have been noticeable only for quiet good conduct and great industry; the laborious, painstaking habit of mind which later on enabled Francis to accomplish more than most other men would deem practicable, was evidently formed in childhood. He was diligently watchful over the use of time, but more careful to do each thing well than to perform large quantities of work. Thus he might be seen spending an hour over two or three Latin phrases, patiently seeking to achieve the best possible translation, before he would pass further on.[1]

When ten years of age Francis was admitted to his First Communion, in the Dominican church at Annecy, and on the same day he was confirmed by the venerable Angelo Giustiniani, then Bishop of Geneva. Already his vocation was clearly developed in his own

---

[1] This habit of mind continued through life. "Make haste slowly," and "Soon enough, if well enough," were favourite sayings of his ("Hâtez vous lentement," "Assez tôt, si assez bien"), and so "Little, but well" ("Peu et bon"). S. Francis's devoted friend, the Bishop of Belley, says: "Whatever he did, and whatever business he undertook, always received his whole attention, as though he had nothing else to think of, or that it were the last act he had to perform in this world. Hurry he was wont to call the greatest enemy of true devotion, and he always urged people to do a little well, rather than a great deal imperfectly. So in devotion he was wont to say it is not by the number of our religious exercises that we advance towards perfection, but rather by the fervour and purity of intention with which each is done."—*Esprit de S. F. de Sales*, iii. 27.

mind, and he entreated his father's permission to receive the tonsure, the first act of consecration to the Priesthood. M. de Boisy had altogether different views for his son's future, and at first refused his consent, but seeing how great the disappointment was, and believing that such pious tendencies would vanish as the boy grew older and knew more of the world, he gave way, and on September 20, 1578, Francis received the tonsure at Clermont. Here again one hails with relief a natural trait which redeems the future saint from the imputation of unreality, or insensibility to the ordinary feelings and weaknesses of mortal boys. Francis was possessed of very beautiful chestnut hair, which, according to the fashion of the day, he wore in long curls about his neck, and a great pang of anguish came over him at the necessity for sacrificing these, as was inevitable before receiving tonsure, but that was speedily overcome, and the golden locks were duly shorn.

These peaceful, happy school days at Annecy, during which Francis delighted to wander about the hills surrounding the lovely little lake with his chosen companions, returning to his dearly-loved home, where three young brothers,[1] Gallois, Louis, and Jean François, looked up to him as a model of all that was

[1] M. and Madame de Boisy's family continued to increase; they had thirteen children in all, six of whom died early.

perfect, only lasted till the year 1580. By that time M. de Boisy, who was bent on a splendid public career for his eldest son, determined on sending him to the College de Navarre in Paris, where all that were foremost amid the nobility of Savoy were wont to finish their education. Fond as he was of study, Francis was most ready to enter upon this larger sphere; but in spite of the fame of the College de Navarre, he shrank from its manifold temptations, and the avowedly worldly tone of its system, and earnestly desired to be allowed to continue his education at the College de Clermont, which was governed by the Jesuit Fathers, and which had an equally good name for science, with a better reputation for religious and moral training. All these misgivings and desires were poured out to his mother, who readily entered into them. The memory of her first fervid dedication of that son of many prayers had not faded from her heart, and her eloquence prevailing with his father, Francis's education was transferred to the College de Clermont. He was accompanied to Paris by the Abbé Déage, the same good priest who had been his first religious teacher, and who remained his tutor till long past the time when modern ideas would suppose such guidance necessary. The Abbé seems to have been a learned and holy man, of strong sense and good judgment, but withal somewhat harsh and imperious in his dealings with his pupil, who continued for many years to submit most absolutely to him, never going out without his leave, and accepting rebukes and even blows with unfailing meekness. All expenditure of money remained in the Abbé's hands to the end of his tutorship, and as late on as when Francis was twenty-one, we are told of his losing his hat during a sea-voyage from Cattolica to Venice, on which occasion the Abbé Déage, not content with a severe reprimand for his carelessness, declared that his pupil should go without till they reached Venice, and obliged him to land at Chiosa with no better head-gear than his night-cap, greatly to the astonishment of the bystanders—an indignity patiently borne by the culprit.

If, however, the Abbé was a somewhat excessive disciplinarian, he appears to have guided his charge's education with wisdom. Francis's devout tendencies and his passion for study were not allowed to put an entire stop to the more worldly accomplishments considered essential to a gentleman's education, and riding, fencing, and dancing all had their share. His natural physical advantages were confirmed by such training, and probably these secular lessons contributed not a little to the grace and dignified ease for which the Bishop of Geneva was remarkable in after life. At this time the temptation to affect the external aspect of piety seems to have come across the youth : " I longed greatly," he said of himself, " to be very saintly, to attain perfection, and accordingly to that end I must needs walk about with my head on one side, saying the Hours, in imitation of a really holy fellow-student who did so. I did this for some time without finding that I became any the holier," and from thenceforward, throwing aside all affectation, his devotion, like all else, took the stamp of perfect simplicity. " I delight in the beauty of simplicity," he said, " and would willingly give a hundred serpents for one dove." [1]

Even at this time Francis habitually carried some spiritual book about with him, frequently reading a few lines, and pondering them as he went through the day's routine. It was some years later that Scupoli, the author of the " Spiritual Combat," visiting Padua, where Francis was studying, gave him a copy of that inestimable book, from which time it was his favourite companion and constant guide. In 1607, the Bishop wrote, " The 'Spiritual Combat' is my dear book [2] which I carry in my pocket, and read continually with ever renewed profit." We are not told who was Francis's director at this time, but subject to guidance, he practised some degree of austerity, and received the sacraments weekly. Being asked why he communi-

[1] *Esprit*, viii. 18.   [2] " Mon cher livre."

cated so often, he replied, "For the same reason that I often talk to my tutor and superior. Our Dear Lord is my Teacher in holiness, and I go continually to Him that I may learn His way; learning without holiness will avail me little." Each Communion, in truth, seemed to strengthen and expand his religious life; and feeling what it was to himself, he already forestalled his apostolic career by trying to lead others to the same Source of Life. Thus a young Savoyard friend having come to see him, Francis invited him to breakfast the next morning, and on the guest's arrival proposed that they should first go together to the neighbouring church for confession and communion; after which the young de Sales said to his friend, "This was the banquet to which I invited you yesterday, now let us go and get some food for our bodies."

Saint Etienne de Grès was his favourite church in Paris, and many an hour was spent there in peaceful, happy devotion by the young student, who never lost sight for a day of what he felt to be his true vocation.

Meanwhile, Francis distinguished himself in his classes, and was more than once appointed prefect; but rhetoric and philosophy, taught as they were by most distinguished professors—Suarez and Dandini—did not satisfy him, and his desire to study theology, with a view to the priesthood, grew daily stronger.

One day—it was Quinquagesima Sunday—the Abbé Déage was struck with his pupil's grave, almost troubled countenance, and attributing it to over-work, kindly proposed that they should go out together and see the humours of the Parisian carnival. But Francis begged to be excused, adding, "Averte oculos meos, ne videant vanitatem." ("Turn away mine eyes, lest they behold vanity.") "What can I do to cheer you?" the Abbé asked; and the boy, raising his earnest face to his tutor's, answered, by quoting from the Gospel for the day the words, "Domine, ut videam!" ("Lord, that I may receive my sight!") "But what is it that you would see?" inquired the Abbé, much moved; and then Francis poured forth his longings after those theological studies, which would, as he believed, enable him to penetrate the deep things of God, and help him to approach the only earthly aim he knew, the priesthood. M. Déage did not reject the petition, and without forsaking his other studies, Francis was now allowed to devote three hours daily to theology, entering with great interest into a course at the Sorbonne which the Abbé was attending himself, and which he regularly transmitted to his pupil. Francis also studied Hebrew and Exegesis under the famous Benedictine, Génébrard, afterwards Archbishop of Aix. His deep studies did not, however, make him a dull or unsympathetic companion among his fellow-students. The Père Binet, who had been among these, used to say that young de Sales was as an angel of light among them; and another says that he never knew whether most to admire the perfect charm of his exterior, or the promise of future greatness his mental qualities gave.

It may have been like S. Paul's thorn in the flesh, sent lest he should be exalted above measure by so many gifts and graces; but so it was, that when seventeen, a season of temptation came over the young man, and he began to fear that he was not in a state of grace, that God's favour had departed from him, and that he should inevitably yield to the first mortal sin which tempted him. Vainly he strove to banish the bewildering thoughts with King David's cry, "Why art thou so heavy, O my soul, and why art thou so disquieted within me? Put thy trust in God. Leave me not, neither forsake me, O my God." Assuredly he was not forsaken of his Dear Lord and Master, but the grateful, soothing sense of His Presence was no longer consciously felt, and his health began visibly to suffer under the strain of mental anguish. Then he resolved, boy as he was, deeply to study what great theologians had written on the vexed question of predestination. But he could not see his way to an entire acceptance of what he read in S. Augustine and S. Thomas Aquinas, and after much study he

c

wrote the following protest, which seems to have given him comfort and strength :—

"Prostrate at the feet of the blessed Augustine and S. Thomas, and willing to abide in ignorance of whatsoever God hides from me, save Christ crucified; believing what I have written to be true, inasmuch as I see no sound cause for doubt; nevertheless, as I cannot perceive everything, and this mighty mystery dazzles my weak sight, should I hereafter believe otherwise, and should I be condemned to hell (which, O Lord Jesus! be far from me), by that holy Will which S. Thomas believes to set forth the justice of God towards sinners, I would with willing submission bow before the Most High, saying with the prophet, 'My soul truly waiteth still upon God.' 'Even so, Father, for so it seemed good in Thy sight.' In the bitterness of my soul I would cry out thus, until He changed His sentence, and answered, 'Be trustful, my son, I have no pleasure in the death of a sinner,—the dead praise not the Lord, neither they that go down into silence,—I made thee for Myself,— the Will of God is thy sanctification,—I abhor nothing which I have made.' Why art thou so heavy, O my soul, and why art thou so disquieted within me? O put thy trust in God, which is the help of thy countenance and thy God. Go not down into hell, but rather go up to the mountain of the Lord, to the house of the God of Jacob. He is not dead but sleepeth; this sickness is not unto death, but for the glory of God. 'Be of good cheer, my lowly child, unworthy indeed, but faithful, in that thy hope is in Me, thy trust in My Mercy. Forasmuch as thou hast been faithful in that which is least, ready to accept damnation were it for My Glory, I will make thee ruler over many things. Forasmuch as thou wouldst glorify My Name, even by the sacrifice of thyself—though in truth that were but a sorry praise to Me, Who Willeth not the loss, but the salvation of men—therefore I will make thee ruler over many things, and thou shalt eternally sing My praises, and enter into the joy of thy Lord.' And to this what else shall I answer save once more, 'Even so, Father, for so it seemeth good in Thy sight; my heart is ready, whether to suffer or to rejoice for Thy Name. Jesus, I am as it were a beast before Thee, nevertheless I am alway by Thee, for Thou hast holden me by my right hand. Be it unto me according to Thy Word.' I will not the death of a sinner, but that he turn from his way and live. In Thy name lift I up my hands. Amen, Jesu, Mary."[1]

---

[1] Ad pedes B. Augustini et Thomæ provolutus, paratus omnia ignorare ut illum sciam qui est scientia Patris, Christum crucifixum, quamquam quæ scripsi non dubito vera, quia nihil video quod de eorum veritate solida possit facere dubitationem, cum tamen non omnia video et tam reconditum mysterium et clarius quam ut fixe ab oculis meis nycticoracis inspici possit, si

Soon afterwards the hour of deliverance came, and while kneeling in Saint Etienne des Grès, the mental chains which oppressed him seemed to fall off, and his soul recovered peace and vigour. S. Francis himself believed that this trial had been sent for his real and truest good, and in after life he was able to thank God for having so proved him. From this time fresh light and grace flowed in upon his soul, and that clear pure love of God, in which perhaps no earthly being ever surpassed him, that infinitely tender love and sympathy for man, which was equally his characteristic,

---

postea contrarium appareret (quod numquam futurum existimo) imo si me damnatum, (quod absit, Domine Jesu) scirem voluntate quam in Deo ponit Thomas ut ostenderet justitiam suam, libenter obstupescens et suscipiens altissimum judicem, post prophetam dicerem : Nonne Deo subjecta erit anima mea? Amen, ita Pater, quia sic placitum est ante Te. Fiat voluntas Tua, et hoc in amaritudine animæ meæ toties dicerem, donec Deus mutans vitam meam et sententiam suam responderet mihi : Confide, fili, nolo mortem peccatoris, sed magis ut vivat ; non mortui laudabunt me, neque omnes qui descendunt in infernum. Te, fili, ut cætera omnia, propter memetipsum feci. Non est voluntas mea nisi sanctificatio tua, nihil odit anima mea eorum quæ feci. Quare tristis est anima tua, et quare conturbat te? Spera in Deo, quia adhuc ei confiteberis ; salutare vultus tui et Deus tuus est. Non descendes in infernum, sed ascendes ad montem Dei, ad tabernaculum Dei Jacob. Non est mortuus, sed dormis : infirmitas hæc non est ad mortem, sed ut conversus glorifices Deum. Euge, serve parve, indigne quidem, sed fidelis, quia sperasti in me, confidens de misericordia mea ; et quia in pauca, scilicet in glorificando me per damnationem, si ita mihi placeret, fuisti fidelis, super multa te constituam ; et quia voluisti mani-

became as a part of his very self. In this severe mental struggle, so early endured, the future Apostle of Christ learnt how to deal tenderly and firmly with the trials and temptations of others, and to say with his whole heart, "Blessed be God, even the Father of our Lord Jesus Christ, the Father of all mercies, and the God of all comfort, Who comforteth us in all our tribulation, that we may be able to comfort them which are in any trouble, by the comfort wherewith we ourselves are comforted of God."[1]

Six years were thus spent at Paris, and at the end of these, the Abbé Déage proposed to M. de Boisy to recall his son, and if he judged well to send him to study jurisprudence at the then famous university of Padua. In truth, the good Abbé saw his pupil's con-

---

festare nomen meum etiam patiendo, si opus esset, quandoquidem in eo parva est magnificatio et glorificatio nominis mei qui non sum damnator, sed Jesus, super multa te constituam, ut beatitudine perpetua laudes me, in qua multa est gloria nominis mei, per memetipsum juravi quia fecisti hanc rem, id est, preparasti cor tuum in obsequium justitiæ meæ et non pepercisti tibi, benedictione perpetua benedicam te, ut intres in gaudium Domini tui. Nec tunc aliter respondere deberem quam prius. Amen, ita Pater, quia sic placitum est ante Te; paratum cor meum ad pænam propter Te, paratum cor meum ad gloriam propter nomen Tuum. Jesu, quasi jumentum factus sum coram Te, et ipse, Domine, sis semper mecum. Fiat mihi secundum verbum tuum. Nolo mortem peccatoris, sed magis ut convertatur et vivat. In nomine ergo levabo manus meas in Sancto. Amen, Jesu, Maria.

[1] 2 Cor. i. 3.

stantly growing religious tendencies, his rapidly developing attraction for prayer and asceticism, with some alarm, fearing lest, if Francis should embrace the monastic life, overthrowing all his father's dreams for a brilliant future, the tutor in whose charge he had been so absolutely trusted would meet with no small share of blame. In the year 1587, accordingly, Francis returned home, greatly to the delight of his parents, who were more than satisfied with his advancement in all respects, and scarce knew whether to be proudest of his personal or mental attractions. They took pleasure in making him known among all their friends, and social claims pressed heavily upon him; but Francis found his chief pleasure at home, where all his childish devotion to his brother Louis was renewed, and the two were never weary of one another's society. Jean François was of a less amiable disposition; and as the elder brother said once, "We three should make a capital salad dressing —Jean François the vinegar, Louis the salt, and poor François, who cares for nothing but gentleness, would do well enough as oil."

Madame de Boisy would fain have had this happy household left undisturbed, but her husband was not equally unambitious, and after a brief holiday he sent his eldest son to Padua, there to study law under Guido Pancirolo, whose fame was world-wide. The Abbé

Déage accompanied him as before, and was satisfied at the ardour with which François devoted himself to study. But the vexed question of his vocation was by no means at rest; François came across an eminent Jesuit Father, Possevin, to whom he felt drawn, and under whose direction he placed himself, setting fully before him both his father's wishes as to his future, and his own ever-increasing attraction to the priesthood. Father Possevin gave mature consideration and much prayer to the subject, and the result was an unhesitating decision that Francis's vocation was a true one, and must be followed. He undertook the young man's theological training himself, and devoted three hours daily to it. Under this wise guidance the future Bishop studied Holy Scripture above all else as the foundation of theology, and, together with that, S. Thomas Aquinas, whose "Summa" was always open at his right hand; S. Bonaventura, and Cardinal Bellarmino, and the Fathers, among whom he was especially well read in the works of S. Chrysostom, S. Augustine, S. Jerome, and S. Bernard, while perhaps his favourite author was S. Cyprian, for whose style he always had a special admiration. As has been already said, Francis met the venerable Scupoli at Padua, and having received the gift of his "Spiritual Combat," that book had henceforth a large share in his affections, and helped in no small degree to form his religious life.

Francis traced out for himself at this time a rule of life which is remarkable for a young man not yet twenty. Beginning with what he calls his "preparation," he looks forward to the day's cares and duties, the dangers and temptations it may present, and the way to meet them with firm resolution, commending his heart and mind, his will, memory, and whole being to God. "My first waking thought," he says, "shall be a thanksgiving, and I will call to mind the shepherds at Bethlehem, and the holy women at the sepulchre, like them dedicating the dawn of day to my risen Lord, the Light of the world. I will daily hear mass with all the earnestness of my soul, crying out, 'O come hither and behold the works of the Lord,' 'Let us now go even to Bethlehem, and see this thing which is come to pass, which the Lord hath made known unto us.' My meditation must be carefully made, and if it is hindered during the day, I must shorten sleep rather than neglect it. If I wake during the night, I will kindle my heart with the words, 'At midnight there was a cry made, Behold the Bridegroom cometh, go ye out to meet Him!' and remembering that He was born amid the darkness of night, I will ask of Him to be born anew in my heart; the shadows of night shall speak to me of the darkness of indifference and sin, and I will pray the Lord to 'lighten our darkness' with His own life-giving light. I will call to mind the Psalmist's words, 'Lift up your hands, and praise the Lord,' and 'I water my couch with my tears.' If any nocturnal terrors beset me, I will remember that my Guardian Angel is at hand, and say, 'He that keepeth Israel shall neither slumber nor sleep. He shall defend thee under His wings, and thou shalt be safe under His feathers, thou shalt not be afraid for any terror by night. The Lord is my light and my salvation, of whom then shall I be afraid?'"

Francis goes on to lay down rules for his meditation; recalling God's loving mercies and goodness toward him, the exceeding hatefulness of sin and worthlessness of this world's treasures, the blessings of holiness, the certainty of death and judgment, dwelling especially on the example of our Dear Lord Jesus Christ, and the Attributes of God, Who has deigned to bid His children aim to be perfect "as I am perfect."

His conduct in the world comes next under consideration. "I must neither despise or seem to shun any one in a proud critical spirit," he says, "but at the same time I must avoid too great freedom even with my best friends. I must neither do or say anything wanting in decorum, and specially avoid whatever may wound or annoy others, giving due honour to all. I will strive to be modest in speech—saying little, so as rather to be thought too silent than too talkative, without affecting austerity or melancholy.

"I will be friendly to all, but intimate with few, for it is hard to turn general intercourse to good account, and not to suffer from contact with impure minds. I will seek to attain unaffected gentleness, simple modesty, ease devoid of all tinge of pride, kindness which absolutely refrains from contradiction, save where it is a duty, honest cordiality and frankness according to the persons I am with.

"I will strive to adapt my intercourse to the position and character of those I meet, giving honour where honour is due."

University life was not free from trial and temptation in Padua or anywhere else, and this Francis de Sales found. His devout life naturally irritated men of licentious habits, and after trying to make him fall into their own evil ways by various temptations, certain of his fellow collegians chose to assume that his gentleness and humility implied cowardice, and accordingly one evening laid in wait and attacked him, first with insult and then with blows. But they found themselves mightily mistaken, for being thus assailed, and looking upon self-defence as lawful, Francis drew his sword, and pursued his assailants until he forced them to give in, and ask his pardon.

Amid all his religious life, however, Francis did not

neglect the secular studies with a view to which he had been sent to Padua, as twelve quarto volumes of notes, long preserved in the de Sales family, testified; and when in the year 1591 he took his Doctor's degree, Pancirolo took occasion to do special honour to the young Savoyard, upon whom he looked as his most distinguished disciple. Forty-eight Doctors were assembled under Guido Pancirolo as President, for de Sales' examination, which was brilliantly successful, and the ceremony of conferring the degree and patent of a doctor in civil and canonical law, was completed with an unusual character of state and éclat. It was at some period before this event that a serious illness threatened to cut short so promising a career—rheumatic fever, induced perhaps by too great carelessness of personal comfort, laid Francis low in exceeding suffering, and at last the poor Abbé Déage, hearing from several physicians whom he had summoned that there was little hope of their patient's recovery, found himself constrained to tell the pupil, whom, in spite of his somewhat pedantic severity, he loved as his child, that his days were numbered. "My son," he said, striving to control his emotion, "if God saw fit to call you to Himself, you would accept His holy Will meekly, would you not?"

Francis instantly caught the Abbé's meaning, and replied, "Most surely; God's Will be done, whether for life or death. It is very sweet to live for Christ, and very sweet too to die for Him." And he quoted the words,

"Sive mori me, Christe, jubes, seu vivere mavis,
Dulce mihi tecum vivere; dulce mori."

After awhile he went on pouring out his soul in the words of holy writ. "O how amiable are Thy dwellings, Thou Lord of hosts—my soul hath a desire and longing to enter into the courts of the Lord. All my days will I wait, until my appointed time come. The Lord is my light and my salvation, of whom then shall I be afraid? Blessed is he whose hope is the Lord his God." Seeing him so calm and restful, the Abbé Déage ventured to ask as to Francis's wishes in the event of his death, which were immediately given, and then the patient received the last Sacraments, and each hour was looked upon as his last. But God willed otherwise—the malady subsided, and Francis recovered perfect health, and with it a firmer conviction than ever in his vocation to the priesthood.

The time for leaving Padua had come, and after visiting Rome, Loretto, Ancona, Venice, and Milan, Francis de Sales crossed the Mont Cenis, and in the spring of 1592 rejoined his family at the Chateau de Thuilles, where his father's residence at that time was, having been for twelve years a student in the great school of the world, and having, according to common parlance, "finished his education."

CHAPTER II.

FRANCIS APPOINTED PROVOST OF GENEVA — ORDINATION: FIRST SERMON—PREACHING—CELEBRATIONS—CONFESSOR AND GRAND PENITENTIARY.

IT is not difficult to imagine the paternal satisfaction with which M. and Madame de Boisy looked upon their eldest son. Every hope which the fondest parent could conceive seemed fulfilled in this bright, handsome, thoroughly accomplished, and singularly attractive young man of twenty-five, whose religious and moral qualities, no less than his other advantages, gave due reason to expect that his future career would be one of usefulness and goodness, as well as of distinction. As eldest son and heir, Francis assumed the title of Seigneur de Villeroget; and shortly after his return home, at M. de Boisy's desire, he went to Chambéry, in order to go through a certain examination, by which he was admitted as advocate of the Senate of Savoy.

Shortly after, he paid a visit to the venerable Bishop of Geneva, Claude de Granier, who was so favourably impressed by Francis's piety and learning that he is reported to have said that he foresaw this youth would one day be his successor. It was about this time that a circumstance occurred which made a vivid impression on Francis's mind in confirmation of his destined vocation. He was riding through the forest of Sonaz when his horse shied, and his sword dropping from its belt fell to the ground, where it lay, forming with the scabbard a perfect cross. Francis barely noticed the fact further than to fasten both belt and sword more securely; but when the same thing occurred a second and a third time, he began to see a serious meaning in it, and told the Abbé Déage, who accompanied him, that he could not but accept it as a sign that God called him to be a soldier of the Cross, and that he would await nothing save his father's consent to devote himself to the priesthood. The worthy Abbé discussed the subject fully with his late pupil, but he still shrank from encountering M. de Boisy's certain displeasure, and declined mentioning it to him. Francis had no reserve with his mother; doubtless she must often have talked to him of those early days of devout expectation, when she had so steadfastly dedicated him to the Lord; and if her maternal pride sometimes led her to share her husband's dreams of earthly greatness for their child, she soon turned back to dwell with more real joy on the hope of seeing him an eminent servant of Christ than aught else.

His cousin, the Canon Louis de Sales, was also a confidant, and he undertook, when a fitting occasion should arise, to open the question with M. de Boisy, who, meanwhile, full of plans and great designs, took his son to visit the Seigneur de Végy, whose only daughter and heiress he wished to become Francis's wife. Courteous and graceful de Villeroget was as ever, but when his father complained that he was cold and restrained with the lady, he could not refrain from declaring that "the Lord Himself is the portion of mine inheritance," and that he could not involve himself in secular ties. While M. de Boisy was combating these—to his mind—most undesirable views of life, there came an offer from the Prince to make his son a member of the Senate—the highest tribute that could be paid to his character and renown, and an opening through which the most brilliant career might fairly be anticipated. M. Antoine Favre, the leading member of that Senate, and an intimate member of the de Sales family, added all his influence to induce Francis to accept this gracious offer, urging upon him that he need not give up his vocation in accepting it, since several eminent ecclesiastics had done good service to both Church and State as senators. But Francis remained unshaken in his decision against all such worldly temptations, answering every argument in the Apostle's words, "No man that warreth entangleth himself with the affairs of this life."

At this time his brother Louis, who was accustomed to consider Francis's judgment well nigh infallible, consulted him anxiously as to his own vocation, and Francis was as clear in advising Louis to serve God faithfully and earnestly in the world, cultivating all secular gifts and graces, and using them all for his Master's service and glory, as he was in putting aside all such in his own case. Still he waited patiently, believing that when God saw fit He would open a way to the fulfilment of his desires, and that ere long he would be able to put on the cassock which his mother had taken delight in preparing against the day when her son should be able openly to follow his holy calling.

Meanwhile, the Canon Louis was watching his opportunity, when at length it appeared to offer itself. The Provost (or Dean) of Geneva died, and he thought that some of M. de Boisy's reluctance to sacrifice his son's worldly advantages might be disposed of, were this office, the most honourable in the country save that of Bishop, conferred upon Francis. Accordingly, having consulted with Bishop Claude de Granier, due application was made to the Pope, in whose gift the appointment rested, and, to Francis's exceeding astonishment, the letters instituting him Provost or

Dean of Geneva were brought to him by his cousin, early in May, 1593, with the intimation that now they might surely hope to obtain M. de Boisy's consent to his ordination. Francis accepted this wholly unsought offer as an indication of God's Will, and as such set it before his father, entreating him no longer to oppose his ecclesiastical career. M. de Boisy, far from convinced, raised every possible difficulty, reproaching his son for wishing to forsake him in his old age; urging the comparative insignificance of the Provostship with the secular dignities he aspired to for Francis, and even at last pleaded with tears against the frustration of his worldly hopes. But the Unseen Hand which beckoned Francis onwards, could not be resisted. Patiently and dutifully he set before his father the firm resolution which had actuated him from the days when, a young child, his golden curls were shorn at Clermont, and with them all worldly hopes and joys were renounced for ever. He reminded him that at Paris and at Padua he had vowed himself to God's service solely, and with holy firmness, tempered with the tenderest filial love, declared that nothing could change his resolution. Overcome, though not convinced, M. de Boisy at length gave way: "If it is indeed God Who calls you, my son," he said, "I must believe what you say. Do as He wills; what am I that I should fight against the Lord?"

That very day S. Francis laid aside his secular dress for the cassock prepared by his mother, replying to an observation that he assumed it as solemnly as though it were a religious habit, that in truth he considered it as such. In after years he loved to refer to that date, May 13, 1593, as the day on which he put on breastplate and helmet as the sworn soldier of the Lord.

There was a great sensation in Annecy when the noble young Seigneur de Villeroget arrived there in cap and cassock, thus proclaiming his irrevocable choice ; and the ceremony of installation, which took place on May 26—Ascension Eve—was a festival to all the country side. After the customary oration (which won all listeners by its humility and grace) the Bishop bade Francis prepare to receive Holy Orders at the coming Trinity, and the young Provost consequently entered upon a retreat, which was only disturbed by one more fruitless effort on the part of M. de Boisy to induce him to accept the office of Senator likewise, on the ground that his predecessor had held both appointments, and that the Duke of Savoy wished Francis to do the like. Obedient to his father's will in all that did not interfere with that of a Higher Will, Francis could not yield this point. "I am convinced," he replied, "that God asks a wholly undivided service of me. I may not give my-

self by halves to Him Who will tolerate no rival."
" It is but time wasted to try and persuade you, I
see!" M. de Boisy exclaimed, passionately. " Be it as
you will; serve God only!"

This was sufficient. Francis hastened to make all
needful arrangements, among other things transferring
the title of Seigneur de Villeroget, together with all his
rights as first-born, to Louis, himself resuming the
name, now so far more illustrious for his sake, of
François de Sales. His next thought was to ask the
assistance of M. Bouvard, a friendly priest, to direct
his retreat, and to instruct him in the formularies and
functions he was about to undertake. But to M.
Bouvard's astonishment, there was little to be taught;
Francis already was familiar with office books and
rubrics, having so long looked upon them as his
destined and desired occupation. Indeed, the venerable priest declared that it was he who received most
edification in this retreat, from the earnestness and
piety of his disciple.

On the 8th of June, 1593, Francis de Sales received
minor orders at the hands of Bishop Granier, and the
following Saturday, being the Eve of the Trinity
Festival, the same Prelate ordained him sub-deacon.
His whole family was assembled at dinner by the
Bishop, in honour of the event, and Francis, turning
to his host, playfully remarked that he seemed to be

playing the part of the Prodigal Son, whose reception was celebrated by a banquet ! The Bishop answered that at all events Francis was his chosen son, and, as such, he required him to preach in the Cathedral in the coming festival of Corpus Christi. The new Deacon would have excused himself on the ground of inexperience and incompetence, but on the Bishop's insisting, he yielded, saying, " I obey, 'in verbo tuo laxabo rete.' " [1] As it happened, a celebrated preacher visited Annecy just then, and, at the last moment, Francis resigned the post to him ; but his own first sermon was preached on the Octave. It is remarkable that, in spite of all his gifts of facility and composure, Francis underwent the most painful nervousness and timidity on this occasion, to such an extent, that when the bell began to sound, announcing the sermon, he was seized with such a fit of trembling as to be unable to stand. There was but one remedy. Falling on his knees before God, the future Saint and Apostle implored God to be with him, to use the weak, human instrument to His Own Glory, and to speak through his lips, and so, rising up calm and strong in the power of the Lord, and losing all self-consciousness and timidity, he went to the Cathedral, where an expectant crowd eagerly awaited one so well known, and so personally interesting to most of them ;

[1] "At Thy word I will let down the net."—Luke v. 5.

and, realizing to the full his responsibility before God, in preaching His Word to Christ's flock, mounted the pulpit with even, unhurried steps, and in that sonorous, exquisitely modulated voice, which was one of his special gifts, fulfilled his appointed office. What more fitting subject for the first dedication of those gifts, than the glories of the Blessed Sacrament of the Holy Eucharist; God ever Present on the Altar, ever offering Himself, veiled beneath the elements of bread and wine, to the faithful members of His Church? Who that has studied the writings of S. Francis de Sales, and pondered their deep, fervent teaching as to Sacramental Grace, will wonder that his loving soul poured forth such a glowing torrent of holy words, as he spoke of the Blessed Sacrament, the Bread of Life, the Precious Blood Which gives life and salvation, ending with so fervent, so intensified a prayer to the Dear Lord Present on His Altar, that the whole multitude was, as it were, wrapt in hushed attention till the sermon ended, a thrill of devotion swept across the congregation, and many a one shed tears of heartfelt devotion. The venerable Bishop went forth to congratulate Monsieur and Madame de Boisy upon the costly gift that they had given to the Lord, and as he went, he could not resist saying to all he met, canons and nobles, "Well, what think you of my son? Are not his words wondrous, and his utterance yet more so? In truth he is an Apostle, marvellous in word and deed, and God has sent him to bring salvation to our people."

The impression made by this beginning was but confirmed by Francis's life in Annecy; his simplicity and modesty, his devotion in church, and the regularity of his external habits, won universal respect, and men, far his seniors in age and position, felt that he was an example to them in every way. It was at this time that he founded a Confraternity, called the Penitents of the Holy Cross, which received formal institution from the Bishop and the Chapter; Francis being the first Prior. It must have been a source of pleasure to him that one of the first members received was his own father, M. de Boisy. This Confraternity gradually spread widely, and later on, the Duke of Savoy, in order to mark his admiration for the work, gave its founder the privilege of setting free a condemned prisoner on every Maundy Thursday, the official acts for which are still preserved.

On September 18 in this same year (1593), Francis de Sales was ordained Deacon, and, on December 18, the desire of his life was fulfilled, and, by the solemn laying on of hands of the venerable Bishop Granier, he received the Priesthood. "From this day," says the Père la Rivière, writing of him, "he gave himself wholly to an interior life of peace.

His intense respect for the sacerdotal office, and his gratitude for the Eternal Goodness Which had brought him to it, inspired him with such a spirit of self-watchfulness, that he seemed wholly transformed, as you might see in his face, his eyes, his bearing, his words and actions, which were all stamped with somewhat well nigh angelic, almost divine, which constrained men to love and venerate him."

It is usual for a newly ordained priest to celebrate his first mass on the day following his Ordination, but with characteristic humility, Francis de Sales preferred to wait until he had still further prepared himself, by a retreat of three days, for this great office. During this retreat, he made three resolutions which influenced his whole life. First, that he would strive to carry the spiritual atmosphere of the Altar into his every action, so that each moment of the day should be a perpetual preparation for the morrow's sacrifice; and that if he were asked why he did anything, he might be able, with truth, to say, "I am making ready to celebrate." His second resolution was always to approach the Altar in such a spirit as he would wish to have on his deathbed, and before the Judgment Seat of God: and the third, to aim at a perpetual union with Jesus Christ through loving imitation and recollection, so as in very deed to be "one with Him." One of his early biographers says that when the newly ordained Priest spoke of these sacred mysteries, his soul was so melted within him by fervent love, that he could not restrain his tears. During this retreat, another priest who had just celebrated his first Mass was mentioned, —" Happy man ! " exclaimed Francis. " Henceforth he can heed nothing save the service of God, and sin seems almost impossible for him." " What do you mean ? " some one asked ; " the Altar does not confer impeccability ; this priest is surely as liable to fall as before ? " " No one can think so," he replied, " who really knows what it is to be a priest, to hold and receive the Body of Jesus Christ daily. No one can be worthy to be a priest who is not as pure as an angel."

Francis de Sales actually celebrated his first Mass on the Feast of S. Thomas, in the Cathedral of Annecy, and, in the afternoon of the same day, he said Vespers, and preached, taking as his subject the Office of the Priesthood. From the first he shunned the prevalent habit of his time in preaching, which was to be rather pedantic than spiritual ; to abound in quotations, especially Latin and Greek, and those as often profane as theological, as in mythological allusions. In all times the uneducated mind is wont to admire what it cannot understand, and then, as now, people seem to have been impressed by what they supposed to be mighty erudition. M. de Boisy himself was rather disappointed at his son's failure in this popular display. "Mine was the best father in the world," Francis de Sales said once to the Bishop of Belley, "but he had spent most of his life in the field or at Court. When I became Provost, I preached perpetually everywhere, in the cathedral, the parish churches, and for every small confraternity. I never refused to preach, on the principle of 'Give to them that ask you.' My dear father used to hear the bells ringing, and ask who preached? 'Who but your son?' was often the answer. One day he took me aside and said, 'Provost, you preach too often. Even on week days the bells go, and it is always the same story, the Provost, the Provost! It used not to be so in my day. Sermons were much rarer. But then to be sure God knows those were something like sermons! full of learning, well got up; more Latin and Greek in one than you stick into a dozen! Everybody admired those, and ran after them as if they were manna hunting! but now you make preaching so common that nobody cares for it or for you!' You see my dear old father spoke to the best of his judgment. He meant no harm, but he looked at the whole thing from the world's point of view. You may be sure of this, there is no fear of our preaching too much, 'nunquam satis dicitur quod nunquam satis discitur,' especially surrounded as we are by heresy, which is mainly spread by means of preaching, and must be counteracted by its own weapon." Francis de Sales acted upon this principle all through life, silencing all remonstrance from those who would have spared his toil, with the reply, "Give to him that asketh." In his most busy days at Paris, when applications to preach inundated him, he was once asked to preach on some particular festival, and, having granted the request, an attendant remarked that he had already promised one sermon for that day. "Never mind," was the answer, "God will multiply the loaves. He is rich in mercy to all those that call upon Him." And to remonstrance on the score of health, he answered, "If God gives one wherewithal to teach, do you doubt that He will also give bodily strength for the needful utterance? Let us cast our care on Him, and He will strengthen us." "But God does not forbid care of our health," was the reply. "Certainly not," the Bishop answered, "but He forbids us to mistrust His goodness." And he closed the discussion by saying, "If I were to be asked to preach a third time that same day, I should suffer less in body and mind by doing it than in refusing. Shall we not give both body and soul for our neighbour, remembering that Our Lord loved him so well that He died for him?"

From these first days of exercising his gifts as a preacher, Francis de Sales laid down certain rules for himself from which he never saw reason to depart. One of these, in spite of what he said about meeting heresy with its own weapon, was to avoid preaching controversy. "He who preaches love is opposing heresy, without saying one controversial word," he was wont to say, and he once said to the Bishop of Belley, that during the thirty-three years for which he had preached Christ's Gospel, he had invariably remarked that sermons on practical duties handled with fervour and zeal were far more efficacious, not only to people in general, but also to heretics and schismatics; and that the pulpit ought never to be made a battle-field for controversy, lest there were less built up than pulled down. Another point on which Francis de Sales' system of preaching was founded, was the importance of always endeavouring to teach some definite point of duty, to inculcate some particular virtue, or correct some particular vice, to explain some special doctrine or mystery of the faith, rather than to generalize, thereby leaving no clear impression, leading to action, on the listener's mind. [1] "Numberless most carefully studied sermons are useless owing to this defect," he said. "My test of the real worth of a man as a preacher is when his congregation go away, saying, not 'What a beautiful sermon!' but, '*I* will do something.' A man may set forth his own learning and eloquence in a

[1] *Esprit*, iii. 5.

fine sermon, but the true sign that God speaks through his mouth is when his words convert sinners, and induce people to leave off bad habits. The only real fruit of preaching is the overthrow of sin and the increase of righteousness. God sends forth His preachers now, as Christ His Apostles, 'that they should go and bring forth fruit, and that their fruit should remain.'" (John xv. 16.)

The simplicity to which M. de Boisy objected, was another thing which his son considered most important. He objected to sermons which drew attention to the eloquence, the learning, the striking action, or personal gifts of the preacher, all of which, he said, appertained rather to the mere worldly orator, than to the Ambassador of Christ teaching the lesson of salvation. Writing to Mgr. de Belley in 1610, who had been preaching a Lenten Course at Chambéry, in which there seems to have been a considerable display of literature and classical acquirement, Francis remarked in his own quaint way, how much he heard of the rich promise of his friend's spiritual garden, how abundantly the vines blossomed, how the parterres bloomed and smiled, "And now," he says, "I await *an flores fructus parturiant.*" Going on to advise Mgr. de Belley to prune his vines of the superfluous branches and tendrils, such as came from mere belles lettres and profane literature, since, although doubtless it was fair to despoil the Egyptians for the service of the tabernacle, all such appropriation must needs be made with a very careful hand, and casting aside simile and metaphor, he adds that Christ's Gospel should be preached with all its own purity and simplicity. He objected to an excessive dwelling on the mystic interpretation of Holy Scripture, to the neglect of its literal meaning, which, he said, was to attempt raising the roof of a house before the foundations were laid; and his deep reverence for the Word of God shrank from distorting it to serve men's purposes. "It is not a stuff made to be cut into garments after everyone's own fashion," he used to say. Brevity was another point at which Francis de Sales aimed. "The more you say, the less people remember; the fewer your words, the greater their profit," he used to say at the end of his career as at the beginning. "The more you overcharge your hearer's memory, the weaker you make it, just as a lamp is extinguished if it is filled too full of oil, or plants killed by overwatering." "When a sermon is too long, the end makes one forget the middle, and the middle the beginning!" He himself had studied the Homilies of the Fathers deeply, and aimed as far as might be at forming his own style on the best patristic models.

But while he estimated the duty of preaching so highly, it was in no degree to the neglect of other priestly offices. He always held it to be the first duty and most blessed privilege of God's priest to serve at His Altar, and nothing short of necessity could induce him to depart from the rule of daily offering the Precious Sacrifice of the Altar. When, during his mission in Chablais, Francis resided at Thonon, where as yet Protestant bitterness and malice made it impossible to offer up the Blessed Sacrament without fear of desecration, he used daily to cross the river Drance, and go to the Church of St. Etienne, in the village of Marin, a small place about equidistant between Thonon and Evian. At one time a sudden, violent flood, brought on by the melting of the snows, carried away an arch of the bridge by which the Drance was crossed, and for a long time the only means of passing was a plank provisionally thrown across the space. During the severe frost which followed, this plank afforded so slippery and dangerous a passage, that the missionary's friends sought to induce him to relinquish his daily visit to Marin; but in vain: nothing could induce him to give up that privilege of his priesthood, whence, as he justly said, he drew all his strength for God's service. In later life a touching story is told of the Bishop of Geneva, bearing on this same point—his strong conviction of the paramount duty and blessing of the daily sacrifice. There was a certain young priest for whom Francis de Sales had a warm affection, who did not appreciate this duty, but was content to celebrate on Sundays and festivals. S. Francis would always "exhort and comfort, and charge everyone, as a father does his children" (1 Thess. ii. 11), rather than rebuke and admonish; and accordingly, instead of remonstrating with this priest, he one day presented him with a beautifully wrought box, saying as he did so, "I have a favour to ask, which I think you will not deny me, as it concerns God's Glory, to which I know you are devoted." The young man made haste to answer that he was ready to obey.

"Oh no," he replied, "I do not command, I would only entreat, and that in the Name and for the love of God." And then, opening the box, he showed the young priest that it contained wafers ready for consecration, saying, "God has called you to the sacred office of the priesthood, He has given you the right to celebrate the Blessed Sacrament every day; why do you not use your privilege? I know, thank God, that there is no weighty hindrance, for I think I am as thoroughly cognizant of the state of your soul as it is possible to be. If you were an artisan, a lawyer, or a doctor, would you be satisfied with exercising your professional duties from time to time only? Accept this little gift, and do not fail to remember me before the Holy Altar."

The young priest, deeply moved, poured out his difficulties and hesitations to the patient, tender listener; his consciousness of secret unworthiness, his infirmity and self-indulgence, and his dread that his daily life was not sufficiently recollected to justify a continual handling of those awful mysteries. "All these excuses," S. Francis answered, "are in fact so many self-accusations, if I saw fit to investigate them. But to leave that for the present, you are willing to submit to my judgment;—Well, I tell you—and I think also that I have the Spirit of God—that all these causes which you allege for your dispensation, are the very reasons why you should rather obey your priestly calling. Nothing will so ripen your character, purify your imperfections, or weaken your temptations, strengthen your weakness, and shed light upon the darkness of your path; and the more you serve God thus, the better you will learn to serve Him. If, like S. Bonaventura, you should be kept back by a humble sense of unworthiness, or feel that you are not profiting as you might do by your privilege, bear in mind that you are public property; your church and your flock, living and dead, need the intercession of the Blessed Sacrifice, and moreover remember that on such days as you abstain from celebrating, you deprive God of some portion of His Glory." One can scarcely wonder to hear that the result was, that for thirty years he to whom this counsel was so lovingly given, had never missed saying Mass daily.

From an early period of his ordination, Francis de Sales also devoted himself specially to the duties of the confessional; and although necessarily at first he had not that experience which made him in later years one of the most eminent guides of the soul ever known, still the practical earnest teaching which he gave from the pulpit, carried out as it was in the personal holiness of his own life, drew numbers to him for the healing ministry of reconciliation; and his early biographers say that he constantly spent the whole morning in his confessional, receiving persons of every description, showing no preference in patience and attention unless it might be to the poorest or the most ignorant, and leading many who came in a hard, formal spirit, to a true spirit of contrition and love. So effectual were the labours of the young Provost, that, although only twenty-seven, the chapter applied to Bishop Granier to appoint him Grand Penitentiary of the diocese, which he accordingly did. As soon as he assumed this office, Francis de Sales put his own confessional immediately within the cathedral door, and when his brethren expressed their surprise at his selecting a position at once the least dignified and convenient, according to their views, he replied that a good shepherd ought to be ever at the door of the sheepfold, ready to call the flock and draw it within the fold; to make the way of repentance as easy to find as possible, for those who were yet without. It is a remarkable fact, and one that seems strange to our present habits, that not only many old friends and dependents of the family put themselves under the Provost's spiritual direction, but his father and mother, who habitually attended his services, loving to receive the Blessed Sacrament from his hand, also became his penitents, and the courtly old soldier, who pretended still to mourn over his son's perversity in rejecting the brilliant worldly career open to him, yet proved his real belief in that son's vocation, by regularly frequenting his confessional, coming over punctually to Annecy at the proper seasons on purpose, when he was not staying there. Probably most men would have shrunk from the duty, but it was part of Francis de Sales' character to refuse no call which came from God, and he appears to have dealt with those most closely allied with him, in the same utterly unselfconscious spirit as in all other cases; quite losing sight of the earthly tie in that of a higher spiritual relationship. His direction was specially useful to his brother Louis, who had always looked up to Francis with more than common reverence, and who delighted in being his constant companion, " the willing disciple of a beloved master." Living necessarily in the world, and exposed to its dangers and temptations, the guidance of this saintly elder brother became the blessing of his life, and kept him pure and religious at a period when such was by no means the type of his fellow nobles in Europe.

Amid all these duties, peculiar to his calling, Francis never would neglect study. He used to say that priests ought not merely to study diligently in preparation for their office, but that those who attempted to teach others, should be continually learning themselves, continually refreshing their acquaintance with all such subjects as tended to promote their usefulness. Accordingly a part of every day was marked out for reading; and his diligence in making notes and analyses of the books he read, and his careful meditation and weighing Holy Scripture and the writings of the Fathers, are testified by the volumes of manuscript to which he was perpetually adding.

It can hardly be a subject of wonder, if amid the success of such a man, who was moreover the avowed favourite friend and counsellor of his Bishop, in spite of his youth, a cloud of jealousy arose. There were men in Annecy who did not care to subject their own lives to a comparison with the pious young Provost, and who dreaded his influence with the Bishop. These persons spared no pains in seeking to weaken this influence, and to persuade Bishop Granier that Francis depreciated him, and lowered his character in the estimation of the diocese; that he aimed at a popularity injurious to his diocesan, and would fain bring in all manner of novelties and reformations, which would be a perpetual trouble to his elders.

The kindly old Bishop did not really believe these imputations, and yet, as we know, a perpetual dropping wears the stone; and without intending it his manner grew colder and less trustful towards his son, as he called Francis. He, on his part, was perfectly conscious that such was the case, but, being equally conscious of the purity of his own motives, he took no heed, going on in tranquil fulfilment of every duty; until at last the Bishop, unable to endure any constraint with one he loved and respected so well, poured out all his grief, and told Francis everything that had been urged upon him. The natural result was that he was more than re-instated in the Bishop's confidence, and it became necessary for him to find excuses for those who had sought to injure him, before he could induce the prelate to reconsider his determination to have nothing more to do with men who had proved themselves guilty of such unworthy jealousy and detraction. It was in the like spirit that in later years, when a friend remarked to S. Francis how he thought no Christian grace so hard to practise as that of loving one's enemies, the saint replied, "I don't know how I was made, or whether God has refashioned me, but somehow I never find that precept so hard. There is such a very special charm and delight in it that I think it would have been more difficult to obey God, if He had commanded us *not* to love our enemies."[1]

Esprit, viii. 25

CHAPTER III.

CHABLAIS MISSION. 1594.

ACTIVE and devoted as Francis de Sales' life in Annecy was, he was destined for a more arduous task. The country round, bordering as it does on Switzerland, could hardly escape the contamination of Calvinistic heresy, and as far back as the year 1536, the Bernese had taken advantage of the Duke of Savoy's being at war with Francis I. to invade the Pays de Vaud, and to take possession of Chablais, putting down the Church with a strong hand, and establishing Protestant ministers in Thonon and the other towns and villages of which they got command. In 1564 the Duke Emanuel Philibert recovered a part of the Chablais, but he was forced to leave it still in the bonds of heresy, and in 1589 fresh warfare occurred during the reign of his successor Charles Emanuel. The unfortunate country was torn hither and thither between the belligerents, until in 1593 a peace was made finally restoring the bailiwicks of Chablais and Ternier to Savoy. The religious condition of the people by this time was pitiable; they had learnt to measure their faith according to their political position, and were for the most part converted to Catholicism by the Duke's warriors, or terrified into Protestantism by Bernese harquebusses. When at length there was a reasonable hope of lasting security, Charles Emanuel wished to see his subjects restored to the Church, and he applied to the Bishop of Geneva, requesting him to exercise his Apostolic zeal for this desirable end. Bishop Granier fully appreciated the necessity though, perhaps, scarcely the difficulty, and at once sent a worthy and learned Priest, François Bouchut by name, to Thonon as Curé, but either through bodily fear or despair of success, he very soon quitted his post, and the Duke wrote to urge that some missionary of a bolder, more persevering character should be sent to fill the post. Bishop Granier was sorely perplexed; the more that whatever the original difficulties might have been, they were increased by M. Bouchut's departure. It was no easy matter to find a man with power and strength for such a task, who would also have the necessary prudence and judgment to carry it out. The Provost was obviously the best fitted man he knew, combining, as he did, with the personal gifts of wisdom, firmness, and gentleness, a family position which commanded respect and consideration throughout the country. But the poor Bishop foresaw how much opposition he would assuredly raise up in the de Sales family by such a proposition, above all in M. de Boisy. After much prayer, he came to the determination that Francis de Sales was the man, but that he, or at least his family, must be taken by guile; an open request to the Provost should not be made, but if possible he should be led to offer himself for the seemingly forlorn hope. Accordingly Bishop Granier summoned the Chapter and whatever ecclesiastics of note he could get together, and put the case before them, producing the Duke of Savoy's letters, and urging that the call was distinctly God's own. He told them that the work clearly was one of intense self-devotion, the toil and the peril great; but if so many men were ever ready to encounter toil and peril of all kinds, by land and by sea, to gain a corruptible crown, how should he think so hardly of his clergy as to doubt that they were not less ready than their secular brethren, in pursuit of one incorruptible? He concluded by saying that he had called them together now, in order to advise with them as to who was able and willing to devote himself to the work?

There was profound silence. Toil, difficulty, dangers, were the only earthly side visible of the mission set before them, and M. Bouchut's failure had discouraged them. All eyes turned to the Provost, and as head of the Chapter, it was his place to speak first. Probably none present more fully appreciated the arduous nature of the work than himself; but amid the disheartening silence, he rose and said in brief words, but with a glowing countenance, "Monseigneur, if you hold me to be capable of this work, and bid me undertake it, I am ready. '*In verbo tuo laxabo rete.*'"

The Bishop expected some such answer to his appeal, and immediately accepted the offer, adding that he considered the Provost the fittest man to lead the enterprise, and had he not come forward, he, the Bishop himself, in spite of age and infirmity, must have undertaken it. This first step, however, was the easiest. Tidings of his son's resolution soon reached the ears of M. de Boisy, who was then at the Chateau de Sales, and, ordering his horse, the old man rode straight to Annecy, and, finding the Provost, poured forth a torrent of remonstrance and entreaty, pleading his seventy-two years, and his desolation at the prospect of parting with his son, probably for ever, with such pathos, that, while unshaken in resolution, Francis wept like a child. "My father," he answered, "I cannot refuse to obey God's call; I must trust to His Mercy for giving you resignation, and courage to make this sacrifice." M. de Boisy bade his son follow him to the Palace, believing that the Bishop's tender heart could not withstand the force of his appeal, and there, kneeling before the prelate, with many tears and sobs, he protested against parting with Francis.

"Monseigneur!" he exclaimed, "I give up this my first-born, the pride and hope of my life, the stay of my old age, to the Church; I consent to his being a confessor, but I cannot give him to be a martyr." Claude Granier was so deeply moved that he could find no words in reply; he was fain to join his tears with those of his aged friend. The sorrowful silence was only broken by Francis's clear voice, saying in touching accents, "Wist ye not that I must be about my Father's business?"

But M. de Boisy recovered his utterance, and urged his views upon the Bishop with so much earnestness, as to make a visible impression upon him; and Francis, fearing that his father's counsel might prevail, burst forth in vigorous words: "Monseigneur!" he exclaimed, "be firm, I implore you; would you have me prove myself unworthy of the kingdom of God? I have put my hand to the plough; would you have me look back, and yield to worldly considerations?"

Bishop Granier reminded M. de Boisy of S. Francis of Assisi, who, like the modern S. Francis, was brought by his father before the Bishop, and who there stripped off his very garments and offered them in token of his entire renunciation of all worldly possessions. And he went on to speak of Abraham, and his ready obedience in giving up Isaac. M. de Boisy would not yield; he could only repeat that he did not wish to defy God's Will, but he was not Abraham, nor was he worthy of an angel's interposition, and therefore he could not consent to sacrifice his son. "As far as I am concerned," he added, "I shall oppose the whole thing; God must do as He wills."

The Provost, taking advantage of this last expression, threw himself on his knees before his father, entreating for his blessing. "My dear son," the old soldier answered, "I have often received your priestly benediction with joy,—and God forbid that I should ever give you anything save a blessing,—but as to this undertaking, nothing can ever make me either sanction or bless it." And so saying, he returned to the Chateau de Sales. From thence he shortly sent an intimate friend, the Marquis de Lullin, in hopes that he might prove more able to convince Francis, and induce him to give up the point. But M. de Lullin, having come to plead the father's cause, was wholly won over to the son's, and returned to M. de Boisy, only to assure him in the strongest terms that Francis was so clearly acting in obedience to God's call, as to make any opposition impossible, and he even ventured to affirm, that not God's Glory alone, but the credit of the de Sales family, and of Savoy generally, were largely promoted by so noble an enterprise.

Meanwhile Francis prepared to enter upon his arduous mission. Several ecclesiastics offered to accompany him, but for the present he judged it wiser to make his undertaking as unostentatious and unobtrusive as possible, and therefore he resolved to take no one with him save his cousin, the Canon Louis de Sales, in whose gentleness and good judgment he had great confidence, while his learning and his gift of preaching fitted him for the task before them.

Before leaving Annecy, they requested all the Chapter and other clergy to promote their undertaking by prayer, and especially by offering the Holy Sacrifice with that intention ; and having received the Bishop's blessing, the two cousins set forth, unattended by any suite, and taking no more luggage than the barest necessaries, with their Bibles, office-books, and Bellarmino's Controversies. They went on the 9th of September, 1594, to the Chateau de Sales, where M de Boisy continued his ineffectual attempts at dissuasion, and after three days' retreat, Francis took leave of his mother, who, though she shared her husband's anxiety, refrained from saying one word in opposition to what she truly believed to be God's call to her child; and then the missionaries departed on their journey. To the last M. de Boisy refused to say farewell to his son, or to supply any funds for his undertaking. It was early in the morning of the 14th of September, the Feast of the Exaltation of the Holy Cross, when the young warriors set forth upon their march, and one cannot but imagine that as they passed through those familiar hills, which the autumn tints were scarce yet tinging with deeper hues, they must have raised the glorious strain,

> "Vexilla regis prodeunt,
> Fulget crucis mysterium,
> . Qua vita mortem pertulit,
> Et morte vitam protulit,"

as doubtless their heart's cry was, "Per signum crucis de inimicis nostris libera nos, Deus noster." As they crossed the boundary of Chablais, we are told that they knelt down, and commended their work specially to God, and to the Guardian Angels, "Ecce ego mittam Angelum meum, qui præcedat te, et custodiat in via, et introducat in locum quem paravi; observa eum, et audi vocem ejus."

The Provost and his companion went first to Allinges, a stronghold which commanded Chablais, where the Governor of the Province, the Baron d'Hermance, was stationed with a garrison. The next morning, after Mass, he took the missionaries over the fortress, from the heights of which the devastation of war was only too visible. "If you can win the hearts of these men," the soldier said, "there will be no more need of our guns to man these walls." It was decided that, for safety, the two priests must return every night to Allinges, where only for the present they could celebrate the Holy Eucharist, save at Marin, across the Drance, or in the little chapel of the monks of the Great S. Bernard, on the lake. M. d'Hermance thought that they might preach at Thonon, where a few church-people were to be found, although afraid openly to declare themselves.

These scattered faithful gathered round Francis de Sales, who took every opportunity of setting forth from Holy Scripture, publicly or privately, the necessity of an apostolic commission for those who would preach and minister in holy things, whereas the Protestant ministers were, of course, utterly without any such commission. Gradually the cousins extended their operations, and staff in hand penetrated into the villages round, preaching three or four times a day, often without any visible success, for the minds of the people were diligently poisoned against the missionaries by their opponents; but not discouraged, and trusting in God to bring forth fruit in His Own good time. A great stir was raised by the Geneva ministers, and every incentive used to kindle opposition. "Never mind," Francis was wont to say to his cousin; "we must be firm, and if you are not afraid, depend upon it we shall hold our own!"[1] To some one who expressed astonishment at the bitterness of the ministers, he answered, "Put yourself into their place; would you not cry out against those who took the bread out of

[1] "Nous ferons prou."

your mouth? It is but natural that they should wish me away, considering how I must damage their work. Let us pray for them, and give them still more cause for complaint in one way, saying with the Emperor Tiberius, 'Satis est nobis si tantum dicant.'"

In truth, it was no easy life which the two de Sales led. They often separated for weeks together, Louis working chiefly in the country, Francis concentrating his labours upon Thonon, which was a sort of stronghold of heresy and schism. Nothing was ever allowed to interfere with his daily work there; however deep the snow or tempestuous the weather (and that winter was one of unusual severity), the Provost never failed to leave Allinges in the early morning, sometimes, his biographers say, scarce able to walk for the broken chilblains which covered his hands and feet, and after celebrating mass at Marin, the rest of the day was spent in preaching and teaching, striving to win a way into the hearts of these poor people, blinded and deluded as they were by the soul-destroying heresy of Calvin. Sometimes his efforts led him into the hills, where with no protection save his staff, his Bible, and breviary, he met with perils and hardships which would have daunted most men. Thus, on one occasion, Francis was benighted in a wood, and found himself tracked along the snow by a number of hungry wolves, from whom he saw no escape save climbing into a tree, where he was fain to bind himself with his girdle to a branch, lest, heavy as he was with weariness and sleep, he should fall. The night was bitter, and the next morning some peasants found the missionary insensible with cold and hunger. They took pity on him, and carried him to their hut, where, in return for their material services, he preached to them the way of life. Another time a certain Genevese who had resolved to kill the Provost, waylaid him, and fired no less than three times upon him; the gun, though carefully selected, missed fire on each trial, and the saintly priest passed on in safety. It is consoling to hear that the intended murderer eventually came to a better mind, and was converted.

Another time, accompanied by a faithful servant, George Rolland (whom at last Madame de Boisy induced her husband to send to their son), he was overtaken by darkness in a thick forest, when returning to Allinges, and after vainly endeavouring to find the way, they resolved to shelter for the night amid the ruins of a chapel on which they had stumbled. There, Rolland used to relate how his master poured out his fervent prayers over the desecrated moss-grown walls, in the plaintive words of David, "Thy holy temple have they defiled, and made Jerusalem a heap of stones; they have laid waste thy dwelling-place. O remember not our sins, but have mercy upon us,

and that soon. Help us, O God of our salvation.
Turn us again, O God; shew the light of Thy Countenance, and we shall be whole. Why hast Thou
broken down our hedge? . . look down and visit this
vine. They break down all the carved work thereof,
with axes and hammers. O God, wherefore art Thou
absent from us so long? why is Thy wrath so hot
against the sheep of Thy pasture? O think upon Thy
congregation, whom Thou hast purchased, and redeemed of old." Once, being surprised by nightfall in
a distant village where no friendly soul would give
the wanderers an asylum, they spent the night in the
village bakehouse, which they found open and still
warm. In some places the villagers refused even to
sell food to the missionary; he was accused of being
a sorcerer, and the report was spread abroad, that
Francis had been seen at a witch's sabbath, and that he
bore the devil's marks upon his body! One day he was
thus surrounded by an excited crowd, who threatened
to pass on from accusations to blows. Francis faced
round upon them with his own placid smile, and making
the sign of the Cross, he said aloud, "This, good friends,
is the only mark which I bear in my body, the only
charm I use; but it is all-powerful, I fear no storm that
man can raise whilst I am defended by it, and in its
strength I am not afraid to meet contending hosts."

Some of his friends who knew the designs made

upon Francis's life, tried to induce him to give up certain duties he had undertaken, but in vain, "Whoso dwelleth under the defence of the Most High, shall abide under the Shadow of the Almighty," was his quiet answer. "His faithfulness and truth shall be my shield and buckler; I trust wholly in Him!" and he pursued his steadfast course. Even M. de Blonay, a pious gentleman who lived near Evian, and who was an earnest supporter of the Faith, expressed his hopelessness of any result among these prejudiced, bigoted people. "My dear friend," Francis replied, "we are but making a beginning. I shall go on in good heart, and hope in God, whatever may be the outward appearance of things."[1]

To these external labours, Francis added the care of the Savoyard soldiers quartered in Allinges, who, though nominally Catholics, were often very ignorant, and beset by the vices common to their time and condition. His manly straightforwardness and kindly sympathy, backed by his well-known personal courage, gave Francis great hold over these men, and he was soon a universal referee in all their concerns. This

[1] "The first ripe fruits are not always the sweetest," he wrote; "and I trust that when once Our Dear Lord cries His 'Ephatha,' we shall reap an abundant harvest. The miller does not lose time while preparing his grindstone, and after all, this work suits me admirably, for I am fit for nothing better than to preach to stone walls."—Lett. ix.

sympathy he turned to good account, getting them together for instruction, and bringing many to confession and a better life. It is told how one of these soldiers, appalled at the sight of his own past life, lost all hope of forgiveness, and came to the Provost in the depths of despair to pour out his griefs. Francis not only received him with the tenderest compassion, and won his fullest confidence, but, fearing lest the dark hour should return, he kept the sorrowful penitent in his own room, made him eat and sleep there, till, having prepared him for the tribunal of penitence, he confessed him, and, deeply touched with his contrition and fervour, laid upon him no heavier penance than one devoutly said *Pater* and *Ave*. The soldier, who expected a life-long penance, exclaimed, marvelling at such indulgent treatment, "Father, would you destroy my soul, that you give me so light a penance for such grievous sins?" "Do not fear," was the reply; "trust in God: His Mercy is more abounding than your sins, and as for your due penance, I will undertake what I do not lay on you." Eventually this man left the army, and went to the Grande Chartreuse, to spend the remainder of his life in devotion to God. Such returns of the wandering sheep no doubt more than made up to Francis for the weary hours of disappointment and seeming useless toil that more commonly fell to his lot.

It was at this time that, in compliance with a suggestion from friends, the Provost wrote his "Controversies," a work setting forth the leading dogmas of the Church, as opposed to the errors of Calvinism.

All this time M. de Boisy continued his vehement opposition to his son's course; the Canon Louis had been obliged once to return to the Chateau de Sales and strive to calm his uncle's alarms, and through him Madame de Boisy secretly supplied Francis with clothes and money. "In those Chablais days," he wrote, "I many a time envied S. Paul, and wished that I could maintain myself with my own hands. But I am a stupid fellow who can do nothing, save sometimes patch my clothes a little, and, when I was quite destitute of everything, my dear mother used to send me linen and money from home."[1] In the summer, Francis went to Annecy for one day's complete retreat, and it was during this that God poured the abundance of His graces and consolations upon His faithful servant, so as to make him cry out, "Domine, contine undas gratiæ tuæ. Domine, recede a me, quia non possum sustinere tuæ dulcedinis magnitudinem, unde prosternere me cogor!"[2] S. Francis has himself recorded this, in a paper headed

---

[1] Mère de Chaugy.

[2] "Lord, withhold Thy floods of grace; draw back, Lord, for I cannot bear the magnitude of Thy sweetness."

"Visitavit Dominus servum suum." No wonder that when, shortly after this, his father renewed the attempt to withdraw him from Chablais, the young priest replied in the words of Holy Writ, "He that endureth to the end shall be saved, and if a man strives for masteries, yet is he not crowned, except he strive lawfully."[1] To the Senator Favre, who also wrote at his father's instigation, persuading Francis to give up his mission, Francis answered: "If my Bishop bids me do so, I shall lay down the burden of this Thonon mission, which is too heavy for my shoulders. But when I consider how it is to be provided for in that case, I cannot at all see my way. Doubtless we are so encompassed with toil and dangers that it is scarce possible even to find sufficient time for that devotion which is absolutely necessary to keep alive the holy fire within us; but one upward glance at Jesus restores our courage. He has said, 'Ye shall hear of wars and rumours of wars; see that ye be not troubled, for all these things must come to pass . . . In your patience possess ye your souls.' Amid all our perplexities, and the troubles of our country, be it ours to fix our eyes on our heavenly country, and remember that it was in a whirlwind that the prophet went up to Heaven."

Upon this there was a conference held by the Bishop, M. Favre, and M. de Boisy, as to the course

[1] Matt. x. 22, and 2 Tim. ii. 5.

to be pursued; the latter urging Bishop Granier to recall his son; M. Favre granting that were Francis himself to despair of success, it were well to do so, but pleading that, so long as he was hopeful, his work ought not to be interfered with. The Bishop tried to touch M. de Boisy's sense of honour, suggesting that, if Francis forsook his undertaking, it would be said of him, "This man began to build, and was not able to finish:" but, failing to make any impression, he actually consented to issue the recall. This seems to have been done in a moment of weakness, for the order was never sent, and when the Senator Favre went shortly after to see Francis, and judge for himself of the state of things, he found his friend working on amid much of trial and even danger, but hopefully, and, in a measure, successfully; while the spirit and earnestness with which he laboured made a most deep impression on the elder man's mind, and, as he says himself, kindled all his best and most fervent zeal. About this time several assaults were really made on the missionary, and the Baron d'Hermance wished to give him a permanent guard; but Francis entirely refused this, saying that S. Paul and the other Apostles had never sought the protection of soldiers or any weapon save the Word of God; and yet with that they had prevailed over emperors and kings, over the power of intellect and the pride of life, and he would strive to do the like. "Endurance and trust in God are worth more than a whole regiment," he added; "and should it after all be God's Will that I seal the doctrine I preach with my blood, what better can I ask?" Shortly afterwards, he left Allinges, and boldly took up his abode at Thoñon, in spite of the danger he incurred by so doing. He went to lodge with a widow lady, Madame du Foug, who was most devout, and who heartily appreciated the privilege of receiving such a guest, although the anxiety that followed was great; as when, for instance, one night some armed men got into the house with the intention of killing the mission priest, who, late as was the hour, was still up reading and praying. Madame du Foug had just time to conceal her cherished guest; and the intruders, after vainly seeking him, had to go away, affirming that he was in league with the powers of evil, and had saved himself by their aid.

Faith and perseverance had their reward, and the tide began to turn in Francis's favour from the time he moved to Thonon. His devoted life, his unfailing gentleness and meekness, the charity with which he met all needs, spiritual and temporal, giving away all but what his very most pressing necessities demanded, even of food and clothing, won the admiration of all save the most prejudiced minds. The monks of Saint Bernard de Montjon gave him the use of their chapel on the shore of Lake Geneva, not far from Thonon, and there Francis daily said Mass, assisted for a time only by some fifteen or sixteen Catholics; heard confessions, and said his offices. Wherever he was admitted, he gladly ministered to the sick and the dying, and there were few days on which he did not preach in one place or another, indifferent as to the number or nature of his listeners, always saying that it was well worth the labour if but one soul profited thereby. Many years afterwards, Monseigneur de Belley was arguing this point with him, and the Bishop referred to those Chablais days. "I speak from the results of thirty years' experience," he said, " and in truth I have always found more real results for God's Glory when preaching to a few than to great congregations. Once in particular at Thonon, on a very wet Sunday, there were only seven persons in church, and it was suggested to me that it was hardly worth preaching to so few. I answered that a large congregation did not excite, or a scanty one depress me, and that if any one person was edified, that was enough. So I went into the pulpit, and I remember that my subject was about the saints. I spoke very simply, without any special pathos or fire, but one of the congregation began to weep, and at last to sob audibly. I really thought he was ill, and I stopped and spoke to him, offering any assistance he might require. However, he begged me to go on, and when the sermon, which was short, came to an end, he came to me, and, throwing himself at my feet, he exclaimed, 'Oh, M. le Prévôt, you have given me new life; you have saved my soul. Blessed be the hour in which I came hither and heard you; blessed to all eternity.' Then he told me how the ministers had persuaded him that the Church taught sheer idolatry with respect to the saints, and had induced him to promise to leave her, and join the Protestant party; but what he had just heard proved how untrue their assertions were, and recalled him to his better mind. This circumstance was of the greatest possible use to our mission; it made a great impression in the whole place, and opened many hearts to receive the words of truth. I could tell you several little incidents, which have all tended to confirm me in my love for little congregations."[1]

From this time, indeed, if the opposition did not diminish, there was a visible increase on the side of friendliness, and the Provost obtained a much more ready hearing. Sometimes he even ventured to preach in the open market-place of Thonon, when the stream of bargainers was arrested, and would cluster round him, some being heard to exclaim as they turned away again, "May God lead us to know what

[1] *Esprit*, ii. 27.

is really His truth!" When Lent of 1596 arrived, Francis mustered a large and important congregation; men who dared not come to him by day, had frequented his house by night, and received instruction in the Faith, and preparation for the Sacraments, and as their belief strengthened, so did their courage. Moreover, a deep impression had been made upon many who were wont to see the imposing figure of the missionary Provost moving along the streets with grave, calm steps, unheeding all who passed, as he bore the Blessed Sacrament (which could not yet be publicly carried without fear of insult) in a silver box on his breast, to the sick and dying. It became known that when he was seen going in this grave fashion, so different from his usual genial ways, that he was bearing that Ineffable Mystery, and the lesson sank deep into the hearts of men. Many began to desire to know the Church's teaching as to her Dear Lord's Presence among them in the Holy Eucharist, and Francis de Sales was not unready to set it forth. During this Lent, accordingly, he announced his intention of preaching upon the subject of the Great Sacrament, and invited any or all Protestants to come forward and prove him wrong, if they were able. The principal minister of Thonon, one Louis Viret, began by depreciating Francis, accusing him of being a mere sophistical rhetorician. "Then why do you not confute him?" was the natural question. So at length the ministers met to confer as to how they should best come forward and argue their own cause against the missionary. But they could not agree among themselves, or put forth any unanimous opinion, and the interview would have come to nothing, if the Baron d'Avully, the leading Protestant noble of the country, had not urged how ruinous it would be to their cause thus to slink out of the field. So the day and place were fixed, but at the last, no one of the ministers save Viret appeared, and he came only to say that he could not take so important a step without the Duke of Savoy's authorization! Of course this was a mere excuse, and it had the natural effect of all unworthy opposition to the truth, of leading men to inquire for themselves, and Francis found his time more and more taken up with seeing people privately, who came to be taught as to the real doctrines of the Catholic faith. Laborious as it was, he greatly preferred this means of teaching to public discussion, in which both sides were likely to wax warm, and, as he said, "Even if those who are in error are proved wrong, it is probable that vexation and irritation combine to harden their hearts, whereas in private intercourse there is no wound inflicted on self-love, and the truth gains a far greater empire over those we wish to convince."

These private interviews were not without their wearisome, sometimes their ludicrous side, and with his ready sense of humour, Francis was quick to seize the latter. One respectable old lady had paid him a multiplicity of visits, returning two or three times in the same day, and during the course of her lengthy interviews, the same difficulties were always poured out, with a most diffuse and endless torrent of talk. The Provost was invariably kind and courteous; he let the good lady go on as she pleased with her confused repetitions, giving her patient and clear replies, till at last all her doubts and perplexities seemed cleared away, and she could find nothing to argue about, save the celibacy of the clergy, which she denounced as an abominable yoke, too heavy to be borne. "Allow me to suggest, madame," the Provost observed, with a half-repressed smile, "that if the clergy were engrossed by family cares, they would have less time, than is now the case, at the disposal of those who seek their aid. For instance," he could not forbear adding, "were I a family man, occupied with household cares, I might scarcely have had time to receive all the visits with which you, madame, have been good enough to honour me."

By degrees one leading person after another returned to the Church. The Baron d'Avully, Pierre Poncet, a well known advocate, and others, whose example had great weight among the people less able to argue and think for themselves. Bishop Granier did not cease to rejoice that he had sent so worthy a representative into Chablais, and even M. de Boisy began to be more reconciled to his son's enterprise. His paternal pride was gratified by a summons from the reigning Duke of Savoy, calling the Provost to Turin, with a view to discussing how best to promote the welfare of Chablais and the surrounding country, a summons in obeying which Francis de Sales nearly lost his life, for in crossing the Great S. Bernard with his faithful servant George Rolland, late in November of this year (1596) they were overtaken by a tremendous storm of snow and wind, and with difficulty reached the hospitable monastery, and its sorely-needed shelter. However, the journey ended prosperously, and at Turin, Francis was most graciously received by the Duke, who went at great length into the question of how best to promote the cause of true religion in Chablais with him. The Provost was unwilling to be absent from his work longer than necessary, and, crossing the Little S. Bernard, returned to Thonon, to make ready the church of S. Hippolyte, in which he hoped to celebrate Midnight Mass, on the coming Christmas festival. The first day on which the workmen gathered at this church, certain bigots stirred up a commotion, and tried by force to hinder the works

There was every prospect of a serious conflict, when Francis de Sales arrived, and with his usual calm dignity, addressed the irritated mob, and before long succeeded in quieting their angry passions. In spite of opposition, he carried out his intentions; the church was made as decent as time and funds admitted, and on Christmas Eve, the Blessed Sacrifice, which had been unknown there for sixty years, was once more offered, followed by the Dawn of day Mass, and High Mass, at which nearly 800 people were assembled. Henceforward, the services of the Church were regularly ministered in Saint Hippolyte, and a great step gained. Day by day more persons were gathered from the outer darkness of Protestantism, and Francis had great reason to thank God for His signal blessing on the work. Naturally such success stirred up the wrath of those who fought on the devil's side; and the Provost met with many a trial yet. Thus a certain number of people chose, first to mock at the ceremony of giving ashes, as observed on the first day of Lent, and, going on to violence, they ended by waylaying the Mission Priest a few days later as he went to preach, intending to seize and maltreat him. Francis escaped from their hands, and showed his confidence in his cause, by taking no steps whatever to protect himself from their assaults, daily celebrating and preaching at Saint Hippolyte, and on Sundays catechizing, and holding classes for both children and elder people. Among other persons who were converted at this time by Francis, Pierre Fournier, Syndic of Thonon, was conspicuous, and his example had great weight with many. It was at this time that the Provost entered upon a controversy with Theodore Beza, which, though unattended by any visible results, is believed, by some historians, to have very considerably shaken that reformer's confidence in his own cause, as it certainly confirmed others in the true faith.

A much larger ecclesiastical staff became necessary under the rapidly increasing labours of the Mission, and Bishop Granier was delighted to send willing workers to assist the Provost, who, however, continued to be the head and mainstay of all that was done; his gentleness and humility contributing doubtless more than his labour, or talent, to his success. Some touching anecdotes are recorded in illustration of this. On one occasion Francis had been preaching from the passage, "If any smite you on the cheek, turn to him the other also," and on leaving the church, a Calvinist came up to him with an insolent gesture, asking in a loud voice whether he would practise his own doctrine, were the blow to be at this moment offered, adding in a scornful tone, "Meseems, you will be of those who say and do not!"

"Friend," was the quiet answer, "I know well enough

what I ought to do, but I know not what I might do, for I am weak and frail; nevertheless, I trust in God, Who can make the frailest reed to be as a strong pillar. But if I were not to endure such an insult as a Christian should, do you bear in mind that the Gospel which you cite, also bids you 'observe and do' what the preacher teaches, but it takes away any excuse for your evil doings by warning you not to do after his works." "Our Saviour did not offer His other cheek to the soldiers who struck Him," the man answered, evading the rebuke. "Then you count Him among those who say, and do not?" replied the Provost. "Say rather that He gave His whole Body to them that smote Him." The Calvinist left Francis, softened and subdued, but his own friends remonstrated with him for his indulgence, urging a sharper and, as they thought, a more dignified treatment of such persons; but nothing could alter the Provost's steadfast resolution to meet all opposition with gentleness. "I never let myself have recourse to invective, or sharp rebuke, without regretting it," he said frequently; "and if God has blessed my labours among those in error, it has been through gentle treatment. Love and affection have more power over souls, be sure, not only than harshness and severity, but than the best and most logical reasoning. Let us never forget the Gracious Gentleness of our Master in dealing with sinners." How closely Francis de Sales studied this great example, his whole life showed. "His gentleness," says the Bishop of Belley, "was inconceivable to those who had not seen it. One might almost say that he was meekness itself, rather than a man gifted with that grace, and this gave him such ascendancy over other men, that everyone yielded to him, while he, on his part, sought to give up everything to others, desiring nothing, save to see them serving God, and saving their souls."[1] He was wont to say to the Bishop, "It is so much easier to adapt ourselves to others, than to seek to bend them to our opinions and wills. The human mind is like a mirror, and easily reflects the images cast upon it. We ought, in all things, to 'bring our gifts before the Altar,' not beyond that, inasmuch as we must not offend God; nor do I mean but that we must rebuke the sinner, only charity requires us to wait for the season in which he is best prepared to receive the remedy we would apply to him. Noisy, immoderate zeal does more harm than good; some people spoil everything by attempting too much; remember the old proverb, 'Chi va piano, va sano.'" S. Francis originated a proverb of his own, "Blessed are the hearts that bend, for they shall never break."[2]

[1] *Esprit*, xiv. 7.
[2] "Bienheureux sont les cœurs pliables, car ils ne rompront jamais."

So little, however, were all his friends able to appreciate this during the days of the Chablais Mission, that some of his colleagues went so far as to represent to Bishop Granier, that the Provost hindered its success by his excessive indulgence towards the Protestants around. As might be supposed, Claude de Granier knew Francis too well to credit such assertions, and contented himself with inculcating unity and mutual love among all who sought to advance the cause of Christ, as the most hopeful way of convincing such as were without of its truth.

CHAPTER IV.

FRANCIS DE SALES APPOINTED COADJUTOR OF GENEVA.—
JOURNEY TO ROME. 1599. — EXAMINATION BY POPE
CLEMENT VIII.—DEATH OF FRANCIS'S FATHER. 1601.—
JOURNEY TO PARIS. 1602.—DEATH OF BISHOP DE GRANIER.
—FRANCIS SUCCEEDS TO THE DIOCESE OF GENEVA. 1603.
—RULE OF THE EPISCOPAL HOUSEHOLD.

THE Chablais Mission might now be considered as successfully established, and a visit from the Duke of Savoy in 1598, accompanied by the Cardinal Legate de Medici, contributed to restore that sorely distraught district to a happier condition, religiously and politically, than it had experienced for many years. The Duke presented Francis de Sales to the Cardinal as the Apostle of the Chablais, he who had really done all the work, and deserved all the credit, of that Mission ; a tribute from which, however deserved, the Provost shrank sensitively. But his humility was about to be put to a severer trial. Claude de Granier was growing old, and daily felt that while in truth his diocese made great progress in true religion, its demands became proportionally heavier, and that he meanwhile had less strength and vigour—mental or bodily—to support the continually increasing weight.

He therefore determined to seek the aid of a coadjutor, and, fully alive to the importance of such an appointment, he spent much time in prayer for right guidance.

The Abbé de Chissé, his nephew, who was already Vicar General, seemed a suitable person for the office, being remarkable for his piety, as well as for his ability and learning, and there was much to lead the Bishop to select his nearest and dearest relation, and the stay of his declining years. But, as he said, his object was to appoint not merely a good man, but the best, and this he decided, and the Abbé de Chissé himself cordially agreed, was Francis de Sales. The Bishop mentioned the subject to the Provost, who however utterly put it aside, and could not be induced to entertain it; but as he was the only person consulted who did not take the same view as the Bishop, the latter communicated with the Duke, who replied that he had already contemplated Francis de Sales as successor to the See, whenever it might please God to take the venerable Claude de Granier to his rest, and therewith he sent his letters patent, to be used when the Bishop saw fit.

It was a subject of ceaseless thought and prayer to that pious man; and one night being greatly disturbed by a dream, in which he saw a flock he was keeping torn to pieces and devoured by some hungry wolves, he cried out for help so loudly, that his chaplain, who occupied the room over the Bishop's, heard him, and hastened to see what was the matter. Rousing himself, though yet shuddering, the Bishop told his dream, adding piteously that his waking thoughts did but coincide too well therewith, and that he felt himself too old and helpless to guard the flock committed to his charge. Seeking to soothe the venerable man, his chaplain enumerated the many causes he had for thankfulness in the diocese, and mentioning the name of Francis de Sales, who was to be his coadjutor and successor, the Bishop burst into tears, exclaiming, "Would to Heaven that it were so, but will he yield? Oh, my son, my son, have pity on these white hairs!"

The next morning the Bishop sent to the Chateau de Sales, where Francis was spending a few days with his parents, to summon him, and, embracing him on his entrance, conjured him, by every claim of religion and friendship, to come now to his aid. "Willingly," was the reply, "but what is it?" "Consent to become my coadjutor," the Bishop answered. The Provost remained silent for a few moments, but then he refused steadily as before, saying, "Monseigneur, I would not reject any toil, but in truth your kindness to me blinds you. I have no qualification for such dignity. You have many priests in your diocese who are infinitely more capable, more enlightened, holier, in every way fitter to bear this burden; I pray you to excuse me." And he took his leave of the Bishop, steadily persisting in this refusal. This time however Claude de Granier was determined not to be refused. He went to the Chateau de Sales, where M. and Madame de Boisy and all their family joined their entreaties to his; he brought to bear the influence of the Chapter, and of all such eminent persons around, whether lay or ecclesiastical, as seemed likely to have weight with the Provost. "This is cruel," Francis said; "you would lade me with golden chains, but chains they will be nevertheless; you wish to expose me to the peril of greatness, but indeed I have not sufficient humility for such a trial, you do not know the vanity of my inmost heart."

At this period a misunderstanding arose between the Duke of Savoy and the King of France, as to whether the town of Geneva was included in the treaty of peace of Vervins, or not, and it was proposed to send the Provost de Sales to Rome, in order that he might solicit the Pope's friendly interference in a matter which so closely affected the welfare of Savoy. But Claude de Granier was unwilling to allow Francis to depart on this mission without having first obtained his consent to become Coadjutor of Geneva. As a last and supreme effort, he therefore sent Pierre

Critain, his chaplain, to the Chateau de Sales, bearing both the letters patent, and a letter from Cardinal de Medici urging the appointment, and further instructing his ambassador to impress forcibly upon the Provost that his conscience ought to forbid any further refusals, and that if he continued to resist the will of his superiors, it would become resistance to the Will of God. The Abbé Critain said nothing concerning his errand on the evening of his arrival, but the next morning, having proposed to Francis that they should go and say their office together in the castle porch, after this was done, he put the matter plainly and strongly before his brother priest, and some few words of discussion having passed between them, the Abbé asked point blank, what further indications of God's Will he could expect? Francis knew not what to reply, but with a heavy sigh he turned away, and for some time walked up and down the terrace, his arms crossed upon his breast, in deep thought. At length he turned to his friend, but it was only to say, "Let us go to Thorens church, and let us each say a Mass, invoking the aid of the Holy Spirit, and then obey His dictates." Thither accordingly the two priests went; the Abbé Critain first said Mass, Francis serving him; and then in his turn he served the Provost, after which Francis knelt for long before the Altar, motionless, wrapt, his face beaming (so the Abbé Critain said), as one in very close communion with God. In truth he was laying his whole heart and its every thought and longing before his Lord, asking with that holy violence, which takes Heaven by storm, to be guided in this most weighty decision; offering up his personal desire to serve God without the responsibilities of a Chief Pastor's office, if such were His Will, and pledging himself that everything, honour, successes, be they what they might, should be but as so many steps, whereby he would come nearer his Lord. The Abbé Critain watched in reverent admiration and wonder. After a while Francis rose, and they left the church together. The chaplain ventured to inquire what answer God had vouchsafed to such fervent prayer? "Say to the Bishop," Francis answered, "that I have always dreaded the Episcopate, but that since he continues to require it of me, I am ready to obey; and if ever I do any good therein, it will be by virtue of his prayers; but I entreat you to say nothing of what has passed." The Abbé told M. and Madame de Boisy and the Canon de Sales of his successful errand, and hastened back to Annecy, where finding Bishop Granier, surrounded by a large company of friends, he could not resist telling his good news in a whisper. But the Bishop, rising up with tears of joy in his eyes, exclaimed out loud, "Hitherto I have done little

enough for my diocese, but now I have indeed done a great work, for I have secured my dear son, Francis de Sales, as my coadjutor and successor."

Possibly the strain of mind attending on this decision was the cause, but anyhow Francis became so seriously ill immediately after it was made, as to oblige him to postpone his intended journey to Rome. His mother hastened to Annecy to nurse him, and her maternal joy in Francis's recent decision was sadly quenched on being told by the physicians that there was little hope of recovery from the fever which had attacked him. Madame de Boisy herself told her son of his danger, and, reproaching himself with a want of sufficiently deep and real contrition, he at once began to recall every slightest sin of omission and commission, crying out partly in the words of Job and David; "I will speak in the bitterness of my soul. Do not Thou condemn me. Have mercy upon me, O Lord, before I go whence I shall not return, even to the land of darkness and the shadow of death. My sins are ever before me, and by reason of my impenitence the fear of death oppresseth me. Lord, be pitiful, for how grievously have I sinned, all my life long! When Thou comest to judge the earth, whither shall I hide myself from Thee? Truly fear hath seized me, and shame hath covered my face!" Often, too, he repeated King Hezekiah's words, "Mine eyes fail with looking up; O Lord, I am oppressed, undertake for me."

While Francis was thus pouring out his soul before God in sorrow at his own want of contrition, those who stood around were filled with silent wonder and admiration at the depth of heartfelt penitence which all who knew him felt was not called for by his outer life, so singular in its holiness and purity; though well knowing that in God's Sight there is none whom penitence does not well befit, no soul that may venture boldly into that Presence Which

"Will gladden thee, but it will pierce thee too."

And as they stood by, they saw the anguish of penitence, the sorrow of deep contrition, pass by, and all the fulness of perfect love pour over and satiate that longing, waiting, trusting soul, which, having laid its burden in simple confidence at the foot of the Cross, now waited in like resting love for the issues of life or death. He had no choice. "The Lord's tender Mercy will keep me, whether I go to Him now or later," he said; "and longer life will but add to my need of mercy. All the ways of the Lord are mercy and truth. I will trust in God, Who is the help of my countenance and my God."¹ Although probably

¹ Some one present lamented that he should die thus in the flower of his age. "Our dear Lord was younger than I," Francis answered. "Our time is in His Hand; He knows the

Francis was the youngest among the Chapter, all its members and many clergy sought to be admitted to his sick room, not merely to take leave of him, but to ask some special word of counsel and guidance, to pour out some private grief or perplexity; and, in spite of his humility, the Provost, who believed himself so nearly closing his earthly career, did not hesitate to give such spiritual warnings and consolations as he knew to be needed. All desired his blessing, and, exhausted by so much mental strain, Francis fell into a swoon which lasted so long that those who were tending him feared lest he should pass away without recovering consciousness. Yet all the time, his intellectual faculties were keenly alive, and, curiously enough, they were wholly absorbed by a speculative difficulty concerning the Blessed Sacrament, which was raised up in his mind during that period of seeming unconsciousness, and which beset him during the weakness of convalescence, so that oftentimes he could only banish it by invoking the Holy Name, with the sign of the Cross. What the special temptation was he

---

fittest season in which to gather the fruit." And a little later he said in reply to some remark, "Do not let us dwell so much upon trifling circumstances. Let us think of nothing save His Holy Will; that is our guiding star, and it will lead us to Jesus Christ, whether in the manger or on Calvary. 'He that believeth on Me shall not come into condemnation, but is passed from death unto life.'"

never told anyone save his brother Louis, believing that to suggest doubts and difficulties, even when counterbalanced by their solution, is often but one way of doing the devil's work. More hope was entertained when Francis rallied from this swoon. Meanwhile, he lay tranquil, asking the Cathedral choir (who had come to inquire after him) to chant the Psalm "Quemadmodum" ("Like as the hart desireth the water-brooks," xlii.), and having listened with tears in his eyes, he turned to the wall, and repeated the Miserere aloud. A little while after, he saw the physician preparing some remedy, and asked what he was doing? The doctor answered in sacred words, "Quod ego facio tu nescis modo, scies autem postea;"[1] whereupon his patient kindly but severely rebuked his seemingly irreverent use of Holy Scripture.

The remedy was one highly esteemed in those days, "or potable,"—a sort of gum made from gold melted in spirits of wine, and mixed with sixteen other carefully prepared liquids. Whether this was the immediate cause of cure or not, may be doubtful, but certainly the sick man began to amend, and by February he was able to go, as originally settled, to Rome. The Abbé de Chissé went with Francis, commissioned by his uncle, Bishop de Granier, to obtain

[1] "What I do thou knowest not now, but thou shalt know hereafter."

the Pope's sanction to the proposed appointment. They went by Turin and Modena, and in Rome they joined Louis de Sales and the Senator Favre, all four taking up their abode in a hotel near San Salvadore in Lauro. The latter records with what enthusiasm and delight his friend visited S. Peter's, and the other hallowed sites so dear to all Christendom. He found Francis once in the catacombs, so entirely absorbed in devotion, and with such streams of tears flowing down his upraised face, that the impression of sorrowful tidings having reached him, led the Senator to disturb his companion, and inquire if it were so. "In truth, no," Francis answered, "but who could find himself thus surrounded with the graves of martyrs who have been privileged to shed their blood for Christ, and not weep over his own unworthiness? Blessed martyrs! enviable lot of which I, a poor weak sinner, am utterly unworthy! What can I do but bow down and weep?" The Apostle of Chablais, as he was called by the Duke of Savoy, was presented to Pope Clement VIII. by the Cardinal de Medici, and transacted the business on which he had been sent. The Abbé de Chissé discreetly reserved his special mission, concerning the Coadjutorship of Geneva, for a separate interview, in which His Holiness expressed himself willing to accept Bishop de Granier's choice, and, having summoned Francis de Sales, bade him prepare to undergo an examination in the Pontifical presence on the following Monday, March 22. It is a characteristic trait, that Francis, with all his reverence for the Holy See, and his freedom from any personal pride, yet was prepared to resist this requisition as an infringement upon the rights of his national church; and accordingly he went to the Ambassador of Savoy, who forthwith represented the case to Clement VIII. The Holy Father granted their claim, and promised that this should not be treated as a precedent, but urged that, having heard so much of the Provost de Sales and his remarkable ability, he wished to judge of it himself, together with the College of Cardinals. Put in this light, the order could not be set aside, and the Ambassador told Francis that he must prepare himself for the ordeal. There was, however, no time for ordinary preparation; some hours of meditation before the crucifix, a night spent in prayer, and the Holy Eucharist offered with special intention—it was thus that Francis de Sales made ready. On his way to the Vatican he entered a church—San Giacomo in Borgo—where he asked of God that if in His All-seeing Wisdom it was known that His servant would be unworthy of the episcopal office—unequal to the solemn trust of souls it involved—he might fail in the coming examination, and, at any cost to his own pride, might be rejected.

The court before which de Sales appeared was no mean assembly. Among the cardinals were Federigo Borromeo, of saintly memory, Baronius, Borghese, Medici, and, though not yet raised to the purple, the future Cardinal Bellarmino also assisted. Archbishops, Bishops, Generals of Religious Orders, and a crowd of men not less intellectually eminent, if less exalted in ecclesiastical rank, sat around, and so imposing was the conclave that a Spanish priest of notable piety and learning who was to come before it with Francis de Sales was altogether overpowered, and had to be carried forth in a fainting fit. Francis de Sales as usual was serene and self-possessed, filled with but one thought—the Glory of God. According to the wonted routine, he knelt down before the assembly, and was asked what sciences he had studied. To this he made answer that he had studied civil law, canonical law, and theology. He was next asked in which science he chose to be examined, a matter which he referred to the Pope; but on being told to choose for himself, he selected theology, as the science specially appertaining to his profession. Then Pope Clement and the other learned assessors put no less than thirty-five questions, more or less abstruse, raising the most subtle objections they could suggest to the Provost's answers. Only two of these questions are recorded; of these, one proposed by Bellarmino, concerned "the formal cause of beatitude of the Saints,"—a question much controverted among theologians—for, while all agree that it consists in the possession of God, there is a great variety of opinion as to the manner by which such beatitude is communicated to the soul. This, which is technically called formal beatitude,[1] may consist, so says the one party, in a clear insight of the Divine Essence, or, according to another view, in the will, *i.e.* love of the soul's Sovereign Good, and joy in possessing it; while others again find it in the understanding and will united. Francis de Sales, adopting this latter view, answered that the beatitude of the elect consists in love of that Sovereign Good which is at length beheld, and in the sight of the Sovereign Being Who is loved,[2] a sentiment one could venture to anticipate from the future author of the "Traité de l'Amour de Dieu."

At the end of this examination Pope Clement, turning to the Cardinals, expressed his supreme content,[3] and, rising from his throne, he went to Francis, and embracing him quoted the words of Solomon: "Drink waters out of thine own cistern, and running waters out of thine own well; let thy

[1] Or constituting cause.
[2] Vie, Curé de Saint Sulpice, i. p. 35-9.
[3] "Non abbiamo avuto cotanta soddisfazione da qualumque abbiamo esaminato."

fountains be dispersed abroad, and rivers of waters in the streets" (Prov. v., 15, 16).[1]

Francis himself regarded with his natural simple humility these fresh proofs of distinction. Writing to his cousin, the Canon Louis de Sales, on March 26, 1599, he says, "I must tell you that it has pleased God not to confound me utterly in this examination, though of myself I could expect nothing else. In truth the Grand Vicar (M. de Chissé) left the consistory more elate than I; and I know that that affectionate friend will be but too eager to publish in Savoy the marks of paternal kindness with which the Pope has honoured me, and which ought to make me a more faithful son of the Church than ever. But whatever you may hear, remember that one's friends are quite as apt to exaggerate one's good as one's enemies that which is evil, and that after all we are in truth neither more or less than that which God knows us to be." There was some strain upon a man's humility, for all Rome contended for the honour of seeking out the Savoyard Provost who combined such rare gifts of personal attractiveness, learning, and holiness. Among the many eminent men who sought him, Francis contracted a lasting friendship with

[1] Vulgate: "Bibe, fili mi, aquam de cisterna tua et fluenta putei tui; deriventur fontes tui foras, et in plateis aquas tuas divide."

Cardinal Borghese, afterwards Pope Paul V.; with Cardinal Baronius, who presented him with the current volume of his celebrated *Annales;* and with Padre Ancina, afterwards Bishop of Saluces, now a venerable priest of S. Philip Neri's Oratory, who had assisted at Francis's examination, and who, on visiting him afterwards, could not forbear exclaiming, "Oh how tenfold I rejoice more now to see you so truly humble than I rejoiced that day to see you so truly learned."

The object of Francis's visit to Rome was achieved; the Holy Father gave him the Apostolic briefs for Chablais which were needed, and signed that which confirmed his appointment as Coadjutor of Geneva, with the title of Bishop of Nicopolis; so having said a last mass in S. Peter's, and received the Pope's parting Benediction, he and the Abbé de Chissé left Rome on the last day of March. So little eager was Francis concerning his episcopal dignities, that he never troubled himself to get the official documents necessary for his consecration, still less to leave the money wanted to pay for them. When he was reproached with this neglect, he answered smiling, "I left no money for the best possible reason; I had none to leave!"

The travellers went by Loretto, Bologna, and Milan to Turin, where Francis was delayed for some time by the Duke of Savoy on business, and by the time he reached Annecy the general enthusiasm had reached a great height, and his entry was a sort of triumph. The venerable Claude de Granier especially rejoiced in this fulfilment of his hopes; but it was in vain that he urged his Coadjutor either to accept half the revenues of the See, or to be consecrated at once. Francis declared that he would remain a humble priest as long as it was possible, and that he would share no part of the episcopal dignity save its labours and cares. Of the latter he had his full share. Claude de Granier would do nothing without him, and to every question that arose he returned the same answer, "You must consult my son." Among the good works of this period of his career was the Sainte Maison, which Francis de Sales founded at Thonon, a sort of university and religious house intended to serve as a centre for the church work and life of the country round. The Sainte Maison was chiefly modelled upon the rules of S. Philip Neri's Oratory. It was to be ruled by a prefect and seven secular priests, who were to supply the parochial needs of Thonon, and educate the seven choir boys, who, it was hoped, would be the beginning of a Seminary. To these priests were added a certain number of Capucin Fathers, whose mission was to preach in the surrounding country, as well as masters for an intended college for public instruction; while a fourth department was provided for the reception of persons desirous of religious instruction, who might also be taught ordinary handicrafts, whereby to maintain themselves. The rules, drawn up by Francis de Sales, provided for the due and reverent administration of the Sacraments and public offices of the Church, as well as for the charge of sick, poor and ignorant, and special care was taken that the priests so engaged should have appointed times for study, and conference upon the duties of their work. Local work pressed heavily, when, as Lent came on, the Coadjutor obeyed Bishop de Granier's summons to preach during that season of penitence at Annecy. Just as he was leaving Thonon, a messenger arrived to inform Francis that his father, now seventy-nine years of age, was dangerously ill, and without delay he hastened to the Chateau de Sales. M. de Boisy was indeed dying, and his greatest comfort was in the thought of being guided and helped by his dearly loved son, to the shore of that dark river where even the tenderest love of natural or spiritual bond must leave the departing soul to Him Who has promised for that moment, as for every other of trial, " I will never leave thee, nor forsake thee."

The aged father made his general confession, and received the Blessed Sacrament three times from his son's hand, listening with childlike earnestness and simplicity to the teaching, which now, in his last hours, he sought from his own child. Fain would they not have parted for the few short hours remaining, but Francis never allowed any claim, however dear, to come between him and his duty to God, and he prepared to leave for Annecy, to preach as appointed. The doctors thought that M. de Boisy's illness was likely to be yet somewhat lingering, and that he might last till Easter; so the father and son separated with a hope possibly yet to meet in this world; but before Francis's departure, he gave his blessing as a Priest to the venerable father who, with an overflowing heart, in return blessed his son with a parent's richest blessing. It is touching to hear how a few days later, his symptoms being worse, the old soldier spirit was kindled to impatience at the sight of his family weeping round his bed, and calling one of his sons, Gallois de Sales, the old man intreated him to "send away all these foolish women, and help him to get up and put on his armour, for it ill beseemed a soldier who had trod the battle-field to die thus, in his bed, surrounded by distracted women!" But the burst of irritation was soon soothed, and, clasping his crucifix, he put away all earthly thoughts and wishes, and having once more bidden all his children comfort their mother and look to their eldest brother as their guide, he blessed them and passed gently to his rest, April 4, 1601.

The messenger who carried these tidings to the

Coadjutor, reached the Cathedral at Annecy just as Francis was quitting the sacristy for the pulpit, and had not discretion to delay the announcement until after the sermon. Francis was deeply moved, but he would not fail in his duty, and, clasping his hands with one upward look of submission to God's Will, he proceeded to preach as usual, without giving way to any of the tender thoughts and memories which swept through his soul. His prepared subject was the death and resurrection of Lazarus, and at the end of a singularly vigorous earnest sermon, he told his listeners in few words that one well known to most of them, to whom he owed everything, had passed away, asking their prayers for the repose of his father's soul. At this point his self-command broke down, and the grief, so steadily repressed at duty's call, had its way. Francis burst into tears, and the whole congregation, deeply touched, remained some time kneeling in reverent devotion.

The Coadjutor went as soon as possible to the Chateau de Sales, accompanied by some of the Annecy Dominicans, who by ancient custom always assisted at the burial of the Seigneurs de Sales, and the last sacred offices of the Church were rendered to his father. The next day Francis confessed and communicated the whole family, and after saying some earnest words to them concerning the duty of fulfil-

ling necessary duties in the spirit of holiness, he returned to complete his Lenten work at Annecy, where the success of his labours was very notable ; and that after the fashion which he himself held to be the true test of preaching, for sinners were led from their evil ways, enemies reconciled, and wrongs repaired. The Senateur Favre says that as he preached, he often saw Francis's face, like that of S. Stephen, "as it had been the face of an angel;" and particularly on one Sunday after Easter, it seemed to him and to many others, that as the Coadjutor was pouring out his fervent words upon the Love of God, the only and overwhelming motive and cause of all good, they could perceive a halo of bright light playing around his animated features.

Francis's pastoral labours were interrupted early in 1602, when Bishop de Granier sent him to Paris to plead the cause of the Diocese of Geneva with Henri IV. ; various political difficulties interfering with the peaceful religious state of that country, as desired by its spiritual rulers. On the 22nd January accordingly the Coadjutor arrived in Paris, and immediately entered upon negotiations with the King and his minister Villeroi. Like most such matters, the business advanced slowly, and all manner of vexatious hindrances arose, so that Francis was detained at Paris until the following autumn. It was not time wasted however. Soon after his arrival, he undertook, at the request of the Duchesse de Longueville, to preach the Lenten course of the Chapel Royal, and it speedily proved too small to accommodate the noble and learned crowd that flocked to hear him—princes of the blood, Sorbonne Doctors, all that was most illustrious in Paris. There was in truth no pandering to fashionable faults and follies in his dealings with the new kind of congregation to whom his Master sent him; his habitual rule was not to deal in generalities, but to press some definite point of doctrine or practice home to his listeners' conscience. "One should aim at building up some special corner in the wall of Jerusalem;" he was wont to say. On one occasion he rebuked the Bishop of Belley for having preached smooth things to a religious community, saying that it was no use merely to give people soft cushions to lean their elbows on, milk instead of bitters; and when the Bishop sought to justify himself by saying that these religious were so pure and holy, the reply was: "If they are standing upright, it is your business to teach them not to fall, to watch against falling from grace, to work out their salvation in fear and trembling."[1]

It was in this spirit that M. de Genève (as he was habitually called, though not as yet consecrated)

[1] *Esprit.*

addressed his fine-world Paris congregation upon the emptiness of this life's pleasures, the delusions of self-love and earthly wisdom, and the inevitable certainty of a judgment to come. He studiously avoided all controversy (with which Paris was naturally rife, owing to political circumstances, and the King's conversion to Catholicism), but several persons of high worldly position were converted, especially by one sermon on the Day of Judgment. "There was not a word in it levelled against heresy," Francis de Sales said himself, "but nevertheless it was antagonistic to heresy by God's Grace, and ever since I have always said that whoever preaches with warm love is really doing enough to root out heresy, without a single controversial word."[1] So many persons sought him out, and were won to repentance and to the Faith by his teaching, that Cardinal du Perron used to say, "God has certainly given M. de Genève the key of hearts: if you only want to convince men, bring them to me by all means, and I will undertake the task; but if you want to convert them, take them to M. de Genève!" "M. de Genève has done me a great deal of good," one eminent statesman remarked, "but he has also done me one evil turn which will not easily be cured —he has disgusted me with all other preachers!" And Henri IV. used to call him "the phœnix of

[1] *Esprit.*

prelates," adding that whereas most men had some weak point—the lack of learning, or piety, or noble birth—M. de Genève had none, adding that were he not already a Catholic, assuredly his conversion would have been effected now. According to the custom of the time, a purse well filled with gold was sent after Easter by the Duchesse de Longueville to Francis, in acknowledgment of his services, and great was the astonishment and edification of the Paris world at his utterly refusing to receive any sort of temporal recompense for his labour.

Among other works performed during this stay in Paris, Francis de Sales delivered the funeral oration of Philippe Emanuel of Lorraine, Duc de Mercœur, who, after fighting successfully against the Turks, died on his way home of fever at Nuremberg. Personally attached to Francis, the widowed Duchess asked his good offices on this occasion, and he would not refuse, though the matter was one of delicacy, the Duke having been an active member of the League, and among the last to come to terms with Henri IV. However Francis set aside the whole question of politics, and treated the subject without human respect, as one calculated to serve the living more than exalt the dead.[1] All that was most distinguished in Paris formed his audience. All his

[1] It was in this oration that Francis de Sales used the striking

time was taken up with preaching and other spiritual works, so that he had scarcely what was necessary for refreshment and sleep. One day just as he was going to preach at Saint Benoit, a friend came in the greatest excitement to announce that the Maréchal de Biron, the Baron de Luz, and others had been arrested as being concerned in a conspiracy with the King of Spain and the Duke of Savoy against Henri IV. Francis de Sales as an intimate friend of de Luz was also denounced as being concerned in it, and his mission to Paris on church matters was supposed to be merely a cloak for these political purposes. He listened to the narration, and then quietly entered the pulpit and preached with all his usual thoughtful energy. His friend remained through the sermon, and when it was over, expressed unbounded amazement at Francis's composure. "You are accused of high treason, and yet you go on in utter indifference!" he exclaimed. "I should be troubled if I were guilty," Francis answered, "and I should no doubt fly if my conscience accused me, but, being innocent, I put my trust in God, and I shall without hesitation go straight to the King. If my good repute is of any importance to the cause of religion, God will take care of it,

phrase, speaking of the Duke's end, "Not knowing when death awaited him, he had learnt himself always to await death."

and, if not, what then does such a thing matter?" Accordingly he went to Henri IV., who was at the Louvre, and was most graciously received. "M. de Genève," the King said, "you need not think of justifying yourself, I never had the slightest suspicion of you." "Sire," Francis replied, "I do not understand state affairs enough to dabble in them, but were it otherwise I should most assuredly not make so unworthy a return for all your Majesty's kindness to me."

Henri IV.'s personal liking for Francis de Sales was characteristically strong, and he did justice to the Coadjutor's straightforward uprightness. One day the king was discussing him with Cardinal du Perron, who remarked that he was tempted to throw away all his controversial books, and study only to imitate Francis de Sales' holiness and gentleness. Henri IV. added, "Yes, and what I like best in M. de Genève is that he does not know how to flatter!" His Majesty made many attempts to induce Francis to remain in France, offering him various honourable and lucrative posts, but the persistent answer was that "he had married a poor bride, and could not forsake her for one wealthier." A pension was pressed on him by the king, and unwilling to offend the monarch, Francis did not refuse it directly, but saying that he had no present need of money, he requested to be allowed to leave it in the royal treasury, for the good of the Church and poor. Henri IV. was much touched by the gracefulness of this virtual rejection of all self-interest. Francis took an active part in Madame Acarie's attempt to restore the Carmelite order in France, which was just set on foot; and other religious communities eagerly sought his assistance in their establishment or reformation. The wise discretion which ruled his conduct in such matters may be traced in a letter to the Abbess of Montmartre. "The door of access to real reformation is narrow, and hard to pass," he says, "and therefore I would beg you to lead your sisters through it gently, and one by one. I do not believe it possible to drive them hastily or collectively through. Some are naturally slower than others, the old are less pliable than the young—mentally as well as physically their nerves stiffen. What you chiefly require for so pious a work, is to be gentle, gracious, considerate, simple, and kindly; and it seems to me, that your age and natural character make this all the more necessary. Harshness does not beseem the young, and believe me that the best care of your spiritual family will be that which most closely resembles God's care for us—a tranquil, peaceful care, calm even in its utmost activity, yet condescending to all, and adapting itself to every most trivial want."

Fine ladies from the Court also sought M. de Genève's guidance; a race with which he would gladly have declined dealing, had it been right. "I do what I can," he said, "but often it is a long time before one can throw in a stray word to the purpose." One young lady who was a prey to pomp and vanity of every description, revelling in the admiration of all who surrounded her, came to Francis de Sales, touched to the heart by some of his uncompromising words of truth, and implored him to undertake her guidance. After some patient, careful dealings with her, he exclaimed, "I see plainly, *ma chère fille*, that you will never go straight on to God, you will always try to reach Him through the creature." Another lady of high birth came to consult him about a suddenly conceived desire to become a religious. "I would not throw one grain into the scale to make you a nun," Francis answered, "quite enough if we can make a good Christian of you!" Both these ladies, however, rewarded his labours in the end.

The months passed on, and the Coadjutor was anxious to get back to his diocese, the more so that the venerable Bishop de Granier became continually feebler. Although he made a great effort to take part in the Jubilee which was celebrated at Thonon, his strength failed when this was over, and having reached the Chateau de Polinge, the property of his nephew, M. de Chissé, the good old Bishop died after only two days' real illness, " without any trouble as to making his will," a biographer remarks, since only six sous were found in his possession, and the sale of his books and scanty furniture barely sufficed to pay the few necessary expenses. The tidings of Bishop de Granier's death reached his Coadjutor at Lyons. Deeply impressed with the weight of responsibility now cast upon him, Francis de Sales went to Annonay to consult Pierre de Villars, a venerable prelate, who, after many years of episcopal labour, had retired to spend his last days in study and prayer. Bishop de Villars had been wont to sum up a Bishop's duties by saying that " he ought to be found daily at the Altar, constantly in the pulpit, never in worldly society or places of public amusement." High as his standard was, when Francis de Sales left the Bishop, having made a general confession of his life, the aged man of God said that " his young brother's confession was enough to put himself to shame as long as he lived."

Francis then went to the Chateau de Sales, where he went into retreat for twenty days, under the direction of a Jesuit Father, Fourrier by name. " I am reviewing my whole soul," he wrote, " and feel from the bottom of my heart a fresh desire to serve God better in holiness and uprightness all the days of my life. I am forcibly impressed with the infinite debt of gratitude I owe Him; I am resolved to devote myself to His service with the most earnest faithfulness possible to me; ever striving to live in His blessed Presence with a calm but true spirit of rejoicing; remembering that nothing in this world is worthy of our love, which should all be centred on that Saviour Who so loved us. All earthly happiness seems to me as nothing compared with this love, for which I would thankfully die, or rather perhaps I should say, live wholly."

During this retreat, Francis de Sales drew up a rule for his own life, and that of his household, which sufficiently proves how he entered into the spirit of S. Paul's question, "If a man know not how to rule his own house, how shall he take care of the Church of God?" No detail is too trifling for his attention. He was never to wear costly raiment, any more than formerly, his rochet, camail, and square cap are to be his regular dress, nothing of silk about it save the girdle—no silk stockings or perfumed gloves.[1] The Episcopal household was not to exceed what was strictly necessary; there was to be no display, no pompous retinue. A chaplain, who would control the

---

[1] At the same time it is recorded that he held cleanliness and neatness of person in special regard, and denounced all slovenliness as a downright vice; nor could he endure to wear any clothes that were dirty, torn, or spotted, and he also liked all he wore to fit well.

household, and assist in saying the offices ; a secretary; two valets de chambre, one for the Bishop, the other to wait on the priests who frequented his house; a cook and his assistant; and a footman;—such was the establishment. The whole household was to be up early, daily to hear mass, every evening to join in prayer and self-examination with the Bishop, and after ten o'clock every one was to retire, and silence be kept. Every room was to have its desk for prayer, its holy water vessel, and some sacred picture. Two apartments only were to be carpeted ; one in which to receive strangers, the other for the transaction of business. Everyone who came to the house was to be received with civility and respect, and admitted without delay to the Bishop's presence. Dinner was to be at ten o'clock, supper at six in the evening; on fast days an hour later, and at those seasons the first meal was to be eaten standing. The episcopal table was to be frugal, but always seemly and well appointed. The priests frequenting it were to take their turn in saying the Benedicite and Thanksgiving, the Bishop himself only offering the prayer, " Benedic, Domine, nos et hæc tua dona quæ de tua largitate sumus sumpturi, per Christum Dominum nostrum ;" except on high festivals, when he was to say all the offices. Some work of piety was to be read during the first part of each meal-time; the rest of the time quiet conversation being permitted. The Bishop was habitually to take part in the services of the Cathedral and of the confraternities belonging thereto.

From such outer details, Francis de Sales proceeds to the regulation of his inner life. Every morning he was to make an hour's meditation, and inasmuch as he desired daily to acquire some fresh knowledge that would promote his usefulness as a Bishop, he allotted from seven to nine o'clock each morning to study, besides an hour devoted to spiritual reading after supper. Habitual remembrance of God's Presence, with pious aspirations and ejaculatory prayer, was nothing new to his way of life. At nine the Bishop would say mass, making a rule not to speak with anyone before that, at all events upon secular matters. His preparation in the sacristy was to be earnest but brief, his celebration solemn and devout as to the exterior, warm and earnest interiorly. When there was any special service in other churches, he would celebrate there, so that the faithful might realize their Bishop's interest in whatever good works might be concerned. He was to keep the Hours punctually, to choose the most helpful confessor available, and not to change him unnecessarily. His confessions were to be frequent, and often to be made in church, so as to set a good example. Fast days were to be carefully observed, and every year the Bishop was to enter into retreat for a week or ten days, reviewing the year past, and examining how far he had kept the resolutions made during his last retreat, taking counsel with his confessor as to his faults, and the hindrances raised by circumstances or natural infirmity towards his advance in spiritual things. The rules Francis de Sales drew up for the government of his diocese have unfortunately not been preserved. This rule when drawn up, was submitted to Père Fourrier, who approved and signed it, so as to give it the additional value of obedience, and the Bishop observed it faithfully, with the exception of minute details of time. In this respect he soon learnt from the press of business, his brother Louis tells us, that only those who are masters of their own time can follow a strict observance, and that, before all other rules, a Bishop must study that of charity. And Francis himself, in a letter to the Archbishop of Bourges, says, "It would doubtless be very desirable that all our episcopal households were conformed to a rule, but I know by experience that it is necessary to adapt oneself to the exigencies of time, place, and circumstance. I break my own rule without scruple when the wants of my flock require it, for charity must prevail over inclination. My object in framing this rule was not to hamper myself, but that I might regulate my life without involving my conscience in scruples. God has given me grace to love freedom of spirit, while I hate licence. It seems to me that we ought to be able to say with the great Bishop of Hippo, '*amor meus, pondus meum.*'"

It is touching to find Madame de Boisy, Francis's pious mother, making a retreat also with a view to her son's consecration, in the preparations for which in the parish church of Thorens she took an active part. It was like the man to choose, as he did, this quiet village church, in which he had been baptized, for his Episcopal Consecration. There, accordingly, he was consecrated, December 8, 1602, by Archbishop Gribaldi (formerly Archbishop of Vienne, then living in retirement at Evian, on Lake Geneva), assisted by Bishop Pobel, of Saint-Paul-Trois-Chateaux, and Maistret, Bishop of Damascus, who was living at Aix. During the consecration, Francis de Sales was at one time so absorbed by the interior grace bestowed upon him, as to become unconscious of all else, realizing ineffably the work of the Holy Spirit within him, and devoting himself even more wholly than before, to God's service and the salvation of souls. "God took me from myself," he said later to Madame de Chantal, in speaking of this season, "making me His own! giving me to His flock, that I might henceforth live for Him and them only."

On the 14th December (having devoted the intermediate days to retreat), the Bishop was installed at Annecy, where the whole town joined the procession, and conducted their new pastor to the Cathedral, where he knelt before the Blessed Sacrament, kissed the Altar, and, after the Te Deum had been sung, gave his Episcopal Benediction for the first time to his flock. It was the beginning of a tie close and fervent, which did but grow warmer and stronger to the end; his whole affections, his time, his strength, every faculty of mind and body, were devoted to the "poor bride" he had espoused, and through her to God. Francis de Sales looked upon the Episcopate as a high honour in one side,—*i.e.*, the spiritual, but all that concerned temporal or personal dignity he steadily rejected, saying that a Bishop was the servant of the Church, and least and lowest among those who served her. "The yoke would be too heavy to bear," he said, "unless our Lord bore the weightiest part; in very truth He bears both us and our yoke." He was wont to observe how many Bishops were to be found among the saints, adding that no condition afforded more abundant means towards sanctification and perfection. Nevertheless, as men look upon the office differently, his humility was watchful. "I ever desired the lowest place," he said once; "and I so greatly feared becoming a Bishop, because of the worldly side of the matter, that I was always glad to be in the company of some prelate of higher position to whom I might yield. In truth, had it been the Will of God, I would rather have been a humble priest carrying holy water and tending a few poor people, than wear the mitre and staff."

This humility was very genuine: Francis de Sales used to say that humility and chastity were virtues which would not endure being spoken of, lest their bloom should be swept away; and consequently, his words were few, his actions being the truer test. Nevertheless, there were occasions on which he could not refrain from giving utterance to his inner mind, as, for instance, when he answered some persons who were flattering him, "Gentlemen, Francis de Sales is a poor man who knows himself better than you know him. God knows what I am." And again, when he was told of the glowing encomiums passed upon him by a brother Bishop, he replied: "I should be grateful to that worthy lord if he would leave me alone: I know what I am; my conscience and my confessor are two witnesses against me who cannot be deceived." It was a habit too, when asked what he would do, or have done, under certain given circumstances, to answer, "I know what I ought to have done, but the question is, should I have done it?"

It was in accordance with this spirit of humility

that on becoming Bishop of Geneva, Francis positively refused to buy an episcopal palace, as he was urged to do. He persisted in having only a hired house, saying it was all needful for a follower of Jesus Who "had not where to lay His Head." He gave up almost all his private revenues, which were considerable, to his brothers, avowing that his "ambition was to die possessing nothing." This ambition was not hard to fulfil, for the revenues of his see were very trifling—scarcely £200 of English money. "The wisdom of this world says, 'Blessed are the rich,'" he writes, "but our Lord said, 'Blessed are the poor,' and in truth, the most blessed state in this life is to be content with what actually suffices us." Some of his friends lamented the poverty of his see: "How much had the apostles?" Francis asked; and he added, "My bishopric is worth as much to me as the Archbishopric of Toledo, for I shall win Heaven or hell through it just as the Archbishop will, according to the way we fulfil our charge. I consider myself quite as well off as any other Bishop, for I have enough for all I want. If one has more, there is more to think of, as well as more to spend. Of course where one has but little, one has little to give, little to think of, little to answer for. No one is really poor who has enough to live on."

We have seen the rule proposed for the Bishop's

household. This was carried out, with but trifling alteration. He gave up having a secretary, on the ground that to admit a third person between himself and his correspondents, was a check on complete confidence, and he preferred sitting up half the night answering letters, to risking any such hindrance to his flock. As might be expected, his correspondence was a large one; every day brought an accumulation of letters, often long and hard to decipher, but nothing was thrown aside, or neglected. A bystander remarked once that he really gave himself too much trouble. The Bishop looked up and smiled, then answered, " What does it matter? While I am about this, I am not obliged to do anything else!" Of the two priests who lived with him as chaplains, one took charge of his purse and all temporal arrangements, and the poor man had rather a hard task, for the Bishop was continually coming to him for money to give away. One day, in despair, the comptroller answered that there was no money left! "So much the better!" the Bishop replied; "we are but the more conformed to our Great Example." "But as a practical matter," the chaplain resumed, "how are we to get wherewithal to live?" "My son," the Bishop answered, "we must use our home resources." "It is all very well to talk of home resources, but there is nothing left!" "I mean that we must sell some of our furniture to buy food," the prelate said. "Surely that will be using our home resources!"

Sometimes Francis was able to conceal sums of money which came to hand unexpectedly, from his comptroller, a little piece of domestic treachery which he greatly delighted in, and would carry out with playful exultation. The grace of hospitality was strong within him, and on great occasions, when the Bishop thought it right and seemly to do honour to some expected guest, he would accept the loan of plate, tapestry, or whatever was wanted; but habitually nothing could be simpler than his whole entourage; he chose for his own sitting room the least attractive chamber in the house, which he used playfully to call "Francis's room," while the better one in which he received his guests, he called "the Bishop's room;" he would not use fine linen either for his bed or his table. The latter was simple, not only in accordance with his rule, but also with his purse, and although anxious that his guests should be fitly served, the Bishop himself took indifferently whatever was put before him, whether hot or cold, well or badly cooked. Nothing disturbed him more than to think that any of his poor clergy put themselves to extra expense when they had to entertain him, and he used expressly to request that no difference might be made for him. Bishop Camus says that Francis held it to be very ill bred to ask for some distant dish, instead of eating the first which came to hand, saying that to do so, betokened a mind set upon sauces and flavours! He used to say that one may be "greedy over cabbages, and ascetic over partridges; but to be indifferent alike to what is coarse or delicate, indicates a really mortified spirit; and to eat dainty food without caring for it, is less easy than to enjoy coarse food." "One day" (that most minute recorder of S. Francis's conversation tells us) "some poached eggs were served to him; he quoted Saint Bernard's saying that we torture this unfortunate comestible in a hundred ways, and then, having finished the eggs, he went on eating bread dipped in the water which had held the eggs. Those around smiled at this unusual sauce, and the Bishop inquired what amused them? On being told, he answered, 'Truly you should not have exposed so agreeable an error, for I assure you this is as good a sauce as any I ever ate; though perhaps my appetite may have something to do with it.'" Elsewhere the Bishop of Belley records: "One day I had helped him to some delicacy, when I remarked that he left it on one side of his plate, and ate something coarser. 'I have caught you,' said I; 'how does this accord with your favourite Gospel precept, Eat such things as are set before you?' He answered most gracefully: 'You don't know what a rustic, working man's digestion I have. I cannot do without strong, coarse food; your delicacies will not support me.' 'It is all very well, *mon père*,' I said, 'to try and impose upon me thus, and to conceal your austerities under such a veil.' 'I really meant no deceit,' he answered; 'I was speaking quite sincerely. In all truth I don't deny that I like delicate food better than that which is common and coarse, but as we eat in order to live, not to indulge our sensuality, I take what I know to be most suitable. I call it living to eat, if one's mind and attention are to be given to the dishes set before one, and their sauces. Nevertheless, I will do honour to your good cheer, if you will have patience; and, having laid the foundation with this solid food, I will tile the roof with the dainties you so kindly press upon me.'" In his own house, if any food of a more delicate kind than usual was set before him, Francis usually sent it to some of the sick people in the place, many of whom looked upon anything coming from his table as a sort of charm or specific for their maladies! He was particular about the due observance of fast days and seasons of abstinence, but without any pedantry or formalism. Directly that any such matter became ostentatious, he preferred setting it aside. Thus, on one occasion, when a brother Bishop was visiting him at Annecy,

Francis went to summon him to supper, and was met with almost a rebuke, and a reminder that it was Friday. Mgr. de Genève said nothing, but sent some food to his guest's room, while he himself went to supper with the assembled chaplains; where those attending the stranger Bishop told how rigidly their lord observed all days of abstinence, refusing to sit down to meals at such times, whoever might be his guest. Francis de Sales commented upon this in his own charitable way to Bishop Camus, saying that it was not well to be so wedded even to the most pious observances of that kind, as never to break through them, lest under the garb of faithful adherence to rule, self-love should creep in. "And moreover," he added, "consideration for others is the offspring of love, and worth more than strictness."

Francis always looked beyond the mere act of abstinence to its object, and both for himself and others objected to whatever injured health. The Bishop of Belley writes: "Noticing that I often fasted, he one day asked whether it did not try me a good deal? I replied that I had seldom any appetite, and almost always sat down to table without any inclination to eat. 'Then you should fast but little,' he said. 'How so, *mon père?*' I replied; 'when Holy Scripture so strongly inculcates the duty of fasting?' 'Yes,' he answered, 'but that is for those who have a better appetite than you have. You should practise some other good work, and mortify your body otherwise.'" "God would have us treat our bodies according to their capacity," he said elsewhere; "we must deal patiently and charitably with them, as poor infirm creatures, and it is often a real mortification to a generous, brave heart to do this. If the course of duty brings on illness, or shortens our days, we must take it patiently and thankfully, but in all other cases it is due to God and to ourselves to avoid all such bodily mortifications as ruin the health. No doubt the spirit cannot get on with an over-fed body, but when the poor body is under-fed, it cannot get on with the spirit; we must treat the body as if it was one's child,—correct it duly, but without overwhelming it."

The same spirit entered into all S. Francis did; when his duties exposed him to the extremes of cold and heat, or bad weather, he accepted all such discomforts patiently; and the same with the many personal inconveniences attending his journeys amid the mountains and forests of his diocese. "I am never better than when ill off," he used to say.[1] But while never seeking any indulgence or luxury for himself, he was always thoughtful and indulgent to others. "When I stayed with him," Mgr. de Belley writes, "he took care

[1] "Je ne suis jamais mieux que quand je ne suis pas bien."

to provide recreation for me after my work—preaching, or whatever it was. He would go with me on the beautiful lake of Annecy in a boat, or walk about its pleasant shores and gardens; and when he came to stay with me at Belley, he did not refuse to do the like things at my request, but he never would have done anything of the sort solely for his own gratification." His country walks, when he had time to take such as a matter of health, were generally occupied by talking to the peasants he met, or in visiting their cottages.

Amid the incessant duties and claims of so busy a life, the secret of S. Francis's great power, and of his unruffled calmness and sweetness, was, that he never allowed himself to be hurried. His natural temperament may have aided the unfailing composure and serenity which meet us at every turn; but certainly there was no lack of energy and eagerness, of life and *verve*, such as we are prone to make the excuse for hurry and bustle. "He took up the matters of business, which came before him, one by one," says one of his biographers, "as though there had been nothing before it, and nothing more were to be done after it; accepting all contradictions with perfect serenity." "Of late," he writes, "I have been beset with troubles and contrarieties, but they have brought nothing save quiet and peace, and lead me to hope that my soul is becoming more stayed upon God, and that is the one desire of my heart." He always found fault with confusion and hurry, which he said were the capital enemies of all true devotion: "Better to do a little and well, than a great deal imperfectly;" "Make haste slowly;"[1] "Soon enough, if well enough;" "Sufficient unto the day is the evil thereof;" were words often in his mouth! and he always reprobated the bustling eagerness which seeks to do several things at once. "It is like trying to thread two needles at once," he said; "people who try to do two things at the same time, will not succeed in either." His rule, too, was to do each separate duty as though it were the last he had to fulfil in this world. His friends sometimes remonstrated at the way in which the Bishop allowed people to consume his precious time about comparative trifles: "But they are important to those whom they concern," he would reply, "and the persons in question want help as much as others. Such work is quite sufficient for me. I care not how I am employed so long as I am at work for God's service. Is that not a sufficiently important work for any one?" Whether for himself or others, S. Francis de Sales always made a point of preferring those duties which God sets plainly before each of us, however uninteresting or unacceptable they may seem, to those which imagination, taste, or self-opinion lean to. "Our great

---

[1] "Hâtez-vous tout bellement."

difficulty," he wrote, "lies in our self-esteem. As soon as we fall into some sin or imperfection, we are straightway astonished, troubled, impatient, because we imagined ourselves to be firm, resolute, substantial, and so finding this to be a mistake, and having tripped, we are downcast and out of heart. But if we really knew ourselves, instead of being astonished at falling, we should rather marvel that we ever stand upright! We need to learn patience with everybody, but most of all with ourselves, being, as we are, more troublesome to ourselves than anyone else is to us."

CHAPTER V.

DIOCESAN WORK.—INTERCOURSE WITH HIS CLERGY.— DEALINGS WITH SOULS.—VISIT TO DIJON.

ONE is fain to linger on the inner life of the holy Bishop of Geneva, and to gather up the words of wisdom concerning its regulation which fell from his lips; but it is time to pass on to the more public doings of his episcopate. Among these duties, one which he esteemed highly was the careful appointment of all ecclesiastical officers, still more the selection and preparation of his clergy for their important work. Failing a regular seminary for the education of priests, which Francis de Sales greatly desired in his diocese, he did his best to supply the deficiency by most careful personal investigation of those who offered themselves as candidates for Holy Orders. It was the Bishop himself who studied, as far as was possible, their character and conduct, their capacity and gifts, and he either examined them finally himself, or presided at the examinations of his chaplains; usually, at all events, receiving the young Ordinands himself for confession at the close of the Ember week. He never appointed to any benefice without a "concours," or examination, so as to be sure of giving each parish the best man attainable; and, once appointed, every priest in the diocese knew that his best friend, his unfailing fatherly guide and counsellor, was always to be found in his Bishop, who, while severe in requiring purity and uprightness of those who ministered at God's altar, was ever sympathising, and tender in encouraging the weak or depressed, the lowly or sorrowful.[1]

Early in his Episcopate, Francis de Sales put forth a sort of pastoral letter to his clergy, in which he places himself thus entirely at their disposal, and at the same time makes sundry useful suggestions as to the right exercise of their sacred functions. He always made a great point with his clergy of study—not content that they should aim only at being saints, he urged that they should also aim at being good theologians, and generally well-informed men. "Those among you," he wrote, "who fill up their time to the exclusion of study, are like people who should refuse solid food, and strive to live on such unsubstantial viands as do not yield needful nourishment. Ignorance is almost worse than faultiness in a priest, since it disgraces, not

---

[1] "Do not fear to trouble me," he writes to one of his clergy. "My life and my soul belong only to God and His church; what matters my trouble, if I can do anything for the salvation of souls? Love heeds no trouble. 'Ubi amatur, non laboratur vel si laboratur, labor amatur !'"

the individual only, but the whole priesthood." And he quotes S. Bernard, "Some there are who study out of mere curiosity, some out of vanity, others for hope of gain—all this is evil; but those who study in order to be useful to others, or to sanctify their own lives, these do well."[1] "All love and no fear,"[2] was the rule S. Francis laid down for a Bishop's government. "Those who like to be feared," he used to say, "are afraid of making themselves loved, and they are really living more in fear than anyone, for while they make other men fear them, they fear everyone." The Bishop of Belley records one of his fanciful sayings,—he loved to deal in quaint similes, "There are no slaves in the royal galley of divine love, every oar is voluntarily worked." "I was complaining to Mgr. de Genève," writes Bishop Camus, "of the opposition I encountered to good works which I sought to establish: 'What an absolute will you have!' he exclaimed; 'you want to walk on the wings of the wind, and give way to your zeal, which carries you to the edge of the precipice! would you do more than God does, and fetter those wills which He has created free? You act as if the wills of all your

---

[1] "Sunt qui scire volunt ut sciant et turpis curiositas est, ut sciantur et vanitas est, ut scientiam vendant et quæstus turpis est; ut ædificent et charitas est, ut ædificentur et prudentia est."

[2] "Tout par amour, rien par force."

diocese were in your hands, yet God, Who really has all hearts of men in His, does not do thus. He bears with resistance, rebellion against light, opposition to His inspirations, and some there are who to the end persist in hardening their hearts, yet He goes gently on, in spite of all. Cannot you do the like?" Francis carried out this principle in his own dealings with recusants. A certain priest in his diocese was imprisoned for vicious and scandalous practices. He urgently requested to be taken before the Bishop, but the officers of the Episcopal Court, knowing that the culprit had already induced Francis to forgive him for past faults, and fearing lest he should again escape a well-merited punishment, refused to promote an interview. At length, however, the guilty man prevailed, and coming before the Bishop, cast himself at his feet, vehemently protesting his repentance, and resolution that for the future "where sin had abounded, grace should much more abound." To the amazement and confusion of the erring priest, his Bishop in turn knelt before him, and interrupted his intreaties by saying, "And I, on my part, implore you by the love of Jesus Christ, in Whom alone we hope, that you will take pity on me, and on all the clergy of this diocese, on the Church, and on our Holy Faith, all of whom you are injuring by your scandalous life, which gives so much cause to the enemy to blaspheme; I implore you to have pity on your own soul, which you are wilfully losing, and I exhort you in the Name of Christ to be reconciled to God by true repentance ; I implore you by all that is sacred in Heaven and earth, by the Precious Blood of Christ which you are trampling under foot, by His Gracious Love which you are crucifying afresh, by that Gracious Spirit, to Whom you are doing daily despite." The victory was gained— this man became a true penitent, and a faithful soldier of Christ.

Mgr. de Belley tells a somewhat similar history of a priest who was put in prison for some scandal, and the ecclesiastical judges intreated the Bishop to let the law take its course. He was punished accordingly, but not long after, this man's conduct was again so bad that, in spite of all his protestations while under fear of sentence, it became necessary to deprive him, and banish him the diocese. At some distance of time another priest was imprisoned under somewhat similar circumstances, and the officials were desirous of treating him in like manner, refusing his request to see the Bishop. Francis bade them bring the offender before him, but the officers demurred. "Very well," Francis said, " then I shall go to him. I cannot allow a brother to appeal to me unheard." The erring priest fell on his knees before the Bishop on his entrance, who turned to the officers, saying, "Can you not plainly see that God has forgiven this sinner? If God forgives him, who shall condemn him? Not I, assuredly. Go, brother," he added, turning to the guilty priest, still kneeling at his feet. "Go in peace, and sin no more. I know that you are truly penitent." The officials mistrusted his penitence, and reminded the Bishop of the previous case, and its evil end. "Perhaps," was the answer, "he too might have been converted, if you had dealt more gently with him. If you like, I will be surety for this man. I most entirely believe him to be sincerely penitent; if he is deceiving me, he will hurt himself more than me." The culprit professed his readiness to undergo any punishment the Bishop might impose, and offered even to resign his benefice. "I should be very sorry for you to do so," was the answer. "I expect the tower, which damaged the church by falling, to adorn it greatly when re-established." This expectation was fulfilled, and when some cognisant of the circumstances were talking of them in the Bishop's hearing, he observed, "It is better to make penitents by gentleness, than to make hypocrites by severity."

But Francis de Sales knew how to carry his tender consideration still further in winning his clergy to holiness. During a Visitation tour he received serious complaints against a priest, who added effrontery to his other faults by presenting himself before his Bishop as though there were nothing amiss. He was received as usual with kindness and dignity, but when he began audaciously to justify his conduct, Francis coloured with shame. This tacit rebuke touched the priest, and, casting aside his assumed boldness, he asked the Bishop to receive him in the sacrament of penance. The request was instantly granted; Francis heard his confession, and before leaving the tribunal, the penitent was altogether changed in heart. Turning to the Bishop, he exclaimed, "Monseigneur, what must you think of the greatest sinner on earth?" "I think, brother, that God has poured out the abundance of His Mercy upon you," was the answer. "You are bright with the light of His forgiveness now." "But, Monseigneur, you know what I am." "You are what I say." "What I was, then." "As to that," Francis replied, "I have forgotten it all; why should I remember what God has blotted out? Would you have me like the Pharisee, who beheld Magdalene at Jesus' Feet, and yet only remembered what her past life had been?" After a few more words, the Bishop went on to require the same service at this priest's hands which he had just rendered to him; and humbled to the very dust by the humility of one whom he believed to be a saint, the absolved penitent took the place of judge, and heard his Bishop's confession. It was a marvellous lesson, and one never to be forgot.

ten. More than once again the Bishop selected this priest as his confessor, in order that it might be known how entirely he considered him re-instated, and those who had watched the change looked upon it as little else than a miraculous conversion.

When his Clergy came with appeals and difficulties to the Bishop, he was wont to remind them that *reason* and *reasoning* were two different things—the former was generally to be trusted, the latter rarely so. His apostolic labours were, however, not confined to his clergy; the Confessional had ever been one of his strongholds, and just as, when Penitentiary General, he had placed his tribunal where it was most accessible to the poor and the timid, so, as Bishop, he claimed as his right to receive those penitents who were likely to be least acceptable in other quarters. The poorest and most repulsive people, whether mentally or bodily, were to be sent to him. "They are the choice part of my flock," he used to say, "and I claim them for my own handling, because they are apt to be neglected, and it is my duty to minister to their wants, both temporal and spiritual." He was no less particular with respect to persons whose position was difficult, either from real or false causes of shame. All such were invariably received and treated with courtesy in his home, and his servants had strict orders never to reject any one who sought his counsel. Sometimes twenty or thirty people would come in the course of a morning with their various wants, and the Bishop would lay aside his occupations, however urgent, to see them, never betraying the slightest annoyance or impatience, save once, when it is on record that, having been engrossed without interval the whole morning till two o'clock, he exclaimed that he could see no more people, and caused the rest to be dismissed.[1] Among these interruptions, a full share, as may be supposed, were feminine, and our old friend the Abbé Déage (who continued his *rôle* of faultfinder long after his former pupil became Bishop of Geneva)

---

[1] On one occasion a gentleman came all the way from Normandy to consult Francis de Sales on certain religious difficulties which hitherto no one had solved for him. He arrived at the Evêché, just as the Bishop was at dinner (probably about 11 a.m.). Francis immediately le t the table, and went to receive the stranger, who plunged at once into the midst of his doubts and perplexities, to all of which the Bishop listened and replied patiently and clearly. The hours passed away, supper time came, and Canon de Sainte Catherine went to announce it to the Bishop; but another hour went by, and still the conference continued. Other messengers summoned him. Francis gently dismissed them saying: "There will be time enough by-and-by to eat and drink—at this moment I must heed only a spiritual hunger and thirst. Do not disturb me again;" nor would he leave his visitor until everything the gentleman wished to say was fully said. After ten hours, the stranger retired, perfectly content, and shedding tears of gratitude. "Oh," he said to M. de Sainte Catherine, who was attending to his material comforts,

thought fit to object to this, declaring that it was not proper for the Bishop to give audience to so many women, and that the world would misinterpret such freedom. "My dear friend," the Bishop replied, "God has given me a task of charity to perform towards all His little ones, specially the weak. I seek only to serve Our Dear Lord in it, and while I hold fast to Him I have no fear—in His Hand the weakest reed becomes a pillar of strength." Some one else, alluding to the same subject, observed that he wondered women sought the Bishop so much, considering how little he generally said to them. "Indeed," the Bishop answered with a smile, "do you call it little to let them say as much as they please? They want one to have ears much more than a tongue—and they say quite enough for themselves and me too—I suppose they come to me because I am such a good listener."

If people were timid and frightened, or found it hard to express themselves through shame or fear, he used to help them patiently and gently, seeking in every

---

"how happy you of Annecy are to have such a saint as pastor and director! I was as one lost, and he has brought me safely home. No one before could give me the slightest comfort. Praised be God for having brought me to your holy Bishop! I had heard great things of him, but they were as nothing to what I have seen for myself; there is as much difference between his fame and his reality, as between a mere effigy and a living man!"

possible way to lead them to open their grief fully and profitably. "I am your Father, remember," he would say; "why should you fear me? God asks nothing but an honest avowal of your faults to forgive you. I hear you in His Name; why should you be ashamed to tell me all, who am myself but a sinner? If you had committed every possible sin, it would not alter my feeling for you; sins which are repented of cannot lessen my affection for my penitents."

Some of his visitors were people of notoriously bad character, and a friend remonstrating with him on this toleration remarked, "Well, I believe that Francis de Sales will go some day to Paradise, but I am more doubtful about the Bishop of Geneva; I think his over-indulgence will stand in his way." "Ah! dear friend," replied Francis, "depend upon it, it will be easier to give account for having been too gentle than for having been too severe. Is not God Himself all Love? the Father of Loving-kindness; the Son a Lamb, and the Holy Spirit a Dove? If anything were more profitable than gentleness, Jesus would have told us, but He bids us learn of Him, because He is Meek and Lowly. Would you have me set aside His own lesson? are you wiser than God?" "But these men are worthless wretches, unworthy of your kindness?" The Bishop's eyes filled with tears, and he exclaimed, "Alas! is there no one that will love these poor sinners? you would have me deal hardly with them because they are sinful, as if that were not the very reason for compassionating them! you would have me ignore that they are my own lost sheep, and refuse tears to men, for whom Christ shed His Blood! To whom would you have me show pity, if not to sinners? No, indeed, they are my children, and I will not treat them harshly— the day may come when they will be converted—perhaps holier far than I; if Saul had been rejected, where would S. Paul have been? I know that I am their Bishop, but I would rather act towards them as a parent. Those who advocate severity may go elsewhere, for I will have nothing to say to it."

The way in which this saintly tenderness was carried out in Francis's dealings with penitents, has been recorded by some of those who experienced it. A woman of high worldly position, who had led a very sinful life, sought him as her confessor, and having poured out her sad tale of profligacy, exclaimed at last, "And henceforth, Father, what will you think of me?" "As a saint," he answered calmly. "That would indeed be in defiance of knowledge and conscience," the penitent replied, in amazement. "Neither one nor the other," the Bishop said. "I do not pretend to be so ignorant of what goes on in the world as not to have known the reports concerning you, and they grieved me, on account of the dishonour to God, as well as for your own reputation, which I knew not how to defend; but now that your soul is reconciled to God by true penitence, I am able to defend you before man or devil, and to contradict whatever may be said against you."

"But, Father, it will be but too true as concerns the past?"

"No pious souls will remember that," he answered; "and as to pharisaical judgments, such as were passed upon Magdalene, like her, you will have Jesus Christ as your Advocate."

"But you yourself," the lady persisted, "what can you think of my past history?"

"Nothing at all," Francis replied. "In the first place, it is not permitted to me to dwell upon such memories, and moreover all the past is blotted out, and has ceased to be, in God's Sight. Try to put away this anxiety as to what I may think; my chief thought of and for you is a thanksgiving to God for having turned your heart to Himself." The same penitent told a friend that Mgr. de Genève shed tears during the confession of her grievous falls, and she, believing that it was because of their exceeding evil, made some remark to that effect. But he set her right: "No," he replied, "my tears are rather those of joy over your resurrection to the life of grace."

Another person told how he had once been to Francis de Sales for confession, with so little compunction or contrition, that he ran through a whole list of sins, boldly and impudently, rather as if telling a story than making a confession. The Bishop did not rebuke him, but soon he began to sigh heavily, and to weep. At last the penitent inquired if he were ill? "No, my son," Francis answered, "I, thank God, am well, but you are very ill, I fear. Go on." The gentleman went on with the same levity, and his confessor's tears flowed freely. At last he again inquired the reason? "Alas, my son, I weep because you do not weep," was the answer. This gentle reproof, so lovingly given, had its desired effect—the barriers of pride and hardihood were broken down, and he who came to make a formal unmeaning act, poured out the bitterness of a truly contrite heart, and submitted to such guidance and discipline as were needful to restore his soul to the ways of godliness. "Other confessors often make their penitents weep," he said, when narrating this scene, "but I made my confessor weep, though in truth he paid me out for it at last!"

A personal friend of the Bishop's, with great effort having made a general confession of his past life, Francis was touched by its earnest sincerity and simplicity, and expressed his satisfaction. "You say this in order to comfort me," the penitent said, "but in your heart you can feel no esteem for so grievous a sinner."

"I should be no better than a mere Pharisee," the Bishop answered, "if I held you as such, after your absolution. You are now white as snow, pure as Naaman coming forth from Jordan. I love you more than ever, and the confidence and trust which drew you to me, make me look upon you as a son begotten in Christ—as one in whose heart Christ vouchsafes to dwell through my feeble ministry; and my esteem is in proportion to my love—how can I but share in the angels' joy over the change and cleansing worked in your heart? In truth I love you dearly, now that you turn to God so sincerely."

Mgr. de Genève was once called in to a condemned criminal, who refused all spiritual consolations, and was plunged in helpless despair, from a consciousness of his sins, which he believed past forgiveness. On the Bishop's arrival the wretched man would only continue to affirm that there was nothing before him but hell, and that he was the devil's victim. Francis de Sales took up his words. "My brother," he said, "were it not better to be the victim of the cross of Christ?"

"He will have none of such as I am!" was the sullen answer.

Then Francis poured out his loving tender soul in prayer, that God would not quench the spark of grace He had once kindled in this poor desolate heart; that He would not break the bruised reed; that He Who wills not the death of a sinner would even yet shed the light of His blessing on the last hours of His guilty creature. And then turning to the criminal he asked, "Would you not at least rather abandon yourself to God than to the devil?"

"Of course," was the answer; "but what would He have to do with such a one as I am?"

"It was for such as you," Francis answered solemnly, "that the Eternal Father sent His Only Son into the world to be crucified; He came not to save the just, but sinners."

"But it would be too hopeless audacity for one so black as I to appeal to His Mercy?"

"No audacity can be so great," the Bishop replied, "as that which mistrusts the depth of His Mercy;" and going on to set forth all the infinite Loving-kindness of God, he gradually softened the poor man's dry hard heart, and after ministering to him to the last, he had the consolation of hearing his parting words, "Oh Jesus, I give myself up wholly and entirely to Thee!"

Mgr. de Belley relates that one day he, together with some other people, waited a long time for his turn to be received, while M. de Genève was hearing the confession of a poor old blind beggar woman. With the freedom he enjoyed towards his friend and master, he made some comment upon this. "I assure you that old woman sees the things of God more clearly than many who have good eyes!" was the answer.[1]

Yet, gentle as Francis de Sales was in dealing with souls, he was never weak; he could use firm and sharp dealing with those who were not to be reached by kindness, and in his familiar intercourse sincerity always prevailed, though for the most part his reproofs were so pleasantly, often playfully given as to be free from all sting. Thus Mgr. de Belley records that once he had been pouring out a flood of complaints about some wrong done to him; his friend listened patiently, and agreed that the offending parties were much to blame. "But," he added, "I only see one thing in the matter really to your disadvantage." Mgr. de Belley eagerly inquired what he meant. "That you should not know how to be wiser than they, and hold your tongue!" was the reply.

Francis de Sales was fond of saying, in his epigram-

[1] Even when vested for the altar, he would turn back to hear any penitent who urgently required his help; nor did he ever refuse to hear little children, or such people as seemed to be taking up his precious time unduly. "Confessors are husbandmen, and must never neglect to reap the harvest," he was wont to say.

L

matic way, that "truth which is not charitable, proceeds from a charity which is not true." Mgr. de Belley asked him once how to know in correcting another, whether the motive was real charity? The answer was promptly given, "If you correct out of pure love of God, and for his good whom you correct, you are moved by real charity." He used to say that it was better to withhold a deserved reproof than to administer it ungraciously, and that judicious silence was sometimes the most effectual rebuke. Mgr. de Belley says that Francis frequently reproved him for his faults, and used to tell him that it was the best proof of his friendship, inviting him on his part to do the like.

One of Francis de Sales' first acts on taking charge of his See, was to establish a system of catechising the young, a means of inculcating clear, definite religious knowledge, which he thought could not be too highly prized. He introduced the custom with a special service, attended by the Chapter, and nearly all the townspeople of Annecy. On Sundays and festivals, he used to send a chorister in violet cassock through the town with a bell, summoning everybody to "come and learn the way to Paradise by means of Christian doctrine." The Bishop made a rule of catechising in person in the Cathedral, whenever it was possible, and when obliged to give the duty into other hands, he always took pains to select such of his clergy as were most likely to replace him satisfactorily. "It was a touching thing," a spectator writes, "to see that good father surrounded by his army of little ones, looking earnestly at his troop, and they at him, setting the principles of our holy faith before them in the clearest, most simple, yet beautiful language, becoming himself, as it were, a child, in order to form them into 'perfect men' in Christ Jesus." He was full of little kindly ways for his young catechumens, often giving them little books or pictures, and writing the lesson they were to learn for the next time with his own hand for them. Madame de Boisy delighted in assisting at these catechisings. One day her son told her that it distracted his attention to see her sitting among the children listening to his instructions in that catechism which she herself had taught him. "Ah, my son," the loving mother answered, "I taught you the outer form, but you teach me the inner mystery of it."

The Bishop's care for the little ones of his flock did not stop here; he took pleasure in special services for their benefit; twice a year he himself led them in procession round the town, chanting litanies; and go where he might he was sure to be surrounded by a swarm of children, anxious to kiss his hand, or to win his blessing; and when, as sometimes happened, they were importunate and really hindered him, so that his attendants would have repulsed them, Francis would never allow it. "Let them come," he used to say, "they are my own little people." Bold in their consciousness of his indulgence, the "little people" would follow the good Bishop wherever they could. A Sister of charity used to tell how one day he came into their parlour, leaving the door ajar. She made some remark about the draught, fearing it might inconvenience the Bishop, and he rose, intending to shut the door, but came back to his place without doing so, saying, "There are such a lot of little children peeping at me so very lovingly, that I have not courage to shut the door in their face."

Another introduction made by the new Bishop was a diocesan Synod, which he held to be most important to the welfare of his flock. It was in the first Synod thus held, that Francis de Sales urged upon his clergy and the faithful laity, that inasmuch as they were surrounded by unbelievers in the Blessed Sacrament, and by those who treated its sacred mysteries with irreverence, it behoved all such as indeed truly believed therein to endeavour to give every possible proof of their love and devotion to that most ineffable of gifts; and he especially invited them to observe Thursdays in special honour of the Blessed Sacrament.

To the end of his life, Francis de Sales called the

Synod together regularly in the second week after Easter. He always carefully prepared for it, and discussed all local arrangements and necessities with the Clergy appointed as "surveillants." The Synod lasted three days, each day beginning with a pontifical celebration and sermon (which the Bishop always preached himself on the first day), the rest of the time being filled up with general conferences and private interviews with his clergy, every one of whom had access to the Bishop, and could seek such counsel and advice as he might require at his hands. It was a labour of love to the Bishop, and one which he never failed to press upon such of his Episcopal brethren as consulted him concerning the rule of their Dioceses.

It was while in the midst of all these internal works that Francis de Sales was called to one external to his Diocese, the result of which was most important, both to himself and the Church; leading as it did to his first acquaintance with Madame de Chantal and the institution of the Order of the Visitation. The authorities at Dijon wrote to request the Bishop of Geneva to preach the Lenten Station of 1604 for them, and he the more willingly consented, that he saw an opening for promoting the welfare of his own country, part of which (the district of Gex) was dependent upon the parliament of Burgundy. Moreover, Henri IV., forgetting that he had assigned the ecclesiastical revenues of Gex to the maintenance of its own parishes, had now bestowed them (after the strange fashion of the times) upon André Fremiot, the newly appointed (as yet not even ordained) Archbishop of Bourges, whose father was President, and himself a councillor of the parliament assembled at Dijon. Francis hoped by a personal interview to get this matter arranged, and to avoid the scandal of legal proceedings. Before going to Dijon the Bishop spent a few days in retirement at the Chateau de Sales, where a most patriarchal family group resided, and where his visits were always hailed as the greatest of blessings and delights. His time was chiefly spent in prayer and preparation for the coming Lent; and one day, while in rapt meditation before the Blessed Sacrament in the Chapel, it pleased God to make known to His servant, how one day he was to found an Order of Religious women, and to show him a vision of one veiled as a widow, accompanied by two other persons, who would be its first-fruits.

Immediately afterwards, Francis went to Dijon, where his Lenten course was like a mission in its effects on those present, and his labours in private teaching, and hearing confessions, increased largely. In the midst of the numerous congregation which crowded the Cathedral of Dijon, Francis de Sales perceived the widow lady veiled in black whom he had seen in his vision, and from that moment he entertained no doubt that she was the person designed by God to help him in the foundation he had long had at heart.

That lady was Madame de Chantal.

CHAPTER VI.

MADAME DE CHANTAL.—DEATH OF JEANNE DE SALES.—VIE
DEVOTE.—DEATH OF THE BISHOP'S MOTHER.

JEANNE FRANÇOISE FRÉMIOT, daughter of the President Frémiot, was born January 23, 1572, and consequently she was now in her thirty-third year. She was married at an early age to Christophe de Rabutin, Baron de Chantal, and no happier life could well be imagined than theirs, devotedly attached to one another, united in the highest and best way through perfect religious sympathy, living to do good, ruling their household, and managing a large property as trusts committed them by God, and looking forward to bright days to come, when their children should have grown up in His love and fear, the joy and comfort of their own declining days. In the earlier part of their married life the Baron de Chantal was frequently obliged to be absent, either at Court, or with the army, and this was a real trial to his wife, who used to spend the time of his absence in strict retirement, refusing to receive any society, and laying aside her usual feminine adornments, saying, "There is no reason why I should bedeck myself, when the only eyes I care to please cannot see me." Home attractions were stronger

than ambition, and the Baron after a time forsook the Court, and it is said, refusing a Marshal's baton, resolved to devote himself entirely to his wife and children. A severe illness which he underwent warned the happy husband and wife of the uncertainty of all earthly joys, and Christophe remained with the strong impression that he would not live long, and that notwithstanding his rapid and satisfactory recovery. He spoke of this to his wife, expressing an earnest wish that whichever might be the survivor, should enter the Religious life. Jeanne recoiled from the idea of separation—she put it away with terror, refusing to accept the thought, and rejoiced to see her husband more vigorous and strong than before his illness, the only visible effect of which was his ever increasing piety and earnestness.

Madame de Chantal was confined to her room, having twelve days before given birth to a little daughter, when it pleased God with one stroke to crush the happiness He had hitherto blessed her with. Christophe de Rabutin went out shooting on his estate of Bourbilly with a cousin, the Baron d'Anlezy, then his guest, and they had scarcely entered the covert, when, by some untoward accident, the latter discharged his gun so that the charge entered de Chantal's thigh, and he fell mortally wounded. His first action was to put out his hand to the unhappy perpetrator of the deed, assuring him of perfect forgiveness, and the next was to send messengers for spiritual help, together with a carefully guarded message to his wife. But no precautions can blind the quick penetration of love: "You are deceiving me!" the young wife exclaimed, when the tidings came that her husband was slightly hurt; "he is mortally wounded. My God, my God, Thy Holy Will be done, but Oh, spare him to me!"

Before the surgeons sent for could arrive, Madame de Chantal had reached the farm-house to which her husband was carried, and it was from his own lips that she received the woeful confirmation of her first dread. The wound was mortal. Calm and unruffled throughout, the Baron was able to notice his unfortunate cousin walking up and down without the house, like one distracted; and calling him in, endeavoured to comfort d'Anlezy, bidding him believe that the accident would not have happened had it not been God's Will, and urging him to be brave, and to bear this terrible misfortune as a Christian should. The surgeons arrived, and while the poor wife hung trembling upon their words, imploring them to say that her husband might yet be restored to her, he stilled her with the touching words, "Dear, unless the Great Physician wills to heal me, it is beyond the power of human skill."

It was indeed beyond that skill; the surgeons did not venture to try extracting two balls which had penetrated de Chantal's body, but believing that death would not immediately ensue, they removed the wounded man to his own house, and for nine precious days the husband and wife were yet together. De Chantal spent the time in most fervent preparation for death. After receiving the last Sacraments he requested the Curé to inscribe in the parish register how purely accidental the fatal shot which cost his life had been, together with his full unconditional forgiveness and that of all his family for it. He bade his wife train up her children in the same mind, and he strove to lead her to accept her bitter trial in patience and submission to God's Will. She, on her part, strove earnestly to obey her husband in this as in all else, and then at times, unable to struggle against the agony of her heart, she would rush to her little Oratory, and prostrate before her Saviour, that poor bleeding heart was fain to cry, as so many have done before and since, "Oh, not this, dear Lord, not this! Anything but this!"

"What I do thou knowest not now, but thou shalt know hereafter." The hours passed by, de Chantal's life ebbed slowly away, and the first words heard to pass his young widow's lips were such as he had striven to teach her: "My God, do all Thy Holy Will in me and mine!" She asked for her little ones, and laid the marble hand of their dead father on the head of each, and clasping her three weeks old baby to her breast, trusted herself and her fatherless children wholly unquestioning, as he who had been the light of her eyes had bidden her, to the God of the orphan and the widow.

Madame de Chantal's great desire henceforth was to give herself solely to God. She put aside everything of state and show in her household, and devoted her life to the care of her children, visiting the sick and poor, and to her religious duties. Although educated piously, she had never been under any definite religious direction, but now, as she herself describes, the need and longing for spiritual guidance became so pressing, that she prayed continually for it, asking God to send her a director who would teach her His Will, and lead her in the ways He destined for her. One day, while wandering about, her mind absorbed in such thoughts and prayers, Jeanne de Chantal saw a priest sitting at the foot of a mound in front of her. He wore a cassock and rochet, and a square cap on his head, unlike anyone she usually saw in those parts; and while she looked curiously at him, a voice within told her that this was "one beloved of God and man, in whose hands she was to place the ruling of her conscience." Immediately the vision disappeared, but the priest's countenance remained clearly impressed upon her memory, and she did not doubt that one day she should again see him. Meanwhile Madame de Chantal's life was spent partly in a trying residence with her father-in-law, M. de Monthélon, partly with her own father, M. Frémiot, who induced her to come frequently and take up her abode once more in her old home at Dijon, where she was at the time that the Bishop of Geneva came there to preach his Lent station.

While at Dijon some intimate friends, hearing of her extreme desire for spiritual guidance, induced Madame de Chantal to put herself under their director, a religious in whom they had the greatest confidence. Jeanne did as they advised her, but she did not recognize the priest of her vision in this reverend Father, neither did she find in his guidance the comfort and help she had hoped for. Yet she submitted meekly to it, and allowed him to bind her by a vow of obedience, as also one prohibiting her from casting off his direction, or consulting any other guide. Under this ill-judged rule, Madame de Chantal's perplexities increased, but her courage also increased, and she felt convinced that in His Own good time God would make her way clear before her. This conviction was powerfully strengthened when, on the first Friday in Lent, 1604, having taken her place near the cathedral pulpit of Dijon, to hear the famous Savoyard preacher, she saw the priest whose exterior was so mysteriously familiar to her in the Bishop of Geneva. His words fell upon her ear with a sense of indefinable rest and comfort. Surely this was the man of God, who was to speak peace to her soul, and her perturbations and mental trials would be at an end! The service over, Mgr. de Genève inquired of the Archbishop of Bourges concerning the lady in black who had attracted his attention, and André Frémiot, who was both fond and proud of his sister, was eager to make her known to him. They met first at the President's table. "I looked on at all he did, and listened to all he said, as if an angel had come down from heaven," Madame de Chantal said afterwards in describing these first interviews. Her conviction that the Bishop could help her, and her extreme longing to obtain his help, grew daily stronger, but fettered as she was by her director she knew not how to satisfy the want. Francis de Sales saw that she was drawn to him, and as was his custom in such cases, often made the way easy, as he thought, supposing her timidity to be the only hindrance. Madame de Chantal had laid aside as much as she thought possible of the world's ordinary gear, but when presiding at her father's or brother's table she still followed the fashions of the day to a certain extent, and the Bishop had probably heard some of the speculations as to her re-marriage, which were rife in the Dijon circles. One day, accordingly, he inquired if she intended to marry again, and upon her eager negative, he answered, "Well, then, you should lower your flag!" The next day they met again at the Archbishop of Bourges' house, Jeanne having laid aside most of her toilette, and the Bishop congratulated her thereon. But willing to test her further, he pointed to a certain lace trimming, and asked, "Would your appearance be unseemly without those laces, Madame?" These last remains of finery were willingly removed, and Madame de Chantal would fain have put herself altogether into the Bishop's hands, but for that unlucky vow. On Wednesday in Holy Week, feeling sorely troubled, and her confessor being absent, she asked her brother to bring about an interview for her with Francis de Sales, which he readily did. This led to his confessing her, and acquiring a complete knowledge of her perplexities with respect to her first director, from whom, however, he was in no haste to separate her.

Francis de Sales left Dijon soon after Easter, promising to pray for Madame de Chantal, as also that he himself might be guided with respect to her, and in the meantime she took counsel with the Rev. Père de Villars, leaving to him, in a great measure, the decision whether she was unduly bound, or whether it was God's Will that she should break her bonds, and accept the guidance she craved for. After a time, the Père de Villars pronounced so clear an opinion to this effect, saying moreover, that he believed she would be resisting the Holy Spirit by longer delay, that Madame de Chantal could not hesitate; and on the feast of S. Bartholomew that same summer, she met Francis de Sales and his mother by appointment at Saint Claude, an abbey in the Jura mountains, at that time a favourite place of pilgrimage. While here, the Bishop formally accepted the charge of her spiritual guidance, and Madame de Chantal thankfully put herself under that paternal rule which was only to end with the saintly prelate's life. As usual Francis de Sales took the line of tranquil waiting on God's Will, and though deeply impressed with the belief that sooner or later his new daughter in Christ was to be employed in some great work for the Church, he made no attempt to hurry any development of plans, but left her to return to the weary monotony of her life at Monthélon, with the crabbed old father-in-law and his overbearing housekeeper, who gave the future Religious abundant opportunities of self-denial and meekness. Some rule of life he planned for her, telling her the while that "all must be done from love of obedience, rather than from fear of disobedience. I would leave you in perfect moral liberty, so that when any of your exercises are rightly hindered by just claims or charity, you may feel the very hindrance to be a kind of obedience, and fill up the deficiency with love." He was stringent as to his penitent's religious observances not entailing discomfort on others; as for instance, finding that when she rose very early for prayer and meditation, one or other of her waiting maids rose too, he forbade this attendance, and henceforth Madame de Chantal dressed herself, lighted her own lamp, dispensing with a fire, and went to her devotions without disturbing any one. Her servants used to say, "Under her former director Madame only prayed three times a day, and yet everybody was inconvenienced and tired, and now M. de Genève makes her pray always, without putting anybody out." She soon cut off her beautiful hair, which had been her husband's pride, but was now valueless in her eyes, and her plain serge dress and linen sleeves and collar were as near an approximation as circumstances admitted to the religious garb she hoped to put on later. Her life had been devoted to good works ever since her widowhood, and there could not be much change in this respect. Already Madame de Chantal was known to the whole country-side as the "Sainte de Monthélon," and whatever of sickness, sorrow, or sin needed consolation or tending, found both without reserve at her hands. In May, 1605, she paid a short visit to the Chateau de Sales, where the Bishop of Geneva met her, and in reply to her earnest petitions that he would take her from the world and from herself, Francis told her that he believed he knew God's designs for her, but that she must wait another year before he should tell her what these were.

The Bishop had indeed been maturely deliberating how best to found a congregation intended to benefit women whose delicacy of health, or their circumstances and age, as widows, prevented from joining the existing Orders, which were unsuitable to such persons, either from the construction of their Rule, or from the asceticism of their practice. He aimed for them at a religious life, which should seek rather to mortify the heart and mind, than the body, which should prefer the attraction of love to the rigour of penitence, interior recollection to multiplied external observances; a life, in short, the outward signs of which should rather be gentleness, simplicity, and holiness, than anything more remarkable to the outward eye. Women, however sickly, even deformed and blind persons, as well as those considered too old for other Orders, were the special objects of this foundation. At length, having appointed a meeting with Madame de Chantal at Annecy, the Bishop developed his plans to her, but not without first testing the readiness of her obedience. "I went to the saintly prelate," writes Madame de Chantal, "with as free and indifferent a mind as I could attain, with no desire save to follow faithfully wheresoever God should lead me through his means, and with a firm conviction that his decision would be the channel of that Divine Will to which I had consecrated my whole being. Up to Whitsuntide he spoke to me about various things, and made me give him an account of all that had been passing through my mind, without telling me anything about his plans, only bidding me pray fervently, and leave myself unreservedly in God's Hands, which I tried diligently to do. At last, the day after the feast of Pentecost, he told me with a grave and recollected manner, that he had come to a decision for me. I fell at his knees, assuring him that I was resolved to obey him absolutely. 'Well then,' he said, in order to try me, 'you shall join the Poor Clares.' 'I am ready, *mon père.*' 'But perhaps you are hardly strong enough for that; you had better be a *Sœur hospitalière.*' 'As you will, *mon père.*' 'Or perhaps a Carmelite?' '*Mon père,* I am ready to obey you implicitly.' Then he said, 'No; God does not require any of these things of you; He destines you to establish an order, which is to be governed by charity and the love of Jesus Christ; an order which will admit such as are infirm or weakly, and which will be occupied in tending the sick and poor.' When he said this, I felt my inner mind go so entirely along with him, and such a peaceful satisfaction and light flamed in upon me, that I was certain this was indeed God's Will, which I had not felt at those first propositions, though I was entirely prepared to submit."

From this time both Francis de Sales and Madame de Chantal considered it a settled thing that the work was to be begun whenever it might be possible, though at present that time did not seem to have arrived, fettered as the latter was by the claims of her children, her own father, and her aged father-in-law. During this visit of Madame de Chantal to Annecy, a marriage was arranged, according to the custom of those times, between her eldest daughter, Aimée, still a mere child, and Bernard de Thorens, the Bishop of Geneva's youngest brother. Before she returned to Burgundy, Madame de Chantal also consented to Madame de Boisy's earnest desire that she should take charge of her only daughter, Jeanne, the youngest child of the de Sales' family. Not long after they reached Monthélon, this young girl, then just fifteen, was seized with violent illness, and died within a few days. It was a sore trouble to Madame de Chantal, thus to lose the child committed to her care, and it was with deep grief that she announced the sorrow to

Francis, who had looked upon this little sister almost as his child. In his reply he says, "We must not only be willing to receive God's strokes, my daughter, but we must be willing that He should strike where He pleases. . . . I see you suffering keenly, with your vigorous heart, which loves and wills strongly, and I am glad of it; as for your poor, half-lifeless hearts, what use are they? But you must make, at least once every week, a special act of love to God's Will above all else, and that not only in things supportable, but also in things insupportable." The Bishop himself felt the trial keenly. "I baptised her with my own hands," he wrote; "she was the first on whom I exercised the trust given me in Holy Orders. I was her spiritual father, and I looked to training her one day into something very choice. . . . This dear little sister, who has departed so suddenly, and in so Christian-like a way, has kindled anew in my heart the love for that sovereign good to which we should refer everything in this brief life."

The sad tidings reached Francis at St. George de Mornex during a visitation tour, and feeling keenly for his mother's grief, he hastened at once to the Chateau de Sales to comfort her. His brother, Jean François, had already made known their sorrow to Madame de Boisy. "My dear mother," the Bishop wrote, "has drunk this cup with the truest Christian steadfastness, and highly as I have ever prized her goodness, I admire her more now than ever. On Sunday night she dreamt that Jeanne was dead, and the next morning, before getting up, she asked my brother if it was really true. 'It is true, mother,' was all he could find courage to say. 'Then God's Will be done!' our dear mother exclaimed, and for a while she wept freely. After that, she called her maid, saying, 'I want to get up and go to the Chapel and pray to God for my child,' which she did. There was never one word of impatience or distrust—a thousand times she blessed God, and resigned her will to His, but I never saw a calmer grief—plenty of tears, but they were all gentle, loving showers forsooth, without any bitterness; yet this was her very dear child."

It was about this time that Francis heard from Rome how his former friend, Alessandro de Medici, now Pope Leo XI., had inscribed his name on a list of proposed Cardinals. Francis felt nothing but reluctance at the thought, and having discussed it with the Chaplain of the Chateau de Sales, he ended by an earnest message to his mother. "Ask her," he said, "to pray and intreat the Lord that He will not raise me to a still higher charge; that which I already bear is too heavy for me. May God not impose this dignity upon me, for in truth I am unworthy of it.

If His Holiness commands, I must obey, but I assure you, if it depended upon me, and I were only three steps from the Cardinal's hat, I would not stir one inch to reach it."

Leo XI. died so soon after his accession, that he was never able to carry out his intention, and the Bishop of Geneva continued undisturbed in his work of love at home. The Visitation, in which he was engaged at the time of his sister's death, was no light labour. In every parish Francis de Sales not only confirmed, but preached and catechised, receiving every one who desired to come to him for confession, acting as arbitrator and universal peace-maker, entering into all the material repairs or wants to be supplied in every church or chapel, giving himself, in short, wholly and unreservedly to his flock. "The affairs of this diocese are not streams merely," he wrote, "they are torrents, and I have had unlimited work during this Visitation." He had troubles too from without, as when, for instance, the Senate of Chambéry sought to make him issue a "Monitory" which he considered unjust, and so declined to do; whereupon they threatened him with the seizure of his temporalities. "That would be a sign that God intends me to be wholly spiritual," he said quietly. But the irate assembly thought better of it, and did not proceed with their unjust attack.

Consolations also were not lacking amid his apostolic labours, among which must be reckoned the appointment of one of his clergy, the Abbé de Fenouillet, who had been early appreciated and brought forward by Francis de Sales, to the Bishopric of Montpellier. The Lent of 1608, too, was one of real satisfaction to the good Bishop. He preached during it at Rumilly, and the results were so fertile that he had to call in the help of some of his Canons to hear confessions and minister to the people. About this time Henri IV. made another effort to draw the Bishop of Geneva to Paris, but he did not alter in his affection for the "poor bride" he had espoused. "I have learnt to love Annecy," he wrote once, "because it is the bark in which I am to cross the ocean of this life," and to all the offers of greater dignity and higher emoluments, Francis only replied that he was satisfied with what he already possessed, and did not consider himself competent to undertake a more influential position, while at the same time he affirmed, without doubt most sincerely, that if it were God's Will to call him to any other work he was ready. "The brief time remaining to me in this life is as nothing compared with eternity." But while refusing exterior dignities, Francis did not reject external labours, and these increased upon him, as the fame of his holiness and wisdom spread abroad.

In this year, October, 1608, he was called into France concerning various affairs, ecclesiastical and other; and profiting by the opportunity, the Bishop went to Monthélon to assist at the betrothal of his brother Bernard and Aimée de Rabutin Chantal.

It was at this time that Francis de Sales finished the book which has made his name as a household word throughout the Church, and which many a grateful soul would call, as he himself called the "Spiritual Combat," "my dear book;" *i.e.* the "Introduction à la Vie Dévote." This is not the place for an analysis of that most valuable work, which indeed should be in the hands of every aspirant to the interior life. It may, however, be well to refer to the circumstances which led to its composition. A certain Madame de Charmoisy, one of the fine ladies of Paris who came under Francis de Sales' influence, was converted by a sermon she heard him preach during the winter of 1603 (where does not seem clear), and in her earnest desire to lead a new life, she cast herself upon the guidance of the saintly Bishop, who had so forcibly arrested her in a course,—not of guilt in the ordinary sense, but of worldliness and self-pleasing. Francis de Sales entered upon the work of forming this soul to higher things with his usual energy, and was much struck with his penitent's strength of character and capacity for a high standard of holiness. His personal interviews with Madame de Charmoisy being necessarily limited, he frequently wrote down the various instructions he wished to convey to her, and also answered fully and carefully the questions she in her turn put to him. This correspondence had continued for some time, when being at Chambery, and under the direction of the Père Forrier (who was once director to the Bishop himself), Madame de Charmoisy showed him the papers she so much prized, and consented to his wish to have a copy of them, a copy which Père Forrier soon multiplied for the benefit of his college. Still this was comparatively a small sphere for the usefulness of such writings, and Père Forrier wrote to the Bishop of Geneva to request him to publish them. Francis was altogether puzzled as to what the good Father meant; he answered that he had no talent for authorship, and no time to write. Nor when the explanation came that his book was in fact already written, did he understand what was meant. Sending for Madame de Charmoisy he asked what it was all about, and when at last he found that Père Forrier had studied and written out what he called his "few miserable notes," he exclaimed, "Truly it is a wonderful thing that according to these good people I have composed a book without knowing it."

Francis was surprised himself to see how numerous the "miserable notes" were when put together, and he wrote to Père Forrier to deprecate printing them in their fragmentary condition, promising to arrange and shape them into a book. About the same time his friend, M. Deshayes, Henri IV.'s secretary, wrote to express the King's earnest desire that M. de Genève would write a Book concerning true religion, such as should set it forth in its rightful beauty, and show the world that holiness of life was not incompatible with a busy, active career, whether at court or in the province, amid the whirl of affairs or the claims of society, a holiness alike free from repulsive severity and treacherous laxity. "No one but Mgr. de Genève could write such a book," the King said. Accordingly the Bishop set to work, and re-wrote his instructions to Madame de Charmoisy, adding to them some of his many letters of direction to Madame de Boisy, and published them at Lyons under the now familiar title of "Introduction à la Vie Dévote." In his preface, which is dated "Annécy, le jour de la Saincte Magdeleine, Juillet, 1608," he says the work has been put together "without any kind of leisure," and with characteristic humility, he adds, "It is true that I write of the devout life, who am not devout myself, yet truly wish to become so ; and this desire gives me courage. For as it has been well said, a good way of learning is to study; a better is to listen; and the best of all is to teach." In one edition of the "Vie Dévote," it is mentioned that the first publisher, a Lyons bookseller, made so considerable a profit upon the book, that he pressed 400 crowns—a very large sum for that time—upon the author. Francis accepted the money, and immediately transferred it in a lump to a poor young woman who wanted to become a Religious, for her dowry. The book made a great stir in the Church world. Henri IV. affirmed that it exceeded his expectations, and his Queen, Marie de Medicis, sent a copy, bound in gold and precious stones, to James I. of England, who is said to have greatly desired to see the writer. On all sides admiration and encomiums poured in upon the book. "Cannot God make fresh-water springs to come forth from the jaw of an ass?" Francis said to Bishop Camus, in allusion to these praises. "These good friends of mine think of nothing but me and my glory, as though we might desire any glory for ourselves, and not rather refer it all to God, Who alone works any good which may be in us. Does not Christ's Gospel teach us that, so far from resting in any worldly applause, we must dread lest pleasing men be but a bad sign as to our pleasing God, for the friendship of the world is enmity with God." "Yesterday," he wrote to Madame de Chantal, "I took a short walk, my eyes full of tears at seeing what I am taken to be, and what I really am. I wish you knew me better; you would say, 'This is a reed on which God bids me lean; I am safe in leaning, if such be His Will, but all the same, the reed itself is worthless.'"

Looking from our far-off point at holy men of God who have fought the good fight, and have entered upon the joy of their Lord, it is sometimes a positive relief to turn from their higher treadings in the ways of perfection, and see them — as in truth we know all men ever must be in this world,—"encompassed with infirmity;" tempted, as we know that One Only has ever been "tempted without sin." The overwhelming distance between oneself and the very lowest of God's saints, seems lessened when we dwell upon that side of their lives, and remember that, although to us they shine as stars in a dark night, they were not exempt from the trials and temptations to evil which beset us here, although earlier trained in resistance to such evil, it may be, than we are. And thus it is with a strong sense of how real Francis de Sales' sympathy was with the faults and frailties of his spiritual children (and is with us who fondly gaze upon his example), that we find him saying in connection with the esteem in which he was held, "I am nought, save vanity;" and again: "The other day, without any forethought, a temptation came over my mind . . . . I saw deep down in the lowest depths of my soul that detestable spirit of self-love and vanity, swelling like a noxious reptile. I defied it, and refused even to think whether I was thinking of it; and so it evaporated, and I saw it no more." "Oh Lord, save me; bid Thou these storms of vanity to cease, and there shall be a great calm. When I am cast down at the foot of the Cross, then, my God, my soul is in peace; but scarcely have I risen up therefrom, and the storm begins anew." His rule to others was doubtless his own likewise. "Put aside all the vainglorious thoughts which come across you in good actions; go on doing what you are about in all simplicity, without pausing to examine whether you are consenting to such thoughts or not." On one occasion the saintly Bishop was seized with a sudden pang of jealousy on hearing another prelate lavishly praised as an incomparable preacher. But so soon as he had acknowledged to himself the humiliating truth, he "seized the evil thought as though it were a vile reptile," he said, "and broke its neck; then bore that other worthy Bishop up to our Heavenly Father's Bosom, asking Him to bless His servant and fill him ever more and more abundantly with His Grace." Francis de Sales had, however, a special abhorrence for professions of humility. "A really humble man does not seek to *seem* humble, but to be really so," he used to say. " Humility is so sensitive that it fears its own shadow, and can scarcely bear itself mentioned without the risk of loss." " He who blames himself, sometimes indirectly seeks to be praised," he said once, "and is like an oarsman, who turns his back to the place he is making for; he would not have you believe the ill he says of himself, and it is out of mere pride that he would fain be thought humble." This exceeding reality made Francis very reticent in speaking of his faults, but on one or two occasions when by so doing he could profit another's soul, he did allude to his own besetting sins, as being too great a tendency to earthly love, which, he said, he could only deal with by an intense seeking after Divine Love, and a temptation to anger and impatience, which must be vigorously dealt with by both hands.[1] Bishop Camus records several occasions on which he was himself caught in the net of mock humility, and playfully but unsparingly dealt with. " He was very much given to take any one who used humble expressions before him at their word, and indeed sometimes to enforce them so as to put the speaker to shame, and teach him or her not to do so again, feeling sure that often their intention was by no means to be taken literally. For instance, when I

[1] " Saisi des deux mains."

first became a Bishop, I thought he required a too high standard of perfection of me, and one day I said to him, 'Mon père, you forget that I am but newly come out from the world, and am called to be a teacher almost before I have learnt myself! You deal with me as with a man who has made good progress in holiness, and capable of leading others therein, while in truth I am as yet still but standing on the threshold.'

"'It is true,' he replied, 'I am quite aware of the fact, and perhaps I see it all still more plainly than you do; I consider you as snatched from utter destruction, saved from out a fire, and still smelling of smoke! But after all you are a Bishop, and you must learn to feel as the father of your flock—you must gather up courage and aim at perfection—you must not be content to drink the waters of your own cistern, you must freely give them to others; God and reason, and your own responsibility, require it of you. You must not look back, unless you would become a mere statue. If you trust in yourself, you will do nothing, but if you trust in God, what can you not do? He vouchsafes to exalt His power by means of our helplessness, His strength by our weakness; He confounds that which is by that which is not. Mistrust of self is a very good thing provided it be accompanied by trust in God, and the more we have of the last, the deeper will be the first. But discouragement is a false humility.' And again, when once a Sister, on being elected Superior of her house, indulged in lavish expressions of her own unworthiness, our dear friend took up her words, and expressed them still more forcibly, saying that among poor concerns there was not much to choose;¹ of course all the Sisters knew her incapacity, her narrow mind, the weakness of her judgment, her want of refined manners, and general imperfections; and that perhaps God had allowed her election with a view to the correction of these faults. She should bear in mind that the government of her community was committed, not to herself, but to God, Who uses the foolish things of this world to confound the wise, and Who saves us through the foolishness of the Cross." Francis de Sales was fond of quoting King Solomon's words, "There is a shame which bringeth sin, and there is a shame which is glory and grace" (Ecclus. iv. 21), and it was a favourite saying of his that to speak of oneself is as difficult as walking the tight rope—one requires such wonderful balance and so much circumspection not to fall in so doing.

It is difficult not to fall into endless digressions, thanks to the copious personal details concerning S. Francis's daily conversations, preserved to us by the good

¹ "Entre fille et feuille il n'y avait pas grande différence."

Bishop of Belley, and in truth there is more real interest and edification in such records of the Saint's words, than in the actual history of his life. It was about this time that family discomforts, which must have been peculiarly trying to the Bishop, arose. M. de Boisy had made arrangements of his property, which did not satisfy all alike; especially the wife of Louis de Sales, the Bishop's favourite brother, who was active among the malcontents. Francis, with his usual unselfishness, conquered these difficulties, and but a short time after the young sister-in-law died. During that same year, 1609, the heavier sorrow of his mother's death came. Madame de Boisy may have felt that her life was fast drawing to a close, or perhaps it was only natural piety which led her to go to Annecy for a month, with the special object of making a retreat in preparation for death, under her son's direction. Touching as their relations were all through life, this last stage seems more peculiarly so than any other, the venerable mother making ready for her last hour under that guide whose earliest lessons of piety it had been hers to give, and saying as she returned to the Chateau de Sales, "I never in all my life received such comfort as I have done now from him who is at once my son and my father." On the Ash Wednesday following Madame de Boisy assisted at all the offices of the church, confessing and communicating devoutly, and after going to bed that night she had three chapters of the "Vie Dévote" read aloud to her. The next morning, while dressing, she was seized with paralysis, and lost the use of one side. Her son Bernard, Baron de Thorens, was instantly summoned, and he sent off to Annecy for his eldest brother, who at once mounted his horse, and rode without delay to the Chateau. Madame de Boisy recognized him, and taking his hand she kissed it, saying, "This is the mark of my respect for my spiritual Father," and then, drawing his face down to hers for a loving kiss, she added, "And this is my dear love for my son." From that time she seemed to have no thoughts for anything save God. Her crucifix was always in her hand, she continually pressed it to her lips, and earnestly repeated after Francis the frequent acts of faith, hope, love, and contrition which he made beside her. This state lasted two days, and then the gentle soul passed to her rest. Francis tended her to the last, and after closing those eyes which had never looked upon him save with such deep love, he let his tears flow unrestrainedly, yet without bitterness. "It has pleased God to take my most excellent and very dear mother from this weary world," he writes, "and He has given her a place in Paradise, I believe; for hers was one of the most lovely, pure souls it would be possible to find. God is ever Good, and His Mercy is never failing. All that He does is holy and true, and I bow beneath the trial of this separation; it is a sharp pang in truth, but a very peaceful grief, and I can say with David, 'I was silent and opened not my mouth, for it was Thy doing.' But for that I should be inconsolable."

It was not long after (May 14, 1609) that Henri IV. fell a victim to the assassin's knife, and Francis de Sales, whose warm loving heart had always gratefully returned the King's cordial liking for him, felt the startling event in its full horror. That was indeed a gloomy year; perhaps the brightest spot in it, as regards the Saint's external history, was, that it saw the beginning of his friendship with Jean Pierre Camus. But the Bishop of Belley is far too important a person to introduce at the end of a chapter, and we must be much too grateful for his faithful records of Francis de Sales not to give him all due honour.

CHAPTER VII.

Bishop of Belley.—Order of the Visitation.—Traite
de l'Amour de Dieu.—Death of Bernard de Sales
and his Wife.

JEAN PIERRE CAMUS was of a Lyonnais family, himself born in Paris, in the year 1583. Endowed with considerable talent and much attractiveness of person and manner, he acquired a reputation in Paris, both as a preacher and an author, at an early age; and he had not completed his twenty-sixth year, when Henri IV. nominated him to the vacant see of Belley, the diocese adjoining that of Geneva on the south-western side. Apparently up to this time M. Camus had only known Francis de Sales by reputation, but he requested him to be the consecrating Bishop, and Mgr. de Genève consenting, the young prelate was consecrated in the Cathedral church of Belley on August 30, 1609. He himself was not without scruples because of his youth, although a papal dispensation had been duly obtained, and these were fully expressed to Francis, who, however, bade him not waste time in looking back, but reach on to those things which were before. "You have come to the

Vineyard in the first hours of your day," he said; "give good heed that you work diligently, and do not let yourself be overtaken by such as arrive later." M. Camus tells us that he once said to the Bishop of Geneva, "Ah, *mon père*, greatly as men esteem you, you were guilty of the crime of consecrating me too early!" to which Francis replied, "Yes, it is true that I did commit that sin, and I am afraid it is an unforgiven sin, inasmuch as I never repented of it! But seriously," he added, "I intreat you by the bowels of our common Master, live so as never to give me cause to repent of it. I have been present at the consecration of many other Bishops, but you are the only one I ever consecrated myself. Let us both try to be worthy of our office, God helping us." The new prelate came almost immediately to stay with Francis, and thenceforward, till death parted them awhile, they never failed year by year to spend a week with one another, part of which was kept as a retreat, and the rest devoted to friendly intercourse, and special discussion concerning those episcopal duties, of which the younger looked to learning so much from his elder brother in the Apostolate. This was by no means their only time of meeting; the distance between Annecy and Belley is not great, and any difficulty or perplexity was apt to bring Bishop Camus over to consult his friend, while in times of sorrow or weariness, it was real refreshment to Francis de Sales to relax his mind beneath the congenial roof of Mgr. de Belley. This familiar intercourse was so valued by the latter, that he continually wrote down the conversations he had had with Francis, and these he eventually gathered into the somewhat diffuse but most valuable work, called " l'Esprit de Saint François de Sales," which, without pretending to be a memoir of that holy man, supplies an infinity of interesting information, and lifelike representations, such as none, save so closely intimate a friend, could have supplied. M. de Belley was so eager in his desire to become acquainted with every minute particle of his friend's way of life, as to adopt means which scarcely seem justifiable to modern ideas—as, for instance, when he caused holes to be bored in the doors or wainscots of the rooms occupied by Francis when visiting him at Belley, in order to observe how he comported himself when alone, whether in prayer or study, dressing or sleeping ! M. Camus (whom one cannot but picture to oneself as a restless, somewhat fidgety personage) was much impressed by the invariable composure and serenity which stamped every action of Mgr. de Genève. " He was always precisely the same alone as when in company; his external manner as placid as his heart. I never saw him use any unusual gestures, whether of head, eyes, or hands;

he always seemed to be conscious of the Presence of God, a practice, indeed, which he inculcated upon all under his direction. When alone, his manner was just the same as when in the largest assembly. When he prayed, it was as though in the presence of all the Saints and Angels, immovable as a pillar, and with a most reverent countenance. I often noticed that he never lounged, never crossed his legs, or leant upon his elbows, and the sweet gravity of his expression filled one with love and reverence."

M. de Belley used to pour out the troubles and perplexities of his charge to the fatherly Bishop, who, however, was a sworn foe to all complaining and murmurs. One of his many epigrammatic sayings was, "Qui se plaint pèche."[1] Every complaining spirit, he said, implied some dissatisfaction with God's decrees, and a good deal of self-love. On one occasion, when the younger Bishop had given way to urgent complaints, Francis de Sales observed, "To another man I might offer some attempt at consolation, but I cannot do so to you, both by reason of your position and of the love I bear you. If I were to pour oil upon your wound, it would probably increase the inflammation. I shall only apply salt and vinegar." He went on to say, "You ended your lamentation by saying that one ought to have a prodigious amount of

[1] "He who complains, sins."

patience to endure such trials silently. At all events you have not got that, since you complain so vehemently!"

"But, *mon père*," M. Camus replied, "I only complain to you in private. To whom may a child have recourse in tribulation, if not to his indulgent father?"

"Oh, you very baby!" Francis exclaimed, "how long will you cling to your babyhood? What right have you, a Father in the Church, to play at being a child? S. Paul says, When I was a child, I spake as a child, but when one is grown up, that which was interesting in the child becomes unseemly. Would you have me feed you on milk and broth, and blow upon your hand when you knock it, like a nurse? Are your teeth not grown strong enough to eat the bread of affliction? You wear a golden Cross on your breast forsooth, but you cannot carry a very little inward cross without complaining, and then you begin to cry out about patience, and expect me to consider you patient all the time you are murmuring! Well, I forgive you this time, but on condition that you are more courageous henceforth, and instead of fretting away all the good sent you by God in your trials, cherish them carefully, and thank God for vouchsafing to give you ever so small a share in His Dear Son's Cross."

Francis de Sales never wearied of pressing upon his friend and pupil, that guidance of souls was the art of arts, and that no one could hope to do his duty in that without much difficulty, and yet, he used to add, where love is, difficulties melt away. From the first he insisted urgently that M. de Belley should fulfil all his ministerial duties, celebrate daily, administer all the Sacraments, visit, preach, catechise; the young Bishop did not like his confessional duties so well as preaching, but Francis would not hear of any such selection, and the poor man was so overwhelmed with penitents, that he wrote to say, "You have made not a confessor, but a martyr of me!" He had been a popular preacher in Paris, and his sermons abounded with the adornments of style and rhetorical flourishes which were more to the taste of the general public than to that of the Bishop of Geneva. M. Camus tells a story against himself with respect to this matter. He was going to preach before a large congregation, including his friend Francis de Sales, and being very anxious to please, he had taken great pains with his preparation.[1] When the sermon was over, the friends being alone together, the preacher looked forward to some expression of approval from the person he most cared to please. Francis observed, "Well, you have given great satisfaction to the good people to-day; they all went away crying *Mirabilia*,

[1] "A dire le vrai, j'avais un peu pensé à moi, et m'étais préparé tout de bon."

after your fine, well got-up panegyric! I only met with one dissatisfied person." "What could I have said to shock that person, whose name forsooth I don't care to hear?" M. de Belley answered. "But I want to tell you," his friend replied. "If I had not great confidence in you, I should hesitate, but as it is I must tell you. I mean myself." "In truth, I would rather have had your approbation than that of the whole assemblage!" poor M. de Belley cried out. And then the Bishop of Geneva went on to explain his mind, as to the real end of preaching—*i.e.* the conversion and strengthening of souls, not pleasing the ears of those who listen.

With amusing honesty, M. de Belley narrates how, in his exceeding love and admiration for Francis de Sales, he tried to imitate him not only in the higher interior gifts of his mind, but in trifling external matters also, his gestures, his action in speaking, even to his pronunciation. The natural temperament of the two men was so very different, that this imitation ended in a most unpleasing result. "I ceased to be myself," M. de Belley says, "and proved a most wretched copy of my model." One day Francis de Sales took occasion to say, "By the way—I hear strange tidings—they tell me that you have taken it into your head to mimic the Bishop of Geneva in preaching?" "Well, and if so?" M. de

Belley replied, "is he such an undesirable example? Does he not preach better than I do?" "Oh yes, of course," Francis answered playfully, "but the worst of it is that I am told you imitate him so badly, that while you spoil the Bishop of Belley, you are not a bit like the Bishop of Geneva. You ought to do like bad painters, and write the name of the person you mean to represent below the effigy!" Francis went on more gravely to urge his friend to lay aside all such affectation, expressing the wish on his own part that he had more of M. Camus' fire and quickness, but still maintaining that each should persevere simply in doing his best according to his own gifts and powers.

The Bishop of Geneva heard that M. de Belley indulged in very lengthy private devotions before and after celebrating mass, and wishing to make him more considerate for others, who were inconvenienced by this habit, he watched his opportunity. It chanced that one day when staying at Belley, Francis was delayed by important despatches, and eleven o'clock arrived before he could say his daily mass. He then came to the chapel, said a short prayer before the Altar, robed, and celebrated the Blessed Sacrament, and after a brief thanksgiving, rejoined the rest of the party, who were waiting to sit down to table. M. de Belley, who as usual was closely observing everything done by his revered friend, was somewhat scandalised at the brevity of both preparation and thanksgiving, and when they were alone together, he ventured to make some remark to that effect. Francis thanked him for speaking his mind, and added that he had a somewhat similar comment to deliver on his side, only it was to the effect that M. de Belley, by his lengthy pauses and delays, fretted those who were assisting at his Mass, or waiting to see him on business afterwards. In the conversation which followed, Francis urged that a priest's morning prayers should be his preparation for the Altar, and that his thanksgiving should be going on all day, and form part of his evening self-examination. Francis thought that M. de Belley was over-strict as to giving dispensations from fasting and the like; and as he was continually asking the Bishop of Geneva's advice upon such matters, at last that prelate asked, "What do you do yourself under similar circumstances?" "I follow the dictates of my conscience," the other answered, " or I consult my ordinary confessor." "Then why not do the same for these people?" "Because neither I nor my confessor is the Bishop of Geneva." "Ah, well," Francis replied; "some day when you consult that Bishop on your own behalf, you will not be so ready to take his advice for yourself as you are for other men." And he went on to say that in proportion as his friend became indulgent to others, so would he become severe with himself; and that generally those who were readiest to overlook their own faults, were most stern in judging another.

In his early days, M. de Belley was sharp and hasty in his dealings, he tells us, and was wont to give reproofs which savoured more of displeasure than compassion. Francis de Sales took him repeatedly to task for this error, pointing out that while in truth those who are in authority have a solemn duty to perform in correcting evil, still it is equally a duty to administer all such correction so lovingly, and with so simple a desire for God's Glory, and the real good of the person corrected, as to take away the sting of reproof. The saintly Bishop went so far as to say that it is better to withhold a deserved rebuke than to administer it ungraciously, and that judicious silence was far preferable to the truth roughly told. "You will catch more flies with a spoonful of honey, than with a whole barrel of vinegar!" he used to say; and "No sauce was ever spoilt by sugar!" "Human nature is so formed, that it always hardens itself against rigorous dealings, but yields to gentleness. Reproof is bitter in itself, and only loving-kindness can make it palatable." M. Camus justified himself by quoting S. Paul's exhortation to Timothy: "Be instant in season; out of season, reprove, rebuke, exhort." "Yes," the Bishop rejoined, "but the point of that passage lies in the concluding words, '*with all longsuffering and doctrine.*'" It was a saying of his that our neighbour's soul is as the tree of the knowledge of good and evil to us, which we are forbidden to touch, God having reserved the right of judging it to Himself. Men are prone to overlook their own inner life, which they ought to examine, while they are very busy about their neighbour's, which they ought to leave alone. He would tell a story of a certain woman who had always been very perverse and done exactly the contrary to what her husband bade her. In course of time this woman was drowned, and the neighbours found the husband looking for her body the contrary way of the stream. They expressed their surprise at his folly, but he quickly replied, "What, do you suppose that she won't still be led by the spirit of contradiction?"

Nevertheless, Francis de Sales did not uphold laxity, or the false kindness which cannot see a neighbour's fault; as we have seen, he was himself ready to reprove where reproof was needed, only ever with a loving spirit. "He often reproved me," says M. Camus, "and he was wont to say that it was the greatest proof of friendship he could give me, and one which I ought to value, intreating me to do the like by him. He used to say that 'an ounce of correction from another hand was worth hundredweights self-administered.'"

The time was coming when the long and patiently awaited work was to be begun, and the Order of the Visitation founded. Francis de Sales went to Monthélon, to perform the marriage ceremony which was to unite his brother Bernard to Aimée de Rabutin, and it was agreed that at the same time her mother's plans should be discussed with her family. So Madame de Chantal knelt in tearful expectancy before her Crucifix, while the Bishop of Geneva went into the subject with her father, the President Frémiot, and her brother, the Archbishop of Bourges. Both of these gave their consent to her adopting the religious life, but they not unnaturally wished the new congregation to be founded either at Dijon or Bourges. Annecy, however, possessed so many superior advantages, and there was so obvious a claim upon Madame de Chantal in being near her young daughter, that this point was ceded, and the foundress of the Visitation left Monthélon with Bernard de Thorens and his young bride, as well as her other children. Her sojourn with the old M. de Monthélon had been rather one of duty than of pleasure, and though moved by his regrets at parting from her, this separation cost Madame de Chantal but little as compared with that which was to come on leaving Dijon, when she parted from her own ever indulgent, tender father, President Frémiot, and from her only son, Benigne. It was in this parting that the often quoted scene took place, when the boy, giving way to a passion of grief at the separation, cast himself down on the threshold of the room, and declared that his mother should only leave by trampling over him. Madame de Chantal paused an instant, and with one cry to Heaven, she passed over her boy, and fled to her father, who was waiting without. Much has been said concerning her want of natural feeling on this occasion, but when one remembers that Bernard de Rabutin was nearly sixteen, and was already entering the world under his grandfather's auspices, while of her three daughters, one was married, and the other two were to accompany their mother to Annecy and remain under her care, this accusation seems scarcely deserved. The little party journeyed on to Annecy, where they spent Easter, and then Madame de Chantal accompanied her young daughter Aimée to the Chateau de Thorens, and remained with her till Whit Suntide, when the Bishop of Geneva hoped to instal her and her few companions in the house which was to be the first home of the Visitation. That house, "the hive I have found for my poor bees, the cage for my little doves," as S. Francis calls it, is still standing, and one cannot look upon its walls without

O

many a reverent memory of those saintly personages who have now so long passed to their rest, while their remembrance is still fresh and sweet as unseen violets among us.[1] It was occupied for the first time on Trinity Sunday, June 6, 1610. Madame de Chantal's first companions were Madlle. de Brechard, a young lady of noble birth, from Nivernois, and Jaqueline Favre, a daughter of the Bishop's old friend, the Senateur Favre. This lady had attracted the attention of Louis de Sales, who desired to win her as his second wife, and, at his request, his eldest brother asked her in marriage for him. But Jaqueline took the opportunity of explaining her real wishes, and the Bishop conveyed tidings to his brother that the bride he sought after had already given herself to another Bridegroom. To these must be added a pious woman named Anne Jaqueline Coste, who had been found by Francis de Sales employed as a servant in the Hotel de l'Écu, at Geneva, some years before. Finding her to be a fervent Catholic, unhappy in her

[1] When visiting the Sisters of the Visitation in the summer of 1870, after seeing various precious relics, and talking of sacred memories with them, the writer made some remark concerning the help it must be to those Sisters in Annecy especially, to live so surrounded by all that is calculated so vividly to recall their saintly founder and his teachiug. "Ah, yes," a Sister answered, "but one had need try to use the help rightly, for it is so easy to lose sight of things merely because they are so very near!"

surroundings, he had brought her to Annecy, where she had also been placed in an inn, but her abiding hope had been that one day she might become a lay sister in the Order she believed her spiritual guide intended to found. The little company went together to their new home, proceeding first to the chapel, where they repeated the Gloria Patri three times, and prayed that above all things their Heavenly Father's Will might be fulfilled in all they did, and then, having read their Rule, prepared for them by the Bishop, they laid aside their secular garments, and the next morning put on those which were henceforth to mark them externally as "Religious of the Order of the Visitation." Francis de Sales said their first Mass at eight the next morning, and thus quietly and simply their work began.

Money did not abound; Madame de Chantal had given up her dowry and everything she possessed to her children, excepting a small annuity ensured to her by her brother the Archbishop of Bourges, and the little community was scantily provided even with necessaries. Madame de Chantal used to tell how one day, when the *tourière* had bought a three sous bag of charcoal, she and her two companions went trembling to open their money-box, doubting whether the three sous would be found, and rejoicing when the exact number proved to be there. During the course of the next few months, five other postulants joined them. The first three members of the community made their profession on the anniversary of their entry into their little home, the Bishop himself having taken continued pains during that interval to teach them, and train their souls for the true religious life. The Sisters were anxious to decorate their little Oratory for the ceremony of their profession, but they had no money excepting some which the Bishop had recently given them for the poor. After much consultation and great hesitation, they determined to make use of this money, and replace it with the first that they might receive; but hardly was the money spent when the Supérieure was conscience-stricken, and wrote in haste to make avowal to the Bishop of what had been done. The next morning, on his arrival, he received her with a grave countenance. "This is your first act of disobedience, my daughter," he said, "and I cannot tell you how it has grieved me."

At last the day arrived, and Francis de Sales professed the three novices. As she returned to her place, Madame de Chantal broke forth without any premeditation in the words of the 132nd Psalm, "This shall be my rest for ever; here will I dwell, for I have a delight therein" ("Hæc requies mea in sæculum sæculi: hic habitabo quoniam elegi eam"), and in consequence this verse has always since been used on similar occasions in the Order of the Visitation. There was great sympathy among many for the new congregation, but it was not without enemies also; those who were disposed to cavil said that the Bishop was founding a hospital rather than a monastery, because he was so indulgent to the feeble and delicate, although the very same people were ready to find fault with more severe religious Orders because they lacked this very indulgence. But Francis de Sales paid little attention to such objectors. "When once we see what is God's Will," he said, "we must go on straightforward, whatever men may say. There is no need to be afraid of obloquy when souls are to be saved, and if this institution were the means of averting but one mortal sin, I should rest satisfied. People say that the whole thing will fall to pieces whenever I die, but I think our Mother in heaven will do as much for it there as I can do here." In truth, the small seed thus planted in lowly faith bore good fruit, and within sixty years the Order contained a hundred and twenty houses.

Very shortly after her profession, Madame de Chantal's good father, the President Frémiot, died. The Bishop carried these tidings to her, and her first question was, "How did he die?" "As a Christian should die," the Bishop answered, "and in the arms of his son, the Archbishop of Bourges." "God be thanked!"

was her reply; but a sharp pang came over the loving daughter's heart, lest grief at parting from her should in any way have hastened his death, as also the inevitable thought that had she delayed her final entrance upon the Religious life a little longer, she might have been permitted to minister to her father's last hours. Such tender but futile regrets could only be dealt with in one way; and in a fervent act of total unquestioning submission to God's Holy Will in all things, "supportable and insupportable" (as Francis had taught her some time before to make), Jeanne de Chantal found rest to her soul. The Bishop sent her to Dijon and Monthélon, in order that she might make all due arrangements for her children's interests. During this absence, which lasted about four months, the Bishop wrote frequently to her: "I intreat you, dear daughter," he says in one letter, "hold fast to Jesus Christ and our Lady, and to your good angel through all your affairs, so that you may not be troubled by their multiplicity, or daunted by their difficulties. If God brings them to a happy result, we will bless Him for so doing: if it should not please Him so to do, we will equally bless Him. And for your part, you must be satisfied with having done your best, inasmuch as our Lord does not require success at our hands, but rather that we should put ourselves faithfully and diligently to such work as He gives us to do. That does depend upon ourselves, the results do not. God will bless your good intentions in this journey, and He will reward you either with the prosperity of your efforts on your son's behalf, or with a holy humility and resignation if you fail." And in another letter he bids her "enter upon these earthly affairs with your eyes fixed on Heaven."

As soon as Madame de Chantal returned, she and her Sisters began to work among the poor, according to their Founder's original intention, and found no lack of employment, especially among the sick, whom they tended in their own houses diligently. One day the Bishop being confined to his room owing to a hurt received in one of his legs, saw two Sisters going past, and called them in. "You are going to tend the sick," he said, "and here is a sick man with a wounded leg; will you take pity on him?" The Sisters were proud to minister to their venerated Founder, but their agitation, half pleasure, half shyness, caused them to set about their work with tremulous hands, and they consequently put the good Bishop to not a little unnecessary pain. He would not betray this, but when the operation was over, and he thanked them for their service, he added, "When you dress the wounds of the poor, my daughters, you must try and steady your hand, and not tremble so much, or be in such a hurry, for it is rather tender work!"

Before long Madame de Chantal fell dangerously ill,

and her life was despaired of. "Our good Mother is very ill," the Bishop wrote, "and I am greatly troubled as to her state, but if the Sovereign Architect of our new Congregation sees fit to remove our cornerstone, to establish it in the New Jerusalem, He will know what to do for the rest of the edifice, and bearing this in mind, I am not anxious about it." He took leave of the patient, saying, with his usual calm and recollected manner, "Well, my daughter, you would have God's Will made perfect in all things, would you not?" And as she assented, "It may be," he said, "that God means to be satisfied with our readiness to do His Will, and that we, like Abraham, are not to finish the work. If it is His Holy Will that we leave it incomplete, at all events, He sees that so far we have done our best; may His Holy Will ever be done." The Mother recovered, to work and suffer more for God in this world; and as their numbers were increasing fast, the community moved into a larger house, just before she was again called away by the death of her father-in-law, to Burgundy. This event set her comparatively free, and on her return, Madame de Chantal entered vigorously into the work of building the first real monastery of the Order, which hitherto had only occupied such houses as could be obtained without much difficulty. The widowed Duchess of Mantua, who was a Daughter of Savoy, laid the first stone of this building, on September 18, 1614, and within a few months a house was established in Lyons, at the request of its Archbishop. Difficulties of all kinds, poverty, opposition, and calumny, attended this undertaking, and Madame de Chantal needed all the Bishop's encouraging counsels to maintain her faith and courage: "God's Providence will aid you, my daughter," he wrote; "invoke that fearlessly in every trouble which surrounds you; bethink you as you advance, that you are pleasing our Dear Lord, and in Him all Paradise. Let us go on gently and happily in the work our Master has given us to do. . . Be sure that the Angels keep their eyes upon you and your little troop, and will never forsake you, who keep steadfast to His Will whom they adore." And again he says, "I gather that you are ill, and also somewhat surprised not to find things at Lyons so smooth as our wishes pictured them. These, dear daughter, are real signs of the worthiness of our work—a hard beginning, some progress, and a blessed end. Do not lose your courage; God will never cease to watch over you and your band, so long as you trust in Him. The gate of consolation is sometimes hard to find, but the end is a sure reward. Do not be disheartened, and do not let your mind be troubled amid all these contrarieties. When was any work done for God free from them, especially in the outset?"

The Archbishop of Lyons, Mgr. de Marquemont, differed from Francis de Sales as to the constitution of the new Order. The latter specially designed his spiritual daughters to be uncloistered, and intended them to go about freely among the sick and poor, combining the vocations of Martha and Mary—a life to which he leaned, as more generally profitable and edifying for women, than one of greater restraint and less activity. His first Religious had, in fact, taken no vows, but only engaged themselves to serve God in community life. But with his wonted gentle readiness to accept the will of others, Francis waived his objections, and consented to alter the governing principle of his new foundation—the Sisters were to take the usual vows, and to be inclosed. "Can anything be more unreasonable," he remarked, after deciding this, "than to call me the founder of the Visitation; I have done exactly what I did not wish to do, and I have undone all I did wish for!"

Nevertheless he took great pains in framing the Rule, studying all those already in use, and consulting all whose opinion was likely to forward his undertaking. The Bishop of the diocese where any house was founded, was to be its Superior; no postulant was to be under sixteen years of age; and if a widow she must have made every due arrangement for her children's benefit before leaving the world. Persons suffering under any infectious complaint, or so infirm as to be incapable of observing the rules and customs of the community, could not be admitted, but with those exceptions neither delicate health nor advancing years were to be any hindrance. No house was to consist of more than thirty-three inmates. There was great simplicity and but little austerity in the daily Rule—the offices, prayer and meditation occupying a large part of it. The spirit of this rule may be found in a letter written by the saintly Bishop to Madame de Chantal, "I would have you be extremely small and lowly in your own eyes," he says, "gentle and tender as a dove. Accept willingly all opportunities of humbling yourself; do not be quick to speak, rather let your answers be slow, humble, meek, and let your modest silence use an eloquence of its own. Bear with and make allowances for your neighbour; do not dwell upon the contradictions which you must encounter; turn from them to see God in all things, and acquiesce simply in all His decrees. Do everything for God, uniting yourself, or maintaining union by means of a simple glance or turning of your heart to Him. Never be hurried, do everything tranquilly and with a restful spirit; do not lose your inward peace for anything whatsoever, not even when all seems going wrong, for what do all earthly things matter, as compared with your heart's peace? Commend all to God, and keep yourself calm and still in the Bosom of His Fatherly Providence. When you find that your spirit has wandered thence, draw it back gently and with perfect simplicity; and never under any excuse entangle yourself in cares, desires, and affections. Our Lord loves you, and would have you wholly His. Seek no other arms save His to bear you up; no breast whereon to lean save that of His Divine Providence; seek not to see beyond Him and His Will. Let your will ever be so bound up with His as to be wholly one, and leave all else unheeded. Be of good courage, and abide humbly, waiting upon His Sacred Majesty. Desire nought save the pure Love of our Lord; refuse nought, however trying, but put on Jesus Christ crucified, and love suffering in Him."

Francis de Sales was not eager to see his Order grow rapidly: "Let us be patient, and we shall do enough, if what we do is acceptable to our Master," he said. "I would rather see growth in the roots of virtue, than in many branches of houses." "It is less easy than people suppose," he said again, "to find good superiors. Often while intending to build up, we really pull down, and hinder instead of forwarding God's Glory. By spreading abroad over much, it is easy to scatter our strength. *Multiplicasti gentem, non magnificasti lætitiam.*"[1]

[1] "Thou hast multiplied the nation and not increased the joy." Isa. ix. 3.

He was anxious that the Visitation should throw open its arms to women whose physical infirmities excluded them from most others, and on this score we find him not unfrequently making even Madame de Chantal go farther than she was inclined. Thus he writes to her: "In what you say about receiving people, there is great danger of holding too fast to human prudence, of building over much on natural inclination, and too little on God's Grace. I see danger lest too great weight be given to constitutional delicacy, or physical infirmity. You would have none that are blind, halt, or weakly come in to the banquet. In short, it is not easy to change human respect into abjection and pure love." While, however, the Bishop was so tender over such difficulties and infirmity, and possessing, as he certainly did, a marvellous power of entering into and adapting his treatment to the feeblest and most timid minds, he yet had a great liking for what was large, open, and straightforward, and an equally decided objection to all that was petty, frivolous, or self-seeking; feminine littlenesses worried him, and he preferred even the faults of a strong, quick feeling character, if they were accompanied with humility, and a ready submission to discipline. "I like independent, vigorous souls, which are not effeminate," he says, "for an excessive softness makes the heart confused and troubled, distracts it from loving prayer, hinders entire resignation, and a perfect death to self." And writing to Madame de Chantal, he alludes to her "vigorous heart, which both loves and wills strongly," adding, "I am glad of it—for your half-withered hearts are of little good in this world." Neither was Francis de Sales strict as to the money each Sister was supposed to bring with her, to aid in the maintenance of the house. "I infinitely prefer gentle humble postulants, though they may be poor, to those who are rich, but neither humble nor gentle. It is all very well for us to go on saying, 'Blessed are the poor;' human prudence will always answer, 'Blessed are the rich monasteries and orders.' We must patiently bear to see our beloved poverty depreciated." One day the reception of a novice was discussed before the Bishop, who said nothing, while Madame de Chantal insisted upon the necessity of her bringing her full dowry; but as soon as he went home, Francis sent her a brief note, saying, "Ma mère, you are rather just than kind, and on these occasions one must be rather kind than just." An only daughter, who possessed considerable independent means, was about to enter the Order, and the Bishop inquired what she had done about her property? The lady replied that she intended to give it to the house. "Not so," Francis answered, "our congregation is not designed to injure family ties; you may give a trifle more to the Order than others who have less at their disposal, but that is all we can allow. What of the rest?" "I will give it to my brother." "Why not to your mother?" "Because she has in several ways given me very serious causes for complaint." "But that in no way dispenses you from the commandment which bids you honour your parents," was the answer, and the Bishop enforced his precept. To attempt any detail of his spiritual guidance in the Order would almost involve the quotation of all his spiritual letters and conferences, which will occupy a separate volume. The patience and minuteness with which he entered into every detail, however apparently insignificant, and the marvellous beauty with which, as the fairy princess turned all she touched to gold, S. Francis turned all he handled to the Love of God, are very remarkable. "The one greatest joy this world can give," he used to say (and his whole life proved the sincerity of his words), "is to win a soul to God."

But we must leave the Order of the Visitation, which continued to spread—new houses being established at Moulins, Grénoble, Bourges, &c.—and trace the saintly Bishop through his more general works. The death of the Comtesse de Sales, Louis's wife, has been mentioned. His worldly position was high, but even in early days Louis had been forcibly impressed by the strong character and holiness of his brother, and now, when the brightness of this world, and the fascinations of its gifts had passed from him, he turned more and more from earthly thoughts, and so admirable was his life in its meekness and piety, that the Bishop would fain have induced him to take Holy Orders, and become his Coadjutor. But Louis's humility could not be overcome, and though aiding his brother in every possible way, it was still as a simple layman.

The year 1610 deprived Francis of that good Abbé Déage, who had remained inseparable from him ever since those early days when he first taught the future Bishop and Saint his catechism, and whose jealous love had maintained an undisputed right to rebuke and interfere to the end. M. Camus tells us that his untempered zeal, and his old habit of rule, made him somewhat intolerable, as it would seem. If the Bishop indulged, as was his habit, in playful words, free as they ever were from the slightest trace of levity, the Abbé would forthwith remind him that a Bishop's demeanour ought to be grave and serious. When he received visitors with his natural winning grace and courtesy, M. Déage was at hand to warn his former pupil that familiarity breeds contempt. When he would not be displeased with some offender, or correct a fault as sharply as the Abbé would have done, he was

told that his over-indulgence was ruinous to everyone. And Francis could never preach in the Abbé's hearing without his sermon being criticised and disapproved; and yet all the time the good old man would wax most wroth, and quite lose his temper if anyone else presumed to find the smallest fault with his beloved pupil; so that Francis used to say, "Why will you be so tender over my reputation? Am I perfect?" Probably the Abbé did really think him so, in spite of his querulous complaints; anyhow, he was a venerated guest, treated with every respect and honour to the end of his days, and when his last illness came, the Bishop tended him lovingly throughout, and himself laid him in the grave. It was noticed that when saying mass for the Abbé's rest, Francis quite broke down at the Pater, and as he finished the service, was almost choked with tears. He told his chaplain afterwards that what had so overcome him was, that as he began to say the Pater, the thought suddenly swept over him how the good man now gone to his rest had first taught his childish lips to utter that sacred prayer.

That same year the Bishop's long-tried friend, Antoine Favre, was appointed President of the Senate of Savoy, and was accordingly obliged to go and live at Chambery. He gave up his house, which was one of the best in Annecy, to the Bishop, and it has continued to be the Episcopal residence ever since.

The Bishop's constant diocesan labours were never intermitted save for some work for the Church, a journey to Turin, Vercelli, and Milan, in 1613, being his longest absence. At Milan he was joyfully welcomed by his old friend and most congenial brother in Christ, Cardinal Federigo Borromeo. Francis returned to Annecy for Whit Suntide, and it was while celebrating the Blessed Sacrament in the Cathedral on that festival, that an incident occurred which is still commemorated in its annals. A structure had been raised, in keeping with the curious taste of those days, meant to represent the clouds, from out which it was intended at the proper moment for flames to issue forth, amid which a dove should appear, in memory of the descent of the Holy Spirit at Pentecost. But the machinery would not work, the flames failed to appear, only the dove escaped her prison, and, bewildered by the crowd and the music, fluttered hither and thither in a perturbed flight until at length, by a touching coincidence, she lighted on the Bishop's head, standing as he did before the altar.[1] How little he himself aspired to any unwonted gifts, may be judged by his

---

[1] A somewhat similar circumstance is recorded as occurring later, when a dove came into the church at an open window, and perched upon the Bishop's shoulder.

remark when some lunatics, supposed to be possessed, were brought to him to be cured. The Bishop looked thoughtfully and silently at them, until his old servant, George Rolland, spoke, and asked him to heal them. "Ah, truly!" Francis then exclaimed, "I am glad M. Rolland should teach me how to work miracles!" It is said, however, that his gentle words and fervent blessing did restore sundry persons suffering from mental disease.

There was little time for study: "I am surrounded with perpetual work, caused by the various affairs of my diocese," the Bishop writes to a gentleman, "and never have a single day for my poor books, which I used to love so well, though now I scarcely dare love them, for fear of suffering more severely under the inevitable divorce which has come to pass between us." And to Madame de Chantal he writes, "You must excuse brevity, for I am so surrounded with business that I scarce know which way to turn. But I am well, I thank our Dear Lord, Who gives me ever fresh courage to love Him, to serve and honour Him more and more, with all my heart, all my soul, all my whole self, as, in truth, I feel that hitherto I have not corresponded with sufficient ardour or faithfulness to His Infinite Grace." Through all this work, however, the Bishop was meditating upon the book which he eventually brought out in 1616—his "Traité de l'Amour de Dieu"—and it was written chiefly in stray moments stolen from sleep at night or early morning. One day—it was the feast of the Annunciation—Francis was preparing to write a chapter of this work, and, kneeling down, he prayed as was his wont that he himself might drink deep of that Heavenly Love concerning which he strove to teach others, when in answer his soul was so abundantly filled with that Divine Love, as to overflow even externally in such a supernatural brightness, that Louis de Sales, who came into his brother's room at the time, was startled. Seldom as the holy man of God would speak of the favours vouchsafed him by his Lord, on this occasion he told Louis what had occurred, bidding him not speak of it, as it was "the secret of the Lord." And in a book which he habitually carried about him, he wrote these words, "Die vigesima quinta Martis, hodie servum suum Franciscum misericorditer visitare dignatus est Dominus."[1] Louis de Sales was so impressed on this occasion that afterwards he said he could never read the "Amour de Dieu" (which he liked to get in manuscript as it was written), save on his knees.

Before it was published, however, the author submitted his writings to M. de Sainte Catherine, a learned Canon of Geneva, to the Archbishop of Lyons,

[1] "To-day, March 25, the Lord in His Mercy has deigned to visit His servant Francis."

and to several other theological authorities; fearing, as he said, lest his imperfect knowledge, and the scant leisure he had to review what he wrote, should have led him into any error or misstatement. Yet that the treatise was carefully written, may be judged from what M. de Belley tells us, *i.e.* that the author himself said, before writing one passage alone of fourteen lines he had studied more than twelve hundred folio pages. Meanwhile nothing that concerned the welfare of his people was neglected, whether it was the introduction of the silk-trade at Annecy, the furtherance of education by means of the Sainte Maison, tending those who were the victims of pestilence, or taking such part as was needful (beyond the actually needful Francis de Sales scrupulously eschewed politics) in political matters. Those were not easy times for ecclesiastics or laity, and politics were entangled then, as now, in many a question which at first sight might have appeared solely spiritual. Suspicion and mistrust were ever afloat, and the jealousies of the Huguenot party stirred up many vexatious troubles. Thus a visit paid by the Cardinal Archbishop of Lyons, Mgr. de Marquemont, to the Bishop of Geneva, was attributed to political motives, and Francis de Sales was accused of intriguing on behalf of France against Savoy. The Duke did not at once dismiss the imputation, as one might have expected, and the

Marquis de Lans, Governor of Savoy, was instructed to inquire into it. The Bishop's reply is very dignified in spite of its humility. After alluding to the beginning of his friendship with the Archbishop, "after the manner of the ancient bishops of the Church, who aided one another to bear their respective burdens, by mutual communication of the inspirations vouchsafed them from Heaven," he goes on to state that the Archbishop's visit was unpremeditated, and he came openly attended by eight horsemen. "And when here, we neither did nor said nor thought anything concerning the world's affairs, for which, I believe I may truly say, neither of us have any attraction, nor even concerning ecclesiastical business, but our intercourse was solely respecting the duties of our calling, and purely spiritual matters. The Archbishop preached two most excellent sermons, one in the Cathedral, the other in the College; he celebrated daily in one place or another, and everything that passed between us had reference to our special vocation. Your Excellency will oblige me by stating this to His Highness, and, with your permission I would also say with all freedom, that I was born, brought up, and trained, and have grown old in a firm fidelity to my sovereign, which is strengthened not only by every human consideration, but also by the duties of my profession. I am every inch a Savoyard and so are all belonging to me; I never could be anything else." Not long after this war broke out between the Duke of Savoy, supported by France, and the Duke of Mantua, backed by Spain, concerning the Duchy of Monferrato. Various complications arose, and the Duke of Nemours threatening to seize Geneva, there was a general stir among the Huguenots and all disaffected people. There was even a threat of besieging Annecy, and every one was in perturbation and dismay. The Bishop only remained unmoved and calm, ready for whatever God might send, but cheering his people with his assurances that the storm would soon pass by, as proved to be the case.

During Advent, 1616, and the following Lent, Francis de Sales preached the usual Stations at Grénoble, where, if possible, his ministrations were still more in request than before, and his work was that of a missionary. He returned gladly, however, to Annecy, saying that "large towns and great honours were not his element." "I am like a statue out of its niche, a something cumbering the way."

The war was destined to bring private as well as public sorrow upon the de Sales family. Bernard de Thorens was summoned with his regiment to Turin, and had scarcely arrived there, when he was seized with an infectious fever, of which he died. Writing to announce this event to the Baron de Villette, his uncle, Francis says, "It seems almost a waking dream, to think that this poor lad should have died so immediately upon his arrival at Turin, before he had time even to see the Prince, for whom he was devoting his life. . . . But he had given himself to a military career, and he might have met with a far more lamentable death. I thank God for preserving him from duels, mutinies, and the innumerable ways of sinning against Him, to which a military life exposes men in this corrupt age. He was very dear to us all, but our will must bow before that of God, and amid one's natural grief there is great comfort in knowing that Bernard died a most happy death, tended by the Barnabite Fathers, and by our Chevalier,[1] having made his general confession, and received Holy Communion and Extreme Unction with great devotion." In another letter the Bishop says, "I leave you to imagine how keenly this sorrow touches me; and the crowning grief is for his poor little wife and her mother, to whom I must now go and take away the faint ray of hope to which they still were clinging after the first tidings of Bernard's illness."

Aimée de Thorens was a devoted wife, and her husband's necessary absences were always a trial to her. Her consolation at such seasons was to take

[1] Janus de Sales, Chevalier de Malte, and a Gentleman in Waiting to the Duke of Savoy.

shelter at Annecy with her mother, and her little room was always kept for her adjoining that of her sister Françoise. At the time of Bernard's death, Aimée was as usual staying in the convent, where as soon as possible after receiving the tidings, her brother-in-law, who was also her confessor, hastened. Aimée was expecting him to hear her confession, which he did, and that ended, he said to her with a tremulous voice, "My child, you have ever given yourself absolutely to God, have you not?" "Yes, Monseigneur, wholly," was the answer. "And now, dear child, that which hitherto has been intention only must be proved: you will receive all things patiently at His Hand, will you not?" "I will," poor Aimée answered steadily—but then there came an exceeding bitter cry, and she fell at the Bishop's feet, "Oh Father, tell me that it is not so—my husband is dead?" "My child, my poor Aimée, Bernard has found that which his soul desired." "Then, my God, henceforth I am Thine only," she exclaimed.

After a few loving words of tender sympathy, the Bishop bade his child-sister follow him into Chapel, where he was about to celebrate the Blessed Sacrament with special intention for their dear one now at rest, telling her that she should communicate with the like intention. The good Sisters took her into the choir, and kneeling there (says one of them, the

Mère de Chaugy), she vowed from that hour to consecrate herself wholly to the Lord. "So soon as she had received the Holy Communion, her heavy sobs ceased, and there she remained with clasped hands, her eyes raised to Heaven, and only gentle tears raining fast from her sad eyes."

"I cannot tell you how good our poor little widow has been in this sorrow," the Bishop writes to a married sister, Madame de Cornillon, "her steadfast earnest faith is most touching. We are extremely thankful on her own account, and for the sake of her unborn babe."

Aimée remained with her mother, earnestly striving to offer up her life's grief to God, and to bear His Will patiently. The Sisters looked on pityingly and tenderly, as she appeared among them in her simple mourning, rejecting all but what was plainest and homeliest, saying that henceforth she needed only to dress her soul. She declined all help at her toilette, and would not allow the kindly Religious to wait upon her as they wished; her great comfort was in devotion, and her only rest seemed to be in church. But in spite of all her efforts to submit her will to that of her Heavenly Father, the poor child could not withstand her grief; or perhaps it would be truer to say that that Loving Father, seeing her entire submission to His Will, accepted the offering, and "made her perfect in a short time." (Wis. iv. 13.) Five months after her husband's death, his young widow was taken prematurely ill, and a babe was

"Just born, baptised, and gone."

For a few moments her little one was laid in her arms, to be covered with its mother's tears and kisses; and then convulsions came on, and the doctors saw Aimée had not long to live. The Bishop was immediately summoned, and remained ministering to her. At times she could not refrain from crying out with pain, but the anguish was forthwith repressed with the thought of Jesus Crucified. "My child," her saintly brother asked, "if it were God's Will, would you not go on bearing all these pains willingly?" "Oh yes, whatever He wills," Aimée answered, "I am His; His only." The Bishop gave her the last Sacraments, after which she intreated him to permit her to die a Religious of the Visitation. He consented, and in the presence of her sorrowing mother, and of all the community, Aimée was admitted first as novice, and immediately afterwards as a professed Sister. A few more loving words of prayer and aspiration, a few more tender exhortations from him who was so closely bound to her by natural and spiritual ties, a last blessing and commendation, and the childlike spirit, hardly less pure than the half-hour old babe gone before, quitted its earthly garment, and the widow's broken heart was healed for ever.

"In patria."

She was scarcely nineteen years of age.

"This dear child had lived so entirely among us," the Bishop wrote to a cousin, Madame de Montfort, "that she had made us all devoted to her, but myself more especially, for she loved me with a really filial affection. But we must love and adore God's Will, as she did, with the whole submission of our hearts. These were almost her last words. Indeed I never saw so holy a death, although the dear child had but five hours' preparation." And to the Mère Favre, who had known Aimée most of her short life, he writes, " It was not the Madame de Thorens that you knew, charming as that one was ; this was a Madame de Thorens wholly dedicated to God, lifted up from this world by her single aim at living to Him, full of light as to spiritual things, of knowledge of God and of herself—such, indeed, that one would have looked to see her become as her own mother over again. I will not dwell upon her holy end ; her exceeding suffering, and her constant cry, ' Oh Jesus, Lord Jesus, take me to Thyself, Oh precious Passion and Death of my Lord, I embrace you, I love you, I adore you, my only hope. Blessed be Jesus and Mary, Whom I love above all things.' And that so sweetly said. During the past year she had advanced in perfection, almost beyond idea, and especially since her widowhood. . . . . I loved her with far more than a brother's love." And to a friend the Bishop wrote, "This year we have lived amid sorrows—the untimely death of my brother and sister—untimely because unexpected, but most blessed in itself, and in the saintliness of the departure, especially my dear little sister, whose death was so happy that one of the doctors who saw her die, said to me that if the angels were mortal, they would surely wish to die such a death. What can we say at such times? Surely only, "Obmutui, et non aperui os meum, quoniam tu fecisti! But in honest truth I can scarcely ever go on to say, 'Amove a me plagas Tuas.'"[1]

As soon as he had rendered the last offices to his departed child, Francis ordered his carriage and left Annecy for Belley. His Chaplain ventured to remonstrate. "Will you leave Madame de Chantal desolate, Monseigneur, at such a trying moment?" he asked. "In truth," the Bishop replied, "she is not more afflicted than I am, but I know the strength of her soul, and the weakness of mine—I need comfort more than she does." And he went to pour out his

---

[1] Vulg. Ps. xxxix. 9, 10. English version, 10, 11: "I became dumb and opened not my mouth, for it was Thy doing. Take Thy plague away from me."

loving grief in the sympathising heart of the Bishop of Belley. Nor was Francis wrong as to the courage with which Madame de Chantal bore this sorrow. She wrote as follows concerning it to a Sister of her Order:

"I bless, I adore and bow every thought of my soul before the Holy Will Which has taken away my most dear and best loved child. Indeed she was, with good reason, the very soul of our heart (*l'âme de notre cœur*) to both our good Father and to me, who am unworthy of watching longer over such early ripe saintliness. But I cannot speak of it, my daughter—for in truth this loss has touched me very deeply, and what can I say? Oh God, Who woundest my heart with such mingled pity and gentleness that I can but bless Thee, give me grace to follow my most precious child both in her life and death! I will not attempt to write about either; our dear Father, whose child she was, will tell you all. But in truth we believe her to be in Paradise. Oh, my daughter, this sorrow turns my mind still more earnestly to Heaven, making me cry out with all my strength, 'Lord, what wilt Thou have me to do? My soul is poured out before Thee; I would live and breathe in and for Thee only. Thy Holy Will be done in me.' I cannot regain my ordinary cheerfulness since this blow, although, thanks be to God, my mind is quite at rest, and satisfied with

His Will, Which I adore in the pain and loss of my darling little one. Oh, dear daughter, we must indeed open our hearts wide to receive whatsoever the Divine Goodness sees fit to pour in."

And in another letter Madame de Chantal says, "It is true, God's Love has pierced my heart through and through with an exceeding sorrow in the loss of my daughter, Madame de Thorens. But what can I do, save lovingly to kiss the Dear Hand Which has dealt this heavy blow? May It ever be blessed! In truth this child was the best and most loveable that ever mother bore; I gazed at her exceeding holiness, and felt an indescribable comfort in seeing her so firmly resolved to give herself wholly to God. Oh, Dear Lord Jesus, I did not deserve such a companion! and perhaps it would not have been well either for her or me to have enjoyed in this life such sweet rest and happiness as we might have had together. Well, she has now entered upon that sovereign blessedness which I desired above all things for her, and God has so tempered this sorrow with mercy and love, that in the midst of it I can but thank and praise Him for His Gracious pity." . . . .

Other deaths followed not long after to swell that store in Paradise, which Francis de Sales knew so well how to prize—the Director of the College at Annecy, a dear friend of the Bishop's, and one of whom it was said that he "seemed like an angel ministering at the altar, and through his intense self-devotion broke down while yet young," went to his rest; as also M. de Sainte Catherine,[1] so often alluded to, who was a Canon, Grand Penitentiary, and more than an ordinary friend to Francis. M. de Sainte Catherine was his confessor, "his right arm and his very eye;" and the Bishop loved him with all the deep love for which his warm strong nature had such intense capacity. When this good priest's last illness began, the Bishop at first desired his recovery with an eagerness proportioned to the value he felt for M. de Sainte Catherine's presence at his side. But seeing that God willed it otherwise, Francis de Sales, as usual, bent his will wholly to his Lord's, and thenceforth his only object was in some measure to return the spiritual benefits done to him by his friend, and help him fitly to prepare for death. During his last hours, the dying man told his brother, the Prior of Talloires, what his knowledge of the Bishop's wishes, as well as the nature of his office as confessor, had hitherto kept silent—that his penitent was "a very saint—a John Baptist in purity, a Carlo Borromeo in humility." It was Francis who ministered the last consolations of religion to his friend, who said

---

[1] He was so called to distinguish him from his brother, M. de Coëx, the Prior of the Abbey of Talloires, on the Lake of Annecy.

the Litanies of the Dying by his side, who spoke the last "Proficiscere" to the parting soul, who gave him the last Blessing, and closed his eyes—and taking his rosary as a memorial, wrote to Madame de Chantal, "God Who gave him to us for His service, has recalled him for His Own Glory. His Holy Name be praised! He will supply this loss, and will raise us up other fellow-labourers to take the place of these two dear friends whom He has called from the vineyard to take their place for ever at His own table."

As the Bishop left his dear friend's death-bed, he was called to one of a very different character—a man of well-known evil life, who, now that all earthly hopes and gains had lost their charm, and death and Judgment alone were before him, was plunged into the most fearful despair. The unhappy man repulsed all attempts to give him spiritual consolation, and refused to see any priest. The Bishop went at once to him, and by his tender, winning persuasions, blended as he knew so well how to blend pity with firmness, he reached the poor sinner's heart, and brought him to feel that God would surely not turn a pitiless ear to one who could kindle so much pity in a fellow-creature's heart. Francis did not cease from his labour of love until the sick man, truly penitent, made public acknowledgment of his faults, and after receiving the Sacraments, passed from this world, reconciled to his God.

CHAPTER VIII.

FRANCIS DE SALES AT PARIS.—HIS BROTHER APPOINTED HIS COADJUTOR. — VISIT TO AVIGNON AND LYONS. — HIS DEATH.

FREQUENTLY as the Bishop of Geneva had been urged to revisit Paris, where his fame as a preacher and director had never been forgotten, he had never gone so far from his diocese since entering upon its charge. But in the autumn of the year 1618, he went there with the Cardinal Prince of Savoy, who was sent to negotiate the marriage of the Prince of Piedmont with Christine de France, and together with the President Favre, took up his abode in the house of Marechal d'Ancre, Rue de Tournon.[1] The Bishop was immediately seized upon to preach on S. Martin's Day for the Oratorians, and all Paris flocked to hear him, the King and both Queens, all the leading ecclesiastics and courtiers, so that when the time came for the preacher himself to arrive, there was no means of getting through the crowd into the church save through a window reached by a ladder. People

[1] Now No. 10, Rue de Tournon.

who had read his books and heard of his repute as an orator went expecting a great display of eloquence, and were much disappointed when, partly, perhaps, as a lesson to those who then, as now, flocked to hear a celebrated preacher as they would an opera-singer; partly from personal humility and dislike of display, Francis kept to a most simple narration of the life of S. Martin. After the sermon he heard people saying how disappointed they were with the "*montagnard*," and that it was not worth the trouble of coming to hear him! Some of the Bishop's friends regretted this very greatly, but S. Vincent de Paul, with whom Francis now became intimately associated, received a quite different impression, and remarked to his brethren that it was after this fashion that true saints repressed the natural clinging to renown and applause which all men possess.

If this first sermon disappointed the world, its disappointment was soon forgotten. Francis de Sales preached through Advent at Saint André des Arts, and the throng which attended him was as considerable as before; cardinals, bishops, princes, fine ladies, all flocked to hear one who was likened to one of the first Apostles. Francis himself could not understand why there should be so much excitement about his sermons. "Are you not astonished," he said to a friend, "to see all these Parisians run after me, with my heavy dull sermons, and tame delivery?" "Yours is Annecy eloquence, or perhaps more truly it comes from Paradise," was the answer.

After Advent was passed, the dignitaries of S. André wished to present the preacher with a handsome service of plate, but he entirely refused any kind of compensation, and continued to preach wherever he was called, saying jokingly, that he would always rather prepare a sermon than say no.[1] The consequence was that during a year which Francis de Sales spent in Paris, he preached no less than three hundred and sixty-five sermons—sometimes preaching twice, or even thrice in the same day. This, however, was by no means the heaviest part of his work. Mgr. de Genève's reputation for personal holiness was so great that as he went through the streets people came near to touch his garments as a saint, and his room and confessional were ceaselessly crowded with applicants for every possible kind of spiritual assistance. Sometimes, it must be owned, the visitors were both intrusive and impertinent, but even then they were always courteously dealt with. Thus on one occasion a man came into the Bishop's room, asking abruptly, "Are you the Bishop of Geneva?" "Yes, sir, I am." "Then I should like to ask you, whom men call an apostolic Bishop, whether the

[1] "J'ai plutôt faict un sermon que de dire nenni."

Apostles went about in carriages?" "Certainly, when it was necessary." " I should like to see that proved from Scripture !" "Then read the eighth chapter of the Acts of the Apostles, and you will find Philip sitting in a carriage with Queen Candace's eunuch." "That is all very fine," the other answered, "but Philip was not in his own carriage, it was the Queen of Ethiopia's —and he did not go about in a carriage all gilding and silk, with splendid horses and liveried servants, as you scandalise the world by doing, you who pretend, forsooth, to be a saint ! 'Tis a nice easy way of going to heaven, indeed !" "To tell you the truth," the Bishop answered quietly, "the good people of Geneva, who have seized my diocesan revenues, pare the ground so closely that it is all I can do to live in the humblest way on what is left. I never yet possessed a carriage of my own, or the means of having one, but while I am here, the King sends one of his carriages for me, as for the other gentlemen, who are in attendance upon the Prince of Savoy." "Then are you really poor?" was the astonished rejoinder.

Among his many visitors, the Bishop had to receive not a few ladies. One day, after he had been preaching, he was surrounded by a whole troop of them, each with some special question to ask or difficulty to be solved, and as in their eagerness all talked at once, M. de Genève turned smiling to them, and said,

"Mesdames, I will gladly answer all your questions, if you will answer one of mine: what is to happen in an assembly where everybody talks and nobody listens?" Whereupon, says Bishop Camus, more truly than civilly, the ladies dispersed like croaking frogs when you throw a stone into the marsh where they abound!

Some of his friends, the learned Père Bourdoise among others, remonstrated with Francis for allowing so much of his time to be taken up by women, expressing regret that he did not rather devote himself to the training of priests, than Religious of the Visitation. His answer was characteristically humble; that doubtless nothing was so important as training good Priests to serve the Church, but that it was a work beyond his capacity, and one which was better done by others, such as M. de Bérulle. Moreover, that the claims of his diocese would not allow of any extensive devotion to such work. "I leave the goldsmiths to manipulate their gold and silver," he said; "potters like me had better stick to their clay moulding!" But he maintained at the same time that it was an important work to train women in holiness, considering how vast their influence in the world and the Church must always be. "Remember, too," he added, "that though women are weak, they are very brave sometimes; the holy women of Jerusalem followed our

Lord even to Calvary, when only one Apostle dared be found at the foot of the Cross." Among the pious women who sought guidance at the Bishop's hands while in Paris, was the celebrated Angélique Arnaud, abbess of Port Royal, whose quick impulsive character, ever aspiring after great things, eager to sound the depths of feeling and fact, passionately moved to indignation at evil doing, ever ready to be made angry or satirical by the " sillinesses, childishness and imperfections of her sisters ;" greedy of sacrifice, impatient of control ;—had a special interest for the skilled director, who evidently felt that he could subdue and guide the strong will which often rebelled against authority, even when wishing to submit. Some fragments of his correspondence with the Mère Angélique lead one to wish for more.

"I see clearly what a swarm of troubles, self-love fosters and pours in upon your heart, my dear daughter," the Bishop says, "and I know well that your subtle, delicate, fertile mind feels the difficulty, but after all, these are but inclinations, and while you are conscious of their importunity and resist them heartily, it is obvious that they have not your deliberate consent. Your soul has accepted the wish God implanted in it to belong wholly to Him ; do not allow yourself to be persuaded that you consent to any of these opposing impulses. Your heart may be buffeted by roving passions, but I do not believe that you are guilty of consenting to them." . . . .

Angélique had complained of her own conscious affectation in speaking and writing; her tendency to *se faire valoir*, and to this the Bishop replies: "In conversation such affectation glides in so imperceptibly, that we are scarcely conscious of it, but of course directly you do perceive it, you must change your tone. As to letters, it is rather—I should say much more insupportable, for you can see what you are doing better, and if you are conscious of any notable affectation, the hand which perpetrated it must be punished by making it write another altered letter."[1]

Affectation was an enemy upon which Francis de Sales always waged unrelenting war. Some one objected, in what he considered an affected spirit, that a lady well known in the world, and known also to be under his direction, continued to adopt many worldly fashions, and to join worldly society. The Bishop cut short all such remark by the answer that the lady in question had a lawful end in view, obedience to her husband. The objector was not satisfied. "She wears earrings!"

"I do not even know whether she has ears!" Francis de Sales retorted, " but anyhow Rebecca, who was

[1] The whole letter will be found among S. Francis's Spiritual Letters in the accompanying volume.

every whit as good, was none the worse for wearing the earrings given her by Isaac!"

Another penitent kept returning restlessly to the troubles already disposed of. "You have more need of submission than of reasoning," was the decisive reply. Lowly beginnings and simple rules were most to his taste. "You cannot attain to high contemplation," he says, "but you can read some good book, and think it carefully over; your health will not bear fasting, but it will be none the worse if you abstain from delicacies; you cannot leave the world, but you may study not to follow its tone; pure love is beyond your grasp, then strive to love God out of gratitude, and for your own sake; you do not feel any lively contrition, try to seek and ask for it more earnestly; you cannot give liberal alms, give a cup of cold water for God's Sake; you have no grievous wrongs to endure, strive to bear little vexations without murmur. You are as yet too weak to bear contempt, but you can bear a passing slight patiently; you are not called upon to sacrifice your life, but you are often called to endure trifling discomforts, and passing annoyances." He could not abide a harsh, stiff, self-asserting piety, or one which made itself disagreeable and inconvenient to others. Goodness, he taught (and his example assuredly illustrated his precept), should always be attractive, ready to adapt itself to the wills and wishes of others; cheerful, bright, well-balanced, free from all singularity and self-consciousness. For instance, Francis had always avoided sitting for his picture, but at last he was persuaded to yield this point; and the painter induced him to grant a further sitting, on the ground that for want of it the portrait would represent him as much handsomer than he really was! "I should say that your reason is more ingenious than ingenuous!" Francis answered, "but I will not be obstinate." So he sat patiently for two hours more, at the end of which the artist released him, exclaiming, "Oh, Monseigneur, you have given me great satisfaction!" "And you have given me great mortification!" the Bishop answered smiling, "but I forgive you, if you will promise never to do it again."

Simplicity, he used to say, means a heart which looks straight to truth, to duty, and to God. He abhorred all equivocation and exaggeration, so that he never would express even humility save when he really felt it, or proffer any kindness unless he meant to fulfil it. One of his spiritual children owned in a letter to experiencing jealousy and envy of another; in reply the Bishop expressed his great satisfaction not at her jealous feeling, but at her honesty in avowing it. "This is the way," he said, "to tear self-love from the inner folds of our hearts. It is a real delight to a loving Father to hear his daughter own that she has been envious and malicious; the envy, followed by so honest a confession, will be blessed to you, and the hand which wrote those lines is as brave as Alexander's own." He liked to speak, as he said, "à l'ancienne gauloise;" "roundly and straight out;" and during the fourteen years that M. de Belley was under his direction, that prelate says he never could observe the slightest singularity or affectation in anything Francis said or did. So much was this the case that some of the Canons of his own Cathedral, while admiring the goodness and purity of their Bishop's life, remarked that nevertheless he would never be canonised, he was so much like other men in his ordinary way of life.

This he persevered in, even during the busy Paris season, seeking to do each duty that came before him amid that whirl of busy life as calmly and quietly as though there were nothing else to do; and as he said, not allowing himself to be distracted from what he had to do by subjects of mere curiosity, not reading books which were not useful to him, and steadily making a duty of order and method in all things. But assuredly the true secret of all this serenity and calmness was the perpetual recollection, to which Francis de Sales had attained from an early period, and which he strove to keep up even when lying down at night to sleep. The activity of his life often hindered his giving any considerable time to uninterrupted prayer and meditation, and when Madame de Chantal asked him if he had been able to find time for his morning prayers, he replied that he had always time for the equivalent, *i.e.* doing all things to and for God in a recollected spirit. "What a blessed thing active prayer is," he said once to a friend; and on being asked to explain what was meant, he said, "I mean by active prayer doing everything in God's Presence and for His Service." He held that all our faults arise from forgetfulness of that Holy Presence, and he considered his yearly retreat, during which that Presence was his sole thought, as absolutely essential to his own soul's welfare, and that of his diocese.

But the fascination of S. Francis's private life must not entirely lead us away from the more public phases of the same; while he was preaching, and confessing, and guiding souls heavenwards, the political affairs for which his journey to Paris had been undertaken went on; the royal marriage was arranged, and the heir apparent of Savoy and Christine of France were duly united. The latter was anxious to secure her husband's illustrious countryman as her Grand Aumonier, or Chaplain, and everyone, except Mgr. de Genève, approved her choice. He had a decided objection to court life in any shape, and as he wrote to Madame de Chantal, he neither directly nor indirectly sought this office, his only wish being to spend the remainder of his days in the service of his Lord. The affectionate earnestness with which Princess Christine urged his acceptance of a post so closely connected with herself overruled the Bishop's difficulties, but before he consented to her wishes, he made two stipulations—one that his duties to Her Royal Highness should not be permitted in any way to interfere with those he owed to his diocese, or with his residence at Annecy; the other that he should not be asked to accept any salary. The Princess agreed, but in doing so she put a valuable ring upon the Bishop's finger. "This, Madame," he immediately said, "will be profitable to our poor at Annecy."

Just at this time the Abbey of Sainte Geneviève, with its large revenues, fell vacant, and the King pressed it upon Francis de Sales; as vainly as a more important position was pressed upon him directly afterwards. Cardinal de Retz used his utmost influence to induce the saintly man (whose singular unworldliness and calm devotion must have presented so strange a contrast to his own troublous political career) to become his coadjutor, and successor as Archbishop of Paris. In vain the Cardinal offered every inducement he could think of—absolute freedom in the government of the diocese, the appointment of his brother to the

Bishopric of Geneva, the immense sphere of usefulness opened to him in so important a charge. All was in vain. "My present diocese," Francis persistently replied, "is the special portion of His vineyard which God has given me to cultivate, and I cannot forsake it. One does not give oneself to the Church with a view to making a worldly position for oneself, but in order to till that piece of ground allotted to one by the householder."

"It is certainly preferable to be poor within the courts of God's House," the Bishop wrote to Madame de Chantal, "rather than to dwell in kings' palaces. I have gone through my novitiate at Court, but I should be very sorry to have to make my profession. . . . But, thank God, I think being at Court has taught me to be more simple and less worldly; when once one has grasped the idea of the Goodness and Power of God, how can one care for the miserable vanities of this world? I was preaching the other day before the Queen, but not with more satisfaction than to our poor little House at Annecy."

The Royal bride and bridegroom left Paris soon after their marriage, and the Bishop of Geneva returned with them to Savoy, visiting Angoulême, Bourges, Moulins and Lyons, inspecting the houses of the Visitation as he passed. He never would take the Princess to visit any of these communities, though he accompanied her to other religious houses ; and when, at Bourges, his spiritual children complained of this disappointment, he would only answer, " I want you to learn to be humble and hidden in your lives, wholly detached from all vain worldly curiosity." Francis was quite in earnest when he stipulated that his office as chaplain to the Princess of Piedmont was not to take him away from Annecy, and accordingly Her Royal Highness requested that his brother, Jean François de Sales, who was also his Vicar General, might be appointed as his deputy. This was done, and two months later the Duke of Savoy obtained a Papal brief making him likewise coadjutor to Francis, under the title of Bishop of Chalcedon, an appointment very acceptable to the Bishop of Geneva, who, though not an old man, began to feel worn and weary, and often unequal to all his work, in which he was as indefatigable as ever. "My brother is a Bishop at last," he writes, "a fact which certainly does not make me a richer man, but it is a great relief, and gives me some hope of being able to withdraw from the pressure of business, and consequently it is worth more to me than a Cardinal's hat." His wish would have been to give up everything to the coadjutor, and himself to retire to a quiet spot on the Lake of Annecy, where he had restored an old chapel, and built a few hermit-like cells. It was close to the Benedictine monastery of Talloires, and Francis told its Prior how he looked forward to coming there, and serving God with his pen and his breviary, during his declining days. He had several spiritual works in his mind, which his present active life gave him no time to write.[1] "And I think that ideas will pour down upon me from above like winter snow-flakes upon our mountains. Oh for the wings of a dove, that I might fly away to that sacred resting-place, and take breath beneath the shadow of the Cross. 'Expectabo donec veniat immutatio mea.'" But God in His Gracious Mercy was preparing to shorten the waiting, and to give His faithful servant a better, surer rest than even his peaceful hermitage on the pleasant shore of that lovely lake.

The Bishop of Chalcedon was consecrated at Turin, January 17, 1621, and came immediately to Annecy, where his saintly brother took every opportunity of

---

[1] S. Francis de Sales proposed to himself to write a Life of our Lord Jesus Christ, a work on the Epistles of St. Paul, one upon the Love of our Neighbour, as the counterpart to that on the Love of God ; and also a Treatise on the duties of Parish Priests, in the shape of a series of pastoral letters. Some one remarked that this was no light prospect of toil, especially at his age, and with his presentiment of coming death. "It is quite true," the Bishop answered, "but if one means to keep up an active mind, one must set oneself more work than it is possible to accomplish, as if there were certainly a long life before one ; while still one must not set one's heart on doing more than if one was to die to-morrow."

putting him into the foremost position, answering the remonstrances of some who did not like to see their beloved Bishop in any way set aside, with the words of John the Baptist, "Oportet illum crescere, me autem minui." To his brother Francis he often said that he should never have asked for so great a blessing as to have so effective a right hand supplied to him, but that God having willed it thus, he heartily thanked His Holy Providence, hoping to throw the part of Martha upon the younger and stronger man, while he accepted that of Mary for himself. The new Bishop, however, could not remain permanently at Annecy, as his special duties called him to Turin, and Francis's labours scarcely seem to have been much lightened. During such seasons as the younger brother could be at Annecy, Francis spent long hours in putting him as completely as possible in possession of all the diocesan affairs,. explaining all his views and intentions for his people, entering even into the detail of personal character among the clergy, and the disposition of parishes, often saying with a cheerful smile, "I want you to know all these things, for who can say how soon my call will come?" Indeed, the conviction that his end was at hand grew daily stronger on Francis's mind. One day two of his brothers came suddenly into his room and found him absorbed in meditation. He asked to be left alone awhile with God, saying that he had been warned of Him to give his most serious attention to a matter of the utmost importance. As the brothers pressed to know what it might be—perhaps some book he proposed to write—the Bishop answered, " It is nothing of that sort. Be patient, you shall soon know." They left him, nothing doubting but that he alluded to his death, and watching him with loving eyes, the impression was confirmed ; for his daily life became more and more as that of one who makes ready for a distant journey, whence he never looks to return. All his temporal affairs were put into the most perfect order ; as to his spiritual life, it seemed as though there could not be much left there to do, and yet the bystanders had an undefined sense of ever increasing beauty and perfection, gathering as it were in a halo around him. Perhaps Francis's exceeding sweetness and sunny brightness were the more noticeable from the natural unlikeness between the brothers. The Bishop of Chalcedon was grave, austere, silent ; his character and manner were severe, his dealings with other men would probably have been harsh, had they not been softened and tempered by his elder brother's gentleness and love. Even so he was sometimes impatient of Francis's indulgent ways, and scarcely thought it fitting that a Bishop should allow himself to be so easily interrupted at every one's beck and bidding. Thus one day, just as they were going to say their office together, Francis was called away to hear a confession. It proved lengthy, and the Bishop of Chalcedon was already discomposed by waiting, when at the end of the first nocturn they discovered they were saying the wrong office. Jean François could not restrain some expression of annoyance, but the Bishop of Geneva gently observed that God was less hard to please than men, and that He would accept the nocturn they had already said, although not the correct one, and so they continued the office without more ado.

Sometimes Francis indulged his natural playfulness at his brother's expense. They were just sitting down to table one day, when a poor servant girl asked for the Bishop of Geneva, and, as usual, he went to her, and listened to all she had to say without hurrying her. Meanwhile the Bishop of Chalcedon fretted and fumed with impatience, and on his brother's return, exclaimed pettishly, "Really, you are enough to drive everybody wild!" "Not everybody," Francis said, smiling, "I and my visitor are somebodies, and we were not driven wild." And then, as they began their meal, he turned upon Jean François, saying, "Do you know, brother, that I think you have really done a very great kindness to one woman! Guess who I mean."

The Bishop of Chalcedon made several wrong

guesses, to each of which Francis shook his head, and at last he said, "I mean the woman who would have been your wife if you had ever married." And he went on to say, more gravely, that Bishops who would be faithful to their duty must never deny themselves to any one, but be like public fountains, at which every creature, man or beast, can freely slake its thirst.

Francis occupied himself also with another member of his family, the only child of his favourite brother, Louis de Sales, whose character was always serious and devout, and of whom his venerable uncle entertained the greatest expectations. "This child is destined for great things," he sometimes said, and to Charles Auguste himself he used to say, "Remember, dear child, that God has made you a chosen vessel of Grace, and that if you are faithful in His service, He has great things for you to do." In this last year of the Bishop's life, he took his young nephew into his own house, telling Louis de Sales that he "meant to pour into the boy's head all that God had put into his own." His opinion was justified, although the time in which Charles was permitted to be under the Saint's guidance was brief. But he was a worthy descendant of S. Francis, and in later years became actually his successor in the See of Geneva.

Day by day the infirmities of the flesh pressed

more heavily upon Francis : his legs swelled painfully, so that he could scarcely walk, and they were also covered with sores, and the oppression on his chest grew so distressing, that at times he would say, putting his hand on his breast, " I feel something here which tells me I have not long to live." His mind was constantly fixed on the thought of death, but not sorrowfully. No one could more heartily have said in the words of the All Saints' Hymn,

"Exsules
Vocate nos in patriam."

One day his brother remarked that he was very thoughtful, and asked if anything troubled him? " Far from it," was the reply, " but I am on the watch to hear the hour of my departure ring out." " I am about to make a review of my conscience," he wrote to Madame de Chantal, "so as to prepare for eternal life. I feel my whole soul tending more earnestly than ever towards God and the life everlasting. Oh, my God, how happy I should be, if some day, after Holy Communion, I could find that my Dear Lord's Heart had taken the place of my own poor wretched heart."

Notwithstanding his physical suffering, Francis would not give up any of his work; when those around intreated him to spare himself, he would reply, with his own gentle smile, " I must die before long, and what matters it, a little sooner or later?" It was remarked that no sign of physical pain ever appeared on his countenance or manner, which was now, as ever, calm and serenely beautiful. In May, 1622, Pope Gregory XV. commissioned the Bishop of Geneva to preside over a Chapter of the Feuillants, who could not agree as to the election of a general; and in spite of the remonstrances of relations and friends Francis went to Pignerol, in obedience to this command, only replying, "What could be happier than to die in obedience. I have but a little while to live, and must strive to do my best for that short time." His obedience cost him dear; at times he was compelled to quit the Chapter, his sufferings were so great; but nevertheless all his spare time was spent in preaching, confessing, or administering his more special episcopal functions. One day, between fatigue and heat, for the weather was oppressive, Francis fainted in the Church. He was carried out, and on his restoration, he observed to the monks who were attending on him, that it "was not well for the members of a thorn-crowned Head to be so delicate."

From Pignerol Francis went to Turin, where he refused the splendid reception the Princess wished to give him, and begged to be allowed to sojourn with the Feuillants. He more than ever shrank from the bondage of Court life, and while the Royal Family of

Savoy pressed him to let his brother fill his place at Annecy, and himself to remain at Turin as Archbishop, his only longing was to return to Annecy and toil to the last for his "dear people." This desire was increased by tidings that the crops had failed, much suffering consequently pressing on the poor. "Ah!" Francis exclaimed, "I will sell my mitre and crosier, and my garments themselves to relieve my poor people." Early in August, the desired return to Annecy took place, and the Bishop kept his word; everything he possessed or could lay hands on was devoted to the poor; among other things a valuable diamond ring, just presented to him by the Princess. Some of the faithful, finding that their Bishop had parted with this, took pains to restore it, when, as might be expected, it was forthwith sold again. This happened several times, till it became a popular saying that it was the beggars' ring rather than the Bishop's.

But the venerable Francis was not destined by God to spend many more days in the diocese he loved so well. The Duke of Savoy was going in state to meet Louis XIII. at Avignon, who had been in Languedoc suppressing a rising among the Huguenots, and was now making a royal progress, accompanied by the two Queens, Marie de Medicis and Anne of Austria; and the Duke's daughter-in-law, the Princess of Piedmont, desired to be accompanied by her Grand

Aumonier, the Bishop of Geneva. Francis's relations and friends were urgent that he should plead the great infirmity of health, which increased daily upon him, as a reason for not obeying this summons; but the Bishop would not hear of this, both because he looked upon his Sovereign's wish as imperative, and also because he hoped to obtain certain benefits for his own diocese, in a personal interview with Louis XIII. of France. "We must go where God calls us as long as we can move at all," he said, "and when we can go no farther, then it will be time to stop." But he believed himself that he should never return, and before leaving Annecy Francis made every preparation as though to die. His departure was fixed for the 9th November, and a few days before he summoned all his available brothers and some few friends, saying that as the hour of his departure drew near he wished to read his will to them. They replied, under the supposition that he alluded to his approaching journey to Avignon, but Francis explained that he meant another journey, "the longest, and the last." Nothing could be simpler than his will. He wished to be buried in the Church of the Visitation at Annecy, unless he died without the diocese, in which case he left the place of his burial to those who might be about him, only, wherever it might be, he expressly forbade any pomp or display in the offices rendered him. On the 7th November the Bishop spent the whole morning in reviewing his own spiritual condition, and made a careful confession, after which he transferred all papers and business matters to the Bishop of Chalcedon, and when this was done, he expressed his great satisfaction. "Truly," he said, "it seems to me as though, by God's Grace, I scarcely tread this earth with one foot, the other is already raised to depart." A Frenchman came that evening to borrow some money of him, and on his promising to restore it faithfully, "You must make haste if so," the Bishop answered, "or your debt will be paid to me by our Eternal King. In truth," he added, "I hope that before long neither you nor I will want for anything." Within two months, the Bishop and this man were both dead. On the 8th November—his last day at Annecy—the Bishop took leave of his relations and friends, as not looking to see them again. To one of his clergy, a parish priest, who came to ask his blessing, the Bishop said, "It matters not where I die, so long as God grants me a holy death. I am going to our Dear Lord, and you and I shall not meet again in this world." And to an intimate friend, the Père Anselme, he said, "This journey will cost me my life, and we shall not see each other again till we meet in Paradise, but we must strive to be obedient, like our Master, to the death."

The Chapter came bodily to take leave of their Bishop, with nearly everyone around, but perhaps the parting which cost him most was that with the Sisters of the Visitation. Madame de Chantal had been for some time absent, superintending the beginning of some new houses, but the Founder carried every individual of the Order in his most inmost heart. He celebrated for the last time in their Chapel, and gave them the gorgeous chasuble he wore (a recent present from the Princess), saying, "When friends part they like to give one another some love-token." Then he spoke some few words of parting admonition, bidding them above all things seek the graces of humility, simplicity, and obedience. "My dear daughters," he said, "ask nothing, and refuse nothing, but be ever ready to do whatever God and holy obedience require of you. Let your only wish be to love God; your only ambition to possess Him. Adieu, my children, till we meet in the next world."

One of the Religious exclaimed, amid her tears, "Oh, Monseigneur, God grant us the blessing of seeing you again!"

"But if it is not His Will that I should return, will you not equally bless Him?" the Bishop said, gently.

The next morning, November 9, 1622, Francis de Sales left Annecy, never to return living. At the last moment, as Francis was mounting his horse, his stern, dignified brother, the Bishop of Chalcedon, was so overcome by feeling, as to throw himself on his knees before him, unable to speak for sobs. All the leading clergy and laity of Annecy went with the Bishop to Seyssel, where he was to take the Rhone boat as far as Belley. The weather was severe, with a bitter wind and icy-cold rain, and his attendants were uneasy at the Bishop's exposure. "Never mind," he said, "you know we are subject in this world to the 'beggarly elements.' Let us think rather of the blessed country to which we are journeying, and where I shall soon arrive. I shall not travel like the army, I shall move without drum or trumpet. I shall be there before men know that I have set off." And so he went on talking gently and calmly of the things of another life.

At Belley, Francis visited the Sisters of the Visitation. One, the Sœur Simplicienne, said that she prayed earnestly that God would spare their spiritual Father to them yet a few years. "I intreat you, do not so!" the Bishop said, almost imploringly. "Can you not rejoice in the thought of my rest? I am so weary, so weary."

From Belley he went to Lyons, and thence by Valence and Saint Andéal to Avignon, where, amid the general excitement caused by the arrival of the King, and the two Queens, and all their brilliant suite, no one was more thought of than the lowly Saint of Geneva. Indeed, so great was the general eagerness to see him, that as he went about the streets, crowds followed him, kissing the hem of his garment, and kneeling down to ask his blessing, much to the humble Bishop's distress. The Royal party made a magnificent entry into the town, and everyone was eager to see the show: Francis meanwhile knelt in his chamber, absorbed in prayer, and when some of his attendants asked him to come and witness the brilliant cortége, he answered gently, " I leave that to you all, who still have your place in the world. I have no more to do with it. I am speeding to my Father in Heaven, and I must do His work, so that I may be ready to render my account."

The Bishop avoided all Court entertainments and gatherings, save such as were a part of his duty, and saw little of anyone save on spiritual matters. He only frequented the different religious houses of Avignon, where everyone was eager to gather up words of counsel and guidance from his revered lips; and was glad to begin the homeward journey on the 25th November. The journey was harassing, and the crowd of travellers made accommodation difficult, so that, as usual, Francis left the best of everything for others, and in spite of his physical sufferings, underwent much discomfort on the way. At Lyons many persons were eager to have so honoured a guest in their homes, but the Bishop declined all invitations, preferring to occupy a little apartment in the gardener's house belonging to the Visitation Convent, which was ordinarily kept for the use of their confessor. The Sisters were distressed at their Founder being so unsuitably lodged, but he silenced all remonstrance, and established himself there. Not even now did he relax in his energetic labours ; he overlooked and arranged everything for the Sisters, giving them many precious counsels and instructions. One day, when he had been doing this, a Sister handed him pen and paper, saying, " Mon père, write down what you specially wish us to cultivate ? " He took the paper, and wrote upon it in large letters the one word, " Humility."

Madame de Chantal, who had not seen him for more than three years,—having been occupied among the more distant foundations of the Order,—came to Lyons, looking forward with the utmost desire to see her beloved Spiritual Father again. She was struck with the alteration since their parting. Looking physically ill as he did, there was a supernatural beauty about his countenance, a gentle brightness altogether of Heaven in his whole manner, which impressed her exceedingly. After the first greetings, Francis remarked that they had two or three hours free for intercourse, and asked Madame de Chantal "which should speak first?" She replied eagerly, "I must, if you please, for indeed I greatly need that you should take my soul's state under consideration."

The Bishop checked her eagerness by saying, "What, ma mère! are you still impetuous and eager? I expected to find you calm as the angels! No, we will not begin to talk yet of you, we will talk about our Congregation." And for four hours they discussed the affairs of the Order. Poor Madame de Chantal, she never had the comfort of that personal manipulation of her soul which she so desired at the Saint's hands! Whether the Bishop considered the affairs of the Order too pressing to be postponed, or whether he thought that the sacrifice of self, and detachment even from spiritual help involved by such obedience, would profit her more than any other help, we cannot judge; but certain it is that, though Madame de Chantal would fain have lingered at Lyons awhile to be near her venerable Director, he would not allow it, but obliged her to continue the appointed round of visits to the Houses at Grénoble and Belley, in spite of severe weather.

It was not only by the Visitation Sisters that the Bishop was sought: persons of every class and age poured in upon him to gather up precious words of instruction and guidance, and the gardener's little cottage was besieged with visitors from the town and from the members of both Courts. But few records are left of these interviews. A Jesuit Father talking with him, observed, "We have three Francis' canonised—S. Francis of Assisi, S. Francis de Paule, and S. Francis Xavier; we only want S. Francis de Sales." "Ah! would to God indeed that he were holy!" the Bishop answered. A Sorbonne doctor ventured to remark that everyone held him to be a Saint, the speaker included; "Sir," Francis said gravely, "may God preserve you from such sorry holiness! You are strangely mistaken. I do indeed desire to please God, and you can do much to forward my progress in holiness by your prayers."

Among his frequent visitors were Monsieur and Madame Olier, he being at that time Intendant de la Justice at Lyons. They brought to the Bishop of Geneva their third son, Jean Jacques Olier, who became in later years the founder of the Seminary of Saint Sulpice. At this time he was a vehement, passionate, ungovernable boy of ten, and his parents, who destined him to be an ecclesiastic, were disposed to fear that he would never be sufficiently disciplined or softened in character for such a life. A friend, Doctor Chaillard, afterwards Curé of Villefranche, describes the occasion on which Madame Olier brought her children to the good Bishop of Geneva, and how she told him that Jean Jacques was not a good boy, but refractory, and so unruly that he often made her and his father very angry.[1] But Francis de Sales bade her have patience, and foretold that the boy would become a light of the Church. If he had lived, the Bishop had promised himself to take Jean Jacques and train him for the priestly life. God did not will that this should be, but certainly the blessing he promised was abundantly granted, as M. Olier's future life and work proved.

On the second Sunday in Advent the Bishop preached at the Jesuit Church; on December 18th and 21st at the Visitation, and on Christmas Eve at the Récollets Church, in compliance with a request from Queen Marie de Medicis. His days were then nearly spent, and that night he suffered severely from the cold, and felt very ill. Yet he celebrated midnight Mass at the Visitation, communicated all the Sisters, and then preached on the Nativity with such glowing fervour, that the Superior, Mère de Bloney, could not refrain from asking him afterwards whether he had not received more than ordinary grace during that Mass. " I could have fancied," she said, "that I

---

[1] "Jean Jacques, le plus jeune, n'était point sage, mais discole, et tellement déréglé en ses déportements, qu'il donnait souvent sujet à son père et à elle-même de pester contre lui."—(Vie de M. Olier.)

saw the angel Gabriel standing beside you when you began the *Gloria in excelsis*." "My dear daughter," the Bishop said kindly, "my heart is very dead to inspirations; I need that the angels should speak very plainly to my material hearing with their holy melody." And when the good Sister pressed the subject, he said, "In truth, I was never more comforted at the Altar; the Holy Child was there, so why not the Angels?"

That Christmas Day the Bishop confessed the Prince and Princess of Piedmont, said the Early Mass (de l'aurore) for them at the Dominican Church, his third Mass not being said till nearly midday. Later in the day he presided at the ceremony of taking the habit at the Visitation, preaching on the Epistle for the Midnight Mass: "Abnegantes impietatem et sæcularia desideria, sobrie et juste, et pie vivamus in hoc sæculo." ("Denying ungodliness and worldly lusts, we should live soberly, righteously, and godly, in this present world." (Titus ii. 12.) After that the Bishop gave a Conference to the Sisters, received sundry visitors, and finally went to pay a parting visit to the Queen Mother, who left Lyons the next morning.

On S. Stephen's Day, the Bishop again did the work of one in strong health, coming about five o'clock in the evening to the Visitation (where he had

s

already said Mass that morning), and giving the Religious an instruction which lasted two hours. He was still teaching them, the good Sisters hanging upon his words, when his servants came with torches, telling the Bishop that it was late. "I could go on all night without remembering that," he said, smiling, "but obedience calls me, and I must go."

The next day, the Feast of S. John, the Bishop was conscious on rising that his sight was very imperfect. He spoke of it to his attendants, saying, "That means that I am going, and I bless God for it; the failing body weighs down the soul." When dressed he made his own confession, said Mass, communicated the Sisters, and, after hearing the Superior's confession, remained some little time in conversation with her. She was struck with the alteration in his face, and asked if he felt worse, but he would only answer that "all things work together for good to them that love God."

Leaving the church, Francis met the Duc de Bellegarde and M. de Villeroy, Governors of Lyons and Burgundy, and he remained some time talking to them, with his head bare, notwithstanding the bitter cold and fog of the atmosphere, and then he went to the Prince of Piedmont, returning home at length quite exhausted. After taking some food, the Bishop began to write letters, until he was interrupted by visitors. His servants noticed that, contrary to his wont, he did not conduct these visitors to the door when they left, but remained sitting in his chair. They were sure by this that the Bishop felt very ill, and were trying to persuade him to postpone leaving Lyons the day following (as he proposed), when Francis fainted. He was moved to his bed, and shortly after a sort of seizure followed, which, however, did not affect his mind. The Rector of the Jesuits kept making acts of faith, hope, love, and contrition for him, and, as he was able, Francis repeated them after him. A friendly Religious came in and expressed his regret at the Bishop's state. "Father," he replied, "I am waiting on God's Mercy: 'Expectans expectavi Dominum et intendit mihi.'"[1]

"If it were God's Will, you would gladly depart at once?" the Religious asked.

"If God wills it, I will it too," the Bishop answered, smiling gently; "now or a little while hence, what does it matter? 'Bonum est sperare in Domino. Dominus est, quod bonum est in oculis suis faciat.'[2] I give myself up to the Lord, let Him do as He will." Another friend, a Jesuit Priest, asked him to say,

---

[1] "I waited patiently for the Lord .... and He heard my calling."—Ps. xl. 1.

[2] "It is better to trust in the Lord."—English ver., Ps. cxviii. 9.

"Transeat a me calix iste;"[1] but Francis answered quickly, "Oh no—I had rather say, 'Thy Will, not mine, be done.'" The same Priest bade him commend himself to the Blessed Trinity. "Most heartily," Francis answered. "I offer and dedicate my whole being to God, my memory and actions to God the Father, my understanding and words to God the Son, my will and thoughts to God the Holy Ghost; my heart, body, tongue, senses, and all my pains to the Most Sacred Humanity of Our Lord Jesus Christ, 'qui non dubitavit manibus tradi nocentium et crucis subire tormentum.'"[2]

After receiving the Sacraments of penitence and extreme unction, the Bishop became very drowsy, and as the doctors were anxious to rouse him at any cost from this dangerous symptom, the Grand Vicaire bethought of asking him, "Monseigneur, what think you of the Catholic Faith? have you any leanings to Calvinism in the depths of your heart?" Francis started into life; "God forbid!" he exclaimed. "I never tampered with heresy, it would have been too grievous an act of faithlessness." And he signed forehead and breast with the Cross. A little later the

---

[1] "Let this cup pass from me."—Matt. xxvi. 39.

[2] "Who was contented to be betrayed and given up into the hands of wicked men, and to suffer death upon the cross for us."—See 1st Collect for Good Friday.

Grand Vicaire asked if he feared death, quoting the words, "O mors, quam amara est memoria tua!" to which the Bishop immediately answered with emphasis, " Homini pacem habenti in substantiis suis," implying that he had no such tie to earth, and therefore death had no bitterness.

Early the next morning the Bishop of Damascus came to see his friend. Francis knew him and gave him his hand, as the other said, " I have come to help you in your last battle. 'Frater qui adjuvatur a fratre quasi civitas firma.' "[1] " Et Dominus salvabit utrumque" (" The Lord shall save both "), the sick man answered. Soon after the Bishop of Damascus spoke again ; " Jacta super Dominum curam tuam."[2] " Et ipse te enutriet ;" Francis completed the quotation, adding, " My meat is to do the Will of my Father."

A little later the Duke of Nemours (Henry of Savoy) came from his own sick bed, which he with difficulty left, to ask a last Blessing for himself and his little son, who had been baptised by Francis in Paris. Madame Olier also brought her children with the same object, and the future founder of the Congregation of Saint Sulpice shared in the Saint's parting

[1] Prov. xviii. 19.—The English version gives quite a different rendering.

[2] "Cast thy burden upon the Lord, and He shall nourish thee."—Ps. lv. 22.

benediction. Among other people, the Père Forrier, once Francis's director, came in, and asked the dying Bishop if he remembered him. "Si oblitus fuero tui," Francis answered earnestly, "oblivioni detur dextera mea."[1] "You must say with Saint Martin, 'Domine, si adhuc populo tuo sum necessarius, non recuso laborem;'"[2] the Father said. "I necessary!" Francis exclaimed; "no, no, I am an altogether useless servant." And he repeated three times, slowly and fervently, "Servus inutilis, inutilis, inutilis!" He often said little kindly words of consolation to his servants and friends, whose grief as they ministered to him sometimes broke forth; and the words of the Miserere were continually on his lips as in his heart. Once, as he murmured the words, "Amplius lava me Domine," some one exclaimed that of a truth his conscience needed no more cleansing, but was pure in God's Sight. "Not so, you are mistaken indeed!" the Bishop said, earnestly. Often he was heard repeating the words, "My soul hath a desire and longing to enter into the Courts of the Lord, my heart and my flesh rejoice in the Living God. . . My song shall be always of the loving-kindness of the Lord.

[1] "If I forget thee, let my right hand forget her cunning." —Ps. cxxxvii. 5.

[2] "Lord, if I am necessary yet to Thy people, I would not refuse toil."

When I am in heaviness, I will think upon God. . . . When shall I come to appear before the Presence of God?"[1] He often, too, repeated the words of the bride in the Canticles, "Tell me, O Thou Whom my soul loveth, where Thou feedest, where Thou makest Thy flock to rest at noon."[2] And hearing some one near his bed begin to say the Sanctus; "Holy, holy, holy," Francis went on, "Heaven and earth are full of Thy Glory."

The fatal drowsiness increased upon him, and when the Archbishop of Embrun came in, Francis did not address him directly, but went on murmuring broken words of the Psalms: "All my desire is before Thee," "Thou knowest all my groaning—my God and my all; I will lift up mine eyes unto the hills from whence cometh my help." Some bystander bade the sufferer unite his pains to those of the Thorn-crowned Saviour and Francis quietly answered, "My pains do not deserve the name compared with His."

Probably it seemed a duty to those who ministered to the sick man, but to us it seems almost a cruelty to read how, knowing that he was dying, they strove to rouse him from the lethargy of death by means of blisters applied to the head, hot irons, and even cauterisation to the spine, besides minor severities. Amid all this torture, some one asked if he felt what was

[1] Psalms lxxxiv., lxxxix., lxxvii., xlii. [2] Canticles i. 7.

being done, when all the while, sheer pain forced tears from his eyes! "Yes, indeed!" Francis answered, with his unfailing patience, "but do what you will with the sick man!" As might be expected, all these barbarous remedies did but hasten the end; he ceased to speak much, not always replying even to questions, though when somebody—not over wisely, as it strikes one—asked him whether he did not grieve to leave his yet undeveloped Order of the Visitation, he answered distinctly, "Qui cœpit opus, ipse perficiet;"[1] adding yet twice again with emphasis, "perficiet, perficiet."

Again some bystander asked whether he feared the last struggle? "Oculi mei semper ad Dominum, quoniam ipse evellet de laqueo pedes meos,"[2] was the reply. "There was one traitor among the Apostles;" some one said. "Expectans expectavi Dominum, et exaudivit preces meas, et eduxit me de lacu miseriæ et de lacu fecis;"[3] he replied; and in a moment he added, "Qui cœpit, ipse perficiet" ("He who began will make perfect his work").

[1] "He which hath begun a good work in you will perform it."—Phil. i. 5.

[2] "Mine eyes are ever looking unto the Lord, for He shall pluck my feet out of the net."—Ps. xxv. 14.

[3] "I waited patiently for the Lord, and He inclined unto me, and heard my calling. He brought me also out of the horrible pit."—Ps. xl. 1, 2.

Not all that well-meant though mistaken kindness could do could trouble him long: In a little while the dying Saint turned round, and pressing the hand of a loving attendant, muttered, "Advesperascit, et inclinata est jam dies."[1] They were the last words he spoke, save that the Name of Jesus hung awhile upon the lips that had so often lovingly named It, and which would next be opened to take part in the Song of the Lamb.

A movement of the eyes and lips showed that till the feeble silver thread was cut, and the golden bowl loosed, there was a loving response to each petition raised Heavenwards by those who strove to go down to the edge of the dark river with him they loved so well. At length, about eight in the evening, they saw that the last moment had really come, and kneeling round, began the last prayers, the last music of praise to fall upon the ear which soon should waken to more joyful strains. The familiar Litanies had not gone far, —the clause :

"Omnes sancti Innocentes, orate pro eo,"

had just been said thrice,—for it was Holy Innocents' Day,—when calmly and peacefully, as he had lived, Francis de Sales died.

"Obdormivit in Jesu."

---

[1] "It is toward evening, and the day is far spent."—Luke xxiv. 29.

The tidings soon spread abroad in Lyons, and then there was one general wail that so great a Saint should have left this earth to mourn his aid; one general tribute of love and veneration to his holiness.

Madame de Chantal was at Grénoble with her Sisters of the Visitation. On the feast of Holy Innocents she was kneeling in prayer, commending the spiritual Father from whom she so lately parted to God's holy keeping, when she distinctly heard a voice say, "He is no more." She did not take the words as implying his death, but answered in her prayer, "Of a truth, my God, it is no more he that lives, but Christ that liveth in him." Yet the echo of those words came back upon her mind with a heavy sense of care, and she was thankful to leave Grénoble for Belley, where the tidings had preceded her. It was not—in those days of slow communication—till the Epiphany, that Madame de Chantal heard of her loss. On that morning some of the Capucin Fathers came to the convent, and of them she eagerly inquired if there were no news of Monseigneur? They replied, "Yes, that he was ill at Lyons." Madame de Chantal expressed her determination to go there, and then the monks gave her a letter from the Bishop of Chalcedon. She foresaw its contents, and offered her heart's grief to God before opening the letter, which was indeed to tell her that anxiety for Francis de Sales had ceased to be. "I knelt down," she says, in telling the tidings to the Supérieure at Dijon, "and adored God's Divine Providence, endeavouring to accept His Holy Will and my own deep grief. I wept all that day and night, until the next day's Communion, but without bitterness, and with great peace and rest in dwelling upon the Will of God, and the blessedness of our dear Saint."

There was a strong desire on the part of the Lyonnese, that the body of the holy man who had passed away in their city might rest there till the Resurrection, and M. Olier went so far as to oppose the departure of the funeral procession. But George Rolland, the faithful attendant who had never left Francis de Sales since he first followed him to the Chablais Mission, ceding the point for the moment, hastened to Annecy, and brought thence the Bishop's will, which empowered those of his household who might be with him at the time of his death to decide as to the place of his burial, should he not be at home. Madame de Chantal was naturally very anxious to lay the beloved body in the Church of the Visitation, and the magistrates of Annecy called upon the Duke of Savoy to represent to the King of France how strong their claim was. The point was established, and Francis de Sales was carried back to his "poor bride," the diocese of Annecy. He was laid to rest in the

Church of the Visitation, until, in the Revolution, it became necessary to remove the venerable remains in order to save them from desecration. When that dark storm had passed away, a new Convent and Church were built, and it is in the latter that S. Francis de Sales now lies, beneath the high altar; a shrine containing various relics, which can be approached from behind, being above it:—

> "The path of the just is as the shining light,
> Which shineth more and more unto the perfect day."

Francis de Sales was solemnly canonised in the year 1665, by Pope Alexander VII.

Much more might be said concerning the interior life of S. Francis de Sales, as well as of his direction of souls, but as this sketch of his life is to be immediately followed by, I. his own Spiritual Letters, and II. a translation of the Bishop of Belley's "Esprit de S. François de Sales," it has been thought better to leave these to develop themselves in his own words, and those of his devoted friend and disciple, from which at best they must be taken. This, however, may be the fittest place for a letter written by Madame de Chantal, at the request of a Religious, who had asked her to put down in writing what she knew concerning the inner life of the Bishop of Geneva.

"Indeed, Rev. Father, you bid me undertake a

task altogether beyond my powers; not but that it was God's Will to give me much closer acquaintance with the inner mind of our dear Father than I deserved, and while his dear presence was yet with us, I was conscious of little save satisfaction and admiration, but now I find no fitting words to say what I would. Nevertheless, out of obedience and loving reverence for your authority, I will strive to write down simply what comes to my mind, as in God's Sight.

"Perhaps the first thing which struck one in our dear Father, was his gift of perfect faith, together with an exceeding clearness, decision, and perfect evenness of temperament. God had poured so clear and bright a light upon his mind, that he was enabled to see the truth and beauty of the Faith with no ordinary vision, and to accept it with a simple and entire act of the will. His one only aim was to live according to the principles of our Faith, and the maxims of the Gospel: he used to say that the true way of serving God was to follow His Law in a perfectly simple spirit, without seeking consolations or lights, and in fact he loved interior mists and desolations.

"He told me once that he was indifferent alike to consolation or desolation; he could receive the former in simplicity, or go without it calmly. But in truth, for the most part he had great inward blessedness, as one could see by the way he turned everything to good for the soul. Such riches of holy thought came upon him, especially when he was preparing his sermons, which he generally did out walking, and he turned all such preparation into prayer. God's Graces pass over one so lightly and delicately, he used to say, that one often cannot define them, only their results abide in the soul.

"During the last years of his life, he had scarcely any time for meditation, and if I asked him whether he had made his meditation, he would say, 'No, but I have done its full equivalent.' He kept up a constant union with God, and used to say that in this life we must cultivate the active prayer of good works. He did not give himself to a selfish enjoyment of God's gifts—rather he loved God's Holy Will alike at all times and in all shapes, and during his last years I believe that he had attained such purity of soul that he desired nothing save to see and love God in all things; he was wholly absorbed in God, and found no rest elsewhere, so that in truth it was no longer he that lived, but Christ in him.

"The evenness of his mind was very remarkable. Who ever saw him waver or falter under difficulty? Not that he could not feel strong and vehement righteous indignation when God was offended, or his fellow men oppressed; at such times one used to see him retire within himself to commune with God in silence, coming forth again with fresh vigour to act firmly and decisively so as might best remedy the evil; in truth, he was the refuge, the help, the stay of all who knew him.

"His peace of heart was quite imperturbable; it was stablished on the absolute mortification of all passion, and complete submission of his soul to God. He undertook all affairs, all business alike, as subject to God's Will, and never felt himself stronger than when he had no other arm to lean upon. 'I do not see my way at present, but I know that God will make it plain;' were words often in his mouth.

"Saint as he was, he was not exempt from earthly feelings and passions, and he used to say that we ought not to wish to be free from them, but treat them as slaves to be vanquished, as means of cultivating grace, and strengthening the soul. He had such complete empire over his own passions that they were altogether subject to his higher will, and during the later years of his life, they ceased to assert themselves entirely.

"His perseverance in all good works was very remarkable. Who ever saw his patience wearied out, or his temper fail? I am certain that he never was guilty of an unkind or malicious act—he was always gentle, humble, gracious and affable to all, and yet with all his wonderful gifts and grace, no one was ever so free from all eccentricities or singularities, or so shunned whatever could attract attention, or make people notice him. He liked to keep to ordinary ways, but he did it after the most heavenly fashion. In prayer, in church, celebrating, you might have taken him for an angel, so saintly was his countenance, but he was absolutely free from all affectation; he eschewed every kind of studied movement, and yet his whole demeanour bore such a stamp of perfect dignity and inward repose, that no one could help being struck by it.

"I do not mean to say that he was free from all imperfections, but such as they were were merely inevitable human infirmity, and assuredly he never allowed the smallest imperfection to cleave to his heart, which was white as snow, and clear as the sun.

"He had a marvellous gift of discerning the hidden secrets of souls and of the spiritual life, and he used this freely for the benefit of others. Indeed, it seems to me that zeal for souls was the distinguishing feature of that saintly character."

BY THE SAME AUTHOR.

THE SPIRITUAL LETTERS
OF
S. FRANCIS DE SALES.

TRANSLATED FROM THE FRENCH.

[*Nearly Ready.*

BY THE SAME AUTHOR.

A DOMINICAN ARTIST; A Sketch of the Life of the Rev. Père Besson, of the Order of St. Dominic. Crown 8vo. 9s.

OPINIONS OF THE PRESS.

"The Author of the life of Père Besson writes with a grace and refinement of devotional feeling peculiarly suited to a subject-matter which suffers beyond most others from any coarseness of touch. It would be difficult to find 'the simplicity and purity of a holy life' more exquisitely illustrated than in Father Besson's career, both before and after his joining the Dominican Order under the auspices of Lacordaire. . . . Certainly we have never come across what could more strictly be termed in the truest sense 'the life of a beautiful soul.' The Author has done well in presenting to English readers this singularly graceful biography, in which all who can appreciate genuine simplicity and nobleness of Christian character, will find much to admire and little or nothing to condemn."—*Saturday Review.*

"It would indeed have been a deplorable omission had so exquisite a biography been by any neglect lost to English readers, and had a character so perfect in its simple and complete devotion been withheld from our admiration. . . . But we have dwelt too long already on this fascinating book, and must now leave it to our readers."—*Literary Churchman.*

"A beautiful and most interesting sketch of the late Père Besson, an artist who forsook the easel for the Altar."—*Church Times.*

"A book which is as pleasant for reading as it is profitable for meditation."—*Union Review.*

"We are indebted to the graceful pen of the translator of Madame Louise de France for another Catholic Life, beautifully written, and full of the spirit of love."—*Tablet.*

BY THE SAME AUTHOR.

" This tastefully-bound volume is a record of the life of Père Besson. From childhood to his premature death in April, 1861, at the age of forty-five, he was pre-eminently suited to a life of self-denial, and so full of love and charity, that his saintly character calls forth the warmest admiration, and we feel sure the perusal of it will give pleasure to our readers."—*Church Herald.*

"Whatever a reader may think of Père Besson's profession as a monk, no one will doubt his goodness ; no one can fail to profit who will patiently read his life, as here written by a friend, whose sole defect is in being slightly unctuous."—*Athenæum.*

" The life of the Rev. Père Besson, who gave up an artist's career, to which he was devotedly attached, and a mother whose affection for him is not inaptly likened to that of Monica for St. Augustine, must be read in its entirety to be rightly appreciated. And the whole tenour of the book is too devotional, too full of expressions of the most touching dependence on God, to make criticism possible, even if it was called for, which it is not."—*John Bull.*

" The story of Père Besson's life is one of much interest, and told with simplicity, candour, and good feeling."—*Spectator.*

" A beautiful book, describing the most saintly and very individual life of one of the companions of Lacordaire."—*Monthly Packet.*

" We strongly recommend it to our readers. It is a charming biography, that will delight and edify both old and young."—*Westminster Gazette.*

" There is much to attract and interest in this biography. Jean Baptiste Besson was a posthumous son, and received early religious training from a loving and attentive mother, noted for her beauty and worth, from whom, doubtless, he inherited much of that gentleness and sensitive humility which distinguished him."—*Examiner.*

" We should advise all who would cultivate the gentleness which is eminently characteristic of the Christian example, to read this earnest adaptation of an earnest art-book."—*Daily Telegraph.*

BY THE SAME AUTHOR.

THE LIFE of MADAME LOUISE DE FRANCE, DAUGHTER OF LOUIS XV., KNOWN ALSO AS THE MOTHER TÉRÈSE DE ST. AUGUSTIN. Crown 8vo, 6s.

OPINIONS OF THE PRESS.

"Such a record of deep, earnest, self-sacrificing piety, beneath the surface of Parisian life, during what we all regard as the worst age of French godlessness, ought to teach us all a lesson of hope and faith, let appearances be what they may. Here, from out of the court and family of Louis XV. there issues this Madame Louise, whose life is set before us as a specimen of as calm and unworldly devotion—of a devotion, too, full of shrewd sense and practical administrative talent—as any we have ever met with."—*Literary Churchman*.

"This is a highly interesting volume, giving an account of the religious life of Madame Louise de France, daughter of Louis XV., who joined the order of Carmelites at the Convent of St. Denis, and was subsequently known as the Mother Térèse de St. Augustin. The memoir is taken from a Life of Madame Louise, compiled by a Carmelite nun, and printed at Autun. The facts are very interesting, from the truly Christian character of Madame Louise, a character that must have been rare in such a profligate court as that of her father; 'a monarch,' as the author observes, 'whose name fills the imagination with visions of diplomatic falsehood, courtly cabal, and sensual profligacy, rather than those of self-devotion and holiness,—whose memory suggests a Pompadour, a Chateauroux, and a Du Barry, rather than a St. Theresa, whose period at once brings before us the school of Voltaire, Diderot, and D'Alembert, whose most notable and best remembered royal saying was, "Après moi, le déluge!"' Those who delight in reading religious biographies will be specially delighted with the present one."—*Public Opinion*.

"On the 15th of July, 1737, Marie Leczinska, the wife of Louis XV., and daughter of the dethroned King of Poland, which Prussia helped to despoil and plunder, gave birth to her eighth female child, Louise Marie, known also as the Mother Térèse de St. Augustin. On the death of the Queen, the princess, who had long felt a vocation for a religious life, obtained the consent of her royal father to withdraw from the world. The Carmelite convent of St. Denis was the chosen place of retreat. Here the novitiate was passed, here the final vows were taken, and here, on the death of the Mère Julie, Madame Louise began and terminated her experiences as prioress. The little volume which records the simple incidents of her pious seclusion is designed to edify those members of the Church of England in whom the spirit of religious self-devotion is reviving. The substance of the memoir is taken from a somewhat diffuse 'Life of Madame Louise de France,' compiled by a Carmelite nun, and printed at Autun."—*Westminster Review.*

'This 'Life' relates the history of that daughter of Louis XV. who, aided by the example and instruction of a pious mother, lived an uncorrupt life in the midst of a most corrupt court, which she quitted—after longing and waiting for years to do so—to enter the severe order of Mount Carmel, which she adorned by her strict and holy life. We cannot too highly praise the present work, which appears to us to be written in the most excellent good taste. We hope it may find entrance into every religious House in our Communion, and it should be in the library of every young lady."—*Church Review.*

"The life of Madame Louise de France, the celebrated daughter of Louis XV., who became a *religieuse*, and is known in the spiritual world as Mother Térèse de St. Augustin. The substance of the memoir is taken from a diffuse life, compiled by a Carmelite nun, and printed at Autun ; and the editor, the author of 'Tales of Kirkbeck,' was prompted to the task by the belief that 'at the present time, when the spirit of religious self-devotion is so greatly reviving in the Church of England,' the records of a princess who quitted a dazzling and profligate court to lead a life of obscure piety will meet with a cordial reception. We may remark, that should the event prove otherwise, it will not be from any fault of workmanship on the part of the editor."—*Daily Telegraph.*

"The annals of a cloistered life, under ordinary circumstances, would not probably be considered very edifying by the reading public of the present generation. When, however, such a history presents the novel spectacle of a royal princess of modern times voluntarily renouncing her high position and the splendours of a court existence, for the purpose of enduring the asceticism, poverty, and austerities of a severe monastic rule, the case may well be different."—*Morning Post.*

BY THE SAME AUTHOR.

THE HIDDEN LIFE OF THE SOUL.
FROM THE FRENCH. Crown 8vo. 5s.

OPINIONS OF THE PRESS.

"'The Hidden Life of the Soul,' by the author of 'A Dominican Artist,' is from the writings of Father Grou, a French refugee priest of 1792, who died at Lulworth. It well deserves the character given it of being 'earnest and sober,' and not 'sensational.'"—*Guardian.*

"Between fifty and sixty short readings on spiritual subjects, exquisitely expressed, and not merely exquisite in expression, but presenting a rare combination of spiritual depth, and of strong practical common sense. We have read carefully a large number of them, for, after reading a few as texts, we could not lay it down without going much further than was sufficient for the mere purpose of reporting on the book. The author was one Père Grou, a native of Calais, born in 1731, who in 1792 found an asylum from the troubles of the French Revolution at Lulworth Castle, known doubtless to many of our readers as the ancestral home of the old Roman Catholic family of Weld, where he died in 1803. There is a wonderful charm about these readings — so calm, so true, so thoroughly Christian. We do not know where they would come amiss."—*Literary Churchman.*

"From the French of Jean Nicolas Grou, a pious Priest, whose works teach resignation to the Divine Will. He loved, we are told, to inculcate simplicity, freedom from all affectation and unreality the patience and humility which are too surely grounded in self-knowledge to be surprised at a fall, but withal so allied to confidence in God, as to make recovery easy and sure. This is the spirit of the volume, which is intended to furnish advice to those who would cultivate a quiet, meek, and childlike spirit."—*Public Opinion.*

"The work is by Jean Nicolas Grou, a French Priest, who, driven to England by the first Revolution, found a home with a Roman Catholic family at Lulworth for the ten remaining years of a retired, studious, devout life. The work bears internal evidence of being that of a spirit which had been fed on such works as the 'Spiritual Exercises,' the 'Imitation of Christ,' and the 'Devout Life of S. Francis of Sales,' and which has here reproduced them, tested by its own life-experience, and cast in the mould of its own individuality. How much the work, in its present form, may owe to the judicious care of the Editor, we are not aware; but as it is presented to us, it is, while deeply spiritual, yet so earnest and sober in its general tone, so free from doctrinal error or unwholesome sentiment, that we confidently recommend it to English Church people as one of the most valuable of this class of books which we have met with."—*Church Builder.*

New Works

IN COURSE OF PUBLICATION BY

Messrs. RIVINGTON,

WATERLOO PLACE, LONDON;

HIGH STREET, OXFORD; TRINITY STREET, CAMBRIDGE.

MARCH, 1871.

DICTIONARY OF DOCTRINAL AND HISTORICAL THEOLOGY.
By VARIOUS WRITERS.
Edited by the Rev. John Henry Blunt, M.A., F.S.A., Editor of 'The Annotated Book of Common Prayer.'
One vol., imperial 8vo. 42s.

The Principles of the CATHEDRAL SYSTEM VINDICATED and FORCED upon MEMBERS of CATHEDRAL FOUNDATIONS.
Eight Sermons, preached in the Cathedral Church of the Holy and Undivided Trinity of Norwich.
By **Edward Meyrick Goulburn**, D.D., Dean of Norwich, late Prebendary of St. Paul's, and one of Her Majesty's Chaplains.
Crown 8vo. 5s.

LONDON, OXFORD, & CAMBRIDGE.

MESSRS. RIVINGTON'S NEW PUBLICATIONS.

ELEMENTS OF RELIGION.
Lectures delivered at St. James's, Piccadilly, in Lent, 1870.
By Henry Parry Liddon, D.D., Canon of St. Paul's, and Ireland Professor of Exegesis in the University of Oxford.
Crown 8vo. [*In the Press.*

A MANUAL OF LOGIC;
Or, a Statement and Explanation of the Laws of Formal Thought.
By Henry J. Turrell, M.A., Oxon.
Square crown 8vo. 2s. 6d.

THE PSALMS translated from the HEBREW.
With Notes, chiefly Exegetical.
By William Kay, D.D., Rector of Great Leighs; late Principal of Bishop's College, Calcutta.
8vo. 12s. 6d.

SERMONS.
By Henry Melvill, B.D., Canon of St. Paul's, and Chaplain in Ordinary to the Queen.
New Edition. Two vols. Crown 8vo. 5s. each.

THE ORIGIN AND DEVELOPMENT OF RELIGIOUS BELIEF.
By S. Baring-Gould, M.A., Author of 'Curious Myths of the Middle Ages.'
PART I. HEATHENISM AND MOSAISM. *8vo.* 15s.
PART II. CHRISTIANITY. *8vo.* 15s.

PARISH MUSINGS; or, DEVOTIONAL POEMS.
By John S. B. Monsell, LL.D., Rural Dean, and Rector of St. Nicholas Guildford.
New Edition. 18mo. *Limp cloth*, 1s. 6d.; *or in cover*, 1s.

LONDON, OXFORD, & CAMBRIDGE.

MESSRS. RIVINGTON'S NEW PUBLICATIONS.

THE WITNESS of ST. JOHN to CHRIST;
Being the Boyle Lectures for 1870.
With an Appendix on the Authorship and Integrity of St. John's Gospel and the Unity of the Johannine Writings.
By the Rev. Stanley Leathes, M.A., Minister of St. Philip's, Regent Street, and Professor of Hebrew, King's College, London.
8vo. 10s. 6d.

THE ELEGIES OF PROPERTIUS,
Translated into English Verse.
By Charles Robert Moore, M.A., late Scholar of Corpus Christi College, Oxford.
Small 8vo. 2s. 6d.

'THE ATHANASIAN CREED,'
And its Usage in the English Church: an Investigation as to the Original Object of the Creed and the Growth of prevailing Misconceptions regarding it.
A Letter to the Very Reverend W. F. Hook, D.D., F.R.S., Dean of Chichester, from C. A. Swainson, D.D., Canon of the Cathedral, and Examining Chaplain to the Lord Bishop of Chichester; Norrisian Professor of Divinity, Cambridge.
Crown 8vo. 3s. 6d.

PRAYERS AND MEDITATIONS FOR THE HOLY COMMUNION.
With a Preface by C. J. Ellicott, D.D., Lord Bishop of Gloucester and Bristol.
With Rubrics in red. Royal 32mo. 2s. 6d.

THE SHEPHERD OF HERMAS.
Translated into English, with an Introduction and Notes.
By Charles H. Hoole, M.A., Senior Student of Christ Church, Oxford.
Fcap. 8vo. 4s. 6d.

LONDON, OXFORD, & CAMBRIDGE.

MESSRS. RIVINGTON'S NEW PUBLICATIONS.

MATERIALS AND MODELS FOR GREEK AND LATIN PROSE COMPOSITION.

Selected and Arranged by **J Y. Sargent**, M.A. Tutor, late Fellow of Magdalen College, Oxford; and **T. F. Dallin**, M.A., Fellow and Tutor of Queen's College, Oxford.

Crown 8vo. 7s. 6d.

THE STAR OF CHILDHOOD.

A First Book of Prayers and Instruction for Children.

Compiled by a Priest.

Edited by the Rev. **T. T. Carter**, M.A., Rector of Clewer, Berks.

With Illustrations. Royal 16mo. 2s. 6d.

THE DOCTRINE of RECONCILIATION TO GOD BY JESUS CHRIST.

Seven Lectures, preached during Lent, 1870, with a Prefatory Essay.

By **W. H. Fremantle**, M.A., Rector of St. Mary's, Bryanston Square.

Fcap. 8vo. 2s.

PROGRESSIVE EXERCISES IN LATIN ELEGIAC VERSE.

By **C. G. Gepp**, B.A., late Junior Student of Christ Church, Oxford, and Assistant Master at Tonbridge School.

Small 8vo. 3s. 6d.

SELF-RENUNCIATION.

From the French. With Introduction by the Rev. **T. T. Carter**, M.A., Rector of Clewer.

Crown 8vo. 6s.

LONDON, OXFORD, & CAMBRIDGE.

MESSRS. RIVINGTON'S NEW PUBLICATIONS.

THE HIDDEN LIFE OF THE SOUL.

From the French. By the Author of 'A Dominican Artist,' 'Life of Madame Louise de France,' etc., etc.

Crown 8vo. 5s.

ANCIENT HYMNS

From the Roman Breviary. For Domestic Use every Morning and Evening of the Week, and on the Holy Days of the Church. To which are added, Original Hymns, principally of Commemoration and Thanksgiving for Christ's Holy Ordinances.

By **Richard Mant**, D.D., sometime Lord Bishop of Down and Connor.

New Edition. Small 8vo. 5s.

THE TWO BROTHERS, and other Poems.

By **Edward Henry Bickersteth**, M.A., Author of 'Yesterday, To-day, and for Ever.'

Fcap. 8vo. 6s.

A HISTORY of the Holy EASTERN CHURCH.

The Patriarchate of Antioch, to the Middle of the Fifth Century.

By the Rev. **John Mason Neale**, D.D., late Warden of Sackville College, East Grinsted.

Followed by a History of the Patriarchs of Antioch, translated from the Greek of Constantius I., Patriarch of Constantinople. Edited, with an Introduction, by **George Williams**, B.D., Vicar of Ringwood, late Fellow of King's College, Cambridge.

8vo. [*In the Press.*

ESSAYS ON THE PLATONIC ETHICS.

By **Thomas Maguire**, LL.D. ex S.T.C.D., Professor of Latin, Queen's College, Galway.

8vo. 5s.

LONDON, OXFORD, & CAMBRIDGE.

MESSRS. RIVINGTON'S NEW PUBLICATIONS.

ST. JOHN CHRYSOSTOM'S LITURGY.
Translated by H. C. Romanoff, Author of 'Sketches of the Rites and Customs of the Greco-Russian Church.'

With Illustrations. Square crown 8vo. 4s. 6d.

DEMOSTHENIS ORATIONES
PUBLICAE.
Edited by G. H. Heslop, M.A., late Fellow and Assistant Tutor of Queen's College, Oxford; Head Master of St. Bees.

De Falsâ Legatione. Forming a new Part of 'Catena Classicorum.'

Crown 8vo. [*In the Press.*

DEMOSTHENIS ORATIONES
PRIVATAE.
Edited by the Rev. Arthur Holmes, M.A., Senior Fellow and Lecturer of Clare College, Cambridge; and Preacher at the Chapel Royal, Whitehall.

De Coronâ. Forming a new Part of 'Catena Classicorum.'

Crown 8vo. [*In the Press.*

THE LIFE OF JUSTIFICATION.
A Series of Lectures delivered in Substance at All Saints', Margaret Street, in Lent, 1870.

By the Rev. George Body, B.A., Rector of Kirkby Misperton.

Crown 8vo. 4s. 6d.

THE ILIAD OF HOMER.
Translated by J. G. Cordery, late of Balliol College, Oxford, and now of H.M. Bengal Civil Service.

Two vols. 8vo. 16s.

LONDON, OXFORD, & CAMBRIDGE.

MESSRS. RIVINGTON'S NEW PUBLICATIONS.

THE SAYINGS OF THE GREAT FORTY DAYS,

Between the Resurrection and Ascension, regarded as the Outlines of the Kingdom of God. In Five Discourses. With an Examination of Dr. Newman's Theory of Development.

By George Moberly, D.C.L., Bishop of Salisbury.

Fourth Edition. Uniform with Brighstone Sermons.

Crown 8vo. 7s. 6d.

DICTIONARY OF SECTS, HERESIES, AND SCHOOLS OF THOUGHT.

By Various Writers.

Edited by the Rev. John Henry Blunt, M.A., F.S.A.; Editor of 'The Annotated Book of Common Prayer.'

(FORMING THE SECOND PORTION OF THE 'SUMMARY OF THEOLOGY AND ECCLESIASTICAL HISTORY,' WHICH MESSRS. RIVINGTON HAVE IN COURSE OF PREPARATION AS A 'THESAURUS THEOLOGICUS' FOR THE CLERGY AND LAITY OF THE CHURCH OF ENGLAND.)

Imperial 8vo.   *[In preparation.*

A PLAIN ACCOUNT OF THE ENGLISH BIBLE,

From the Earliest Times of its Translation to the Present Day.

By John Henry Blunt, M.A., Vicar of Kennington, Oxford; Editor of 'The Annotated Book of Common Prayer,' etc.

Crown 8vo. 3s. 6d.

The CHURCH of GOD and the BISHOPS :

An Essay suggested by the Convocation of the Vatican Council. By Henry St. A. Von Liaño. Authorized Translation.

Crown 8vo. 4s. 6d.

LONDON, OXFORD, & CAMBRIDGE.

MESSRS. RIVINGTON'S NEW PUBLICATIONS.

THE POPE AND THE COUNCIL.
By **Janus**. Authorized Translation from the German.
Third Edition, revised. Crown 8vo. 7s. 6d.

LETTERS FROM ROME on the COUNCIL.
By **Quirinus**. Reprinted from the *Allgemeine Zeitung*.
Authorized Translation.
Crown 8vo. 12s.

THE AMMERGAU PASSION PLAY.
Reprinted by permission from the *Times*. With some Introductory Remarks on the Origin and Development of Miracle Plays, and some Practical Hints for the use of Intending Visitors.

By the Rev. **Malcolm MacColl**, M.A., Chaplain to the Right Hon. Lord Napier, K.T.
Second Edition. Crown 8vo. 2s. 6d.

The FIRST BOOK OF COMMON PRAYER
OF EDWARD VI. AND THE ORDINAL OF 1549;
Together with the Order of the Communion, 1548.

Reprinted entire, and Edited by the Rev. **Henry Baskerville Walton**, M.A., late Fellow and Tutor of Merton College.

With Introduction by the Rev. **Peter Goldsmith Medd**, M.A., Senior Fellow and Tutor of University College, Oxford.
Small 8vo. 6s.

THE PURSUIT OF HOLINESS.
A Sequel to 'Thoughts on Personal Religion,' intended to carry the Reader somewhat farther onward in the Spiritual Life.
By **Edward Meyrick Goulburn**, D.D., Dean of Norwich.
Second Edition. Small 8vo. 5s.

LONDON, OXFORD, & CAMBRIDGE.

MESSRS. RIVINGTON'S NEW PUBLICATIONS.

APOSTOLICAL SUCCESSION IN THE CHURCH OF ENGLAND.

By the Rev. **Arthur W. Haddan**, B.D., Rector of Barton-on-the-Heath, and late Fellow of Trinity College, Oxford.

8vo. 12*s.*

THE PRIEST TO THE ALTAR;

Or; Aids to the Devout Celebration of Holy Communion; chiefly after the Ancient Use of Sarum.

Second Edition. Enlarged, Revised, and Re-arranged with the Secretæ, Post-communion, etc., appended to the Collects, Epistles, and Gospels, throughout the Year.

8vo. 7*s.* 6*d.*

NEWMAN'S (J. H.) PAROCHIAL AND PLAIN SERMONS.

Edited by the Rev. **W. J. Copeland**, Rector of Farnham, Essex.

From the Text of the last Editions published by Messrs. Rivington.

Eight vols. Crown 8vo. 5*s.* *each.*

NEWMAN'S (J. H.) SERMONS, BEARING UPON SUBJECTS OF THE DAY.

Edited by the Rev. **W. J. Copeland**, Rector of Farnham, Essex.

From the Text of the last Edition published by Messrs. Rivington. With Index of Dates of all the Sermons.

Printed uniformly with the 'Parochial and Plain Sermons.'

Crown 8vo. 5*s.*

BRIGHSTONE SERMONS.

By **George Moberly**, D.C.L., Bishop of Salisbury.

Second Edition. Crown 8vo. 7*s.* 6*d.*

LONDON, OXFORD, & CAMBRIDGE.

MESSRS. RIVINGTON'S NEW PUBLICATIONS.

The CHARACTERS of the OLD TESTAMENT.
In a Series of Sermons.
By the Rev. **Isaac Williams**, B.D., late Fellow of Trinity College, Oxford.
New Edition. Crown 8vo. 5s.

FEMALE CHARACTERS of HOLY SCRIPTURE.
In a Series of Sermons.
By the Rev. **Isaac Williams**, B.D., late Fellow of Trinity College, Oxford.
New Edition. Crown 8vo. 5s.

THE DIVINITY OF OUR LORD AND SAVIOUR JESUS CHRIST:
Being the Bampton Lectures for 1866.
By **Henry Parry Liddon**, D.D., Canon of St. Paul's, and Ireland Professor of Exegesis in the University of Oxford.
Fifth Edition. Crown 8vo. 5s.

SERMONS PREACHED BEFORE THE UNIVERSITY OF OXFORD.
By **Henry Parry Liddon**, D.D., Canon of St. Paul's, and Ireland Professor of Exegesis in the University of Oxford.
Third Edition. Crown 8vo. 5s.

A MANUAL FOR THE SICK;
With other Devotions.
By **Launcelot Andrewes**, D.D., sometime Lord Bishop of Winchester.
Edited, with a Preface, by **Henry Parry Liddon**, D.D., Canon of St. Paul's.
With Portrait. Second Edition. Large type. 24mo. 2s. 6d.

LONDON, OXFORD, & CAMBRIDGE.

MESSRS. RIVINGTON'S NEW PUBLICATIONS.

WALTER KERR HAMILTON: BISHOP of SALISBURY.

A Sketch, Reprinted, with Additions and Corrections, from the *Guardian.*

By **Henry Parry Liddon**, D.D., Canon of St. Paul's.

Second Edition. 8vo. *Limp cloth*, 2s. 6d.

Or, bound with the Sermon, 'Life in Death,' 3s. 6d.

THE LIFE OF MADAME LOUISE DE FRANCE,

Daughter of Louis XV., also known as the Mother Térèse de S. Augustin. By the Author of ' A Dominican Artist,' etc.

Crown 8vo. 6s.

JOHN WESLEY'S PLACE IN CHURCH HISTORY DETERMINED,

With the aid of Facts and Documents unknown to, or unnoticed by, his Biographers.

With a New and Authentic Portrait.

By **R. Denny Urlin**, M.R.I.A., of the Middle Temple, Barrister-at-Law.

Small 8vo. 5s. 6d.

THE TREASURY OF DEVOTION:

A Manual of Prayers for General and Daily Use.

Compiled by a Priest. Edited by the Rev. **T. T. Carter**, M.A., Rector of Clewer, Berks.

Third Edition. 16mo, *limp cloth* 2s.; *cloth extra*, 2s. 6d.

Bound with the Book of Common Prayer, 3s. 6d.

LONDON, OXFORD, & CAMBRIDGE.

MESSRS. RIVINGTON'S NEW PUBLICATIONS.

THE GUIDE TO HEAVEN:

A Book of Prayers for every Want. (For the Working Classes.) Compiled by a Priest. Edited by the Rev. T. T. Carter, M. A., Rector of Clewer, Berks.

Second Edition. Crown 8vo, limp cloth, 1s.; *cloth extra,* 1s. 6d.

A DOMINICAN ARTIST:

A Sketch of the Life of the Rev. Père Besson, of the Order of St. Dominic.

By the Author of 'The Life of Madame Louise de France,' etc.

Crown 8vo. 9s.

THE REFORMATION OF THE CHURCH OF ENGLAND;

Its History, Principles, and Results. A.D. 1514-1547.

By **John Henry Blunt**, M.A., Vicar of Kennington, Oxford, Editor of 'The Annotated Book of Common Prayer,' Author of 'Directorium Pastorale,' etc., etc.

Second Edition. 8vo. 16s.

THE VIRGIN'S LAMP:

Prayers and Devout Exercises for English Sisters, chiefly composed and selected by the late Rev. J. M. Neale, D.D., Founder of St. Margaret's, East Grinsted.

Small 8vo. 3s. 6d.

CATECHETICAL NOTES AND CLASS QUESTIONS, LITERAL & MYSTICAL;

Chiefly on the Earlier Books of Holy Scripture.

By the late Rev. **J. M. Neale**, D D., Warden of Sackville College, East Grinsted.

Crown 8vo. 5s.

LONDON, OXFORD, & CAMBRIDGE.

MESSRS. RIVINGTON'S NEW PUBLICATIONS.

SERMONS FOR CHILDREN:

Being Thirty-three short Readings, addressed to the Children of St. Margaret's Home, East Grinsted.

By the late Rev. J. M. Neale, D.D., Warden of Sackville College.

Second Edition. Small 8vo. 3s. 6d.

THE WITNESS of the OLD TESTAMENT TO CHRIST.

The Boyle Lectures for the Year 1868.

By the Rev. Stanley Leathes, M.A., Professor of Hebrew in King's College, London, and Minister of St. Philip's, Regent Street.

8vo. 9s.

THE WITNESS of ST. PAUL to CHRIST:

Being the Boyle Lectures for 1869.

With an Appendix, on the Credibility of the Acts, in Reply to the Recent Strictures of Dr. Davidson.

By the Rev. Stanley Leathes, M.A., Professor of Hebrew in King's College, London, and Minister of St. Philip's, Regent Street.

8vo. 10s. 6d.

HONORÉ DE BALZAC.

Edited, with English Notes and Introductory Notice, by Henri Van Laun, formerly French Master at Cheltenham College, and now Master of the French Language and Literature at the Edinburgh Academy.

(BEING THE FIRST VOLUME OF 'SELECTIONS FROM MODERN FRENCH AUTHORS.')

Crown 8vo. 3s. 6d.

LONDON, OXFORD, & CAMBRIDGE.

MESSRS. RIVINGTON'S NEW PUBLICATIONS.

H. A. TAINE.

Edited, with English Notes and Introductory Notice, by **Henri Van Laun**, formerly French Master at Cheltenham College, and now Master of the French Language and Literature at the Edinburgh Academy.

(BEING THE SECOND VOLUME OF 'SELECTIONS FROM MODERN FRENCH AUTHORS.')

Crown 8vo. 3s. 6d.

DEAN ALFORD'S GREEK TESTAMENT.

With English Notes, intended for the Upper Forms of Schools, and for Pass-men at the Universities.

Abridged by **Bradley H. Alford**, M.A., late Scholar of Trinity College, Cambridge.

Crown 8vo. 10s. 6d.

ELEMENTARY ALGEBRA.

By **J. Hamblin Smith**, M.A, Gonville and Caius College, and Lecturer at St. Peter's College, Cambridge.

New Edition, Revised and Enlarged. Crown 8vo. 4s. 6d.

ELEMENTARY TRIGONOMETRY.

By **J. Hamblin Smith**, M.A., Gonville and Caius College, and Lecturer at St. Peter's College, Cambridge.

New Edition, Revised and Enlarged. Crown 8vo. 4s. 6d.

ELEMENTARY STATICS.

By **J. Hamblin Smith**, M.A., Gonville and Caius College, and Lecturer at St. Peter's College, Cambridge.

Royal 8vo. 3s.

LONDON, OXFORD, & CAMBRIDGE.

ELEMENTARY HYDROSTATICS.

By **J. Hamblin Smith**, M.A., Gonville and Caius College, and Lecturer at St. Peter's College, Cambridge.

New Edition, Revised and Enlarged. Crown 8vo. 3s.

EXERCISES ADAPTED TO ALGEBRA.
PART I.

By **J. Hamblin Smith**, M.A., Gonville and Caius College; and Lecturer at St. Peter's College, Cambridge.

Crown 8vo. 2s. 6d.
Copies may be had without the Answers.

ELEMENTS OF EUCLID,

Arranged with the Abbreviations admitted in the Cambridge Examinations, and with Exercises.

By **J. Hamblin Smith**, M.A., Gonville and Caius College; and Lecturer at St. Peter's College, Cambridge.

Crown 8vo. [*In the Press.*

ARITHMETIC, THEORETICAL AND PRACTICAL.

By **W. H. Girdlestone**, M.A., of Christ's College, Cambridge, Principal of the Theological College, Gloucester.

New and Revised Edition. Crown 8vo. 6s. 6d.
Also an Edition for Schools. *Small 8vo. 3s. 6d.*

CLASSICAL EXAMINATION PAPERS.

Edited, with Notes and References, by **P. J. F. Gantillon**, M.A., sometime Scholar of St. John's College, Cambridge; Classical Master in Cheltenham College.

Crown 8vo. 7s. 6d. Or interleaved with writing-paper for Notes, half-bound, 10s. 6d.

LONDON, OXFORD, & CAMBRIDGE.

MESSRS. RIVINGTON'S NEW PUBLICATIONS.

THE STORY OF THE GOSPELS.

In a single Narrative, combined from the Four Evangelists, showing in a new translation their unity. To which is added, a like continuous narrative in the Original Greek.

By the Rev. **William Pound**, M.A., late Fellow of St. John's College, Cambridge; Principal of Appulddurcombe School, Isle of Wight.

Two vols. 8vo. 36s.

THE LYRICS OF HORACE,

Done into English Rhyme.

By **Thomas Charles Baring**, M.A., late Fellow of Brasenose College, Oxford.

Small 4to. 7s.

A PLAIN AND SHORT HISTORY OF ENGLAND FOR CHILDREN.

In Letters from a Father to his Son. With a Set of Questions at the end of each Letter.

By **George Davys**, D.D., late Bishop of Peterborough.

New Edition, with Twelve Coloured Illustrations.

Square Crown 8vo. 3s. 6d.

A Cheap Edition for Schools, with portrait of Edward VI.

18mo. 1s. 6d.

HISTORY OF THE COLLEGE OF ST. JOHN THE EVANGELIST, CAMBRIDGE.

By **Thomas Baker**, B.D., Ejected Fellow.

Edited for the Syndics of the University Press, by **John E. B. Mayor**, M.A., Fellow of St. John's College.

Two vols. 8vo. 24s.

LONDON, OXFORD, & CAMBRIDGE.

MESSRS. RIVINGTON'S NEW PUBLICATIONS.

HELP AND COMFORT FOR THE SICK POOR.

By the Author of 'Sickness; its Trials and Blessings.'

New Edition. Small 8vo. 1s.

THE DOGMATIC FAITH:

An Inquiry into the relation subsisting between Revelation and Dogma. Being the Bampton Lectures for 1867.

By Edward Garbett, M.A., Incumbent of Christ Church, Surbiton.

Second Edition. Crown 8vo. 5s.

SKETCHES OF THE RITES & CUSTOMS OF THE GRECO-RUSSIAN CHURCH.

By H. C. Romanoff. With an Introductory Notice by the Author of 'The Heir of Redclyffe.'

Second Edition. Crown 8vo. 7s. 6d.

HOUSEHOLD THEOLOGY:

A Handbook of Religious Information respecting the Holy Bible, the Prayer Book, the Church, the Ministry, Divine Worship, the Creeds, etc., etc.

By John Henry Blunt, M.A.

New Edition. Small 8vo. 3s. 6d.

CURIOUS MYTHS OF THE MIDDLE AGES.

By S. Baring-Gould, M.A., Author of 'Post-Mediæval Preachers,' etc. With Illustrations.

Complete in one Volume.

New Edition. Crown 8vo. 6s.

LONDON, OXFORD, & CAMBRIDGE.

MESSRS. RIVINGTON'S NEW PUBLICATIONS.

MEMOIR OF THE RIGHT REV. JOHN
STRACHAN, D.D., LL.D., First Bishop of Toronto.
By A. N. Bethune, D.D., D.C.L., his Successor in the See.
8vo. 10s.

THE PRAYER BOOK INTERLEAVED;
With Historical Illustrations and Explanatory Notes arranged parallel to the Text.

By the Rev. W. M. Campion, D.D., Fellow and Tutor of Queen's College, and Rector of St. Botolph's, and the Rev. W. J. Beamont, M.A., late Fellow of Trinity College, Cambridge.

With a Preface by the **Lord Bishop of Ely.**

Fifth Edition. Small 8vo. 7s. 6d.

CONSOLING THOUGHTS IN SICKNESS.
Edited by **Henry Bailey**, B.D., Warden of St. Augustine's College, Canterbury.

Large type. Fine Edition. Small 8vo. 2s. 6d.

Also a Cheap Edition, 1s. 6d.; or in paper cover, 1s.

SICKNESS; ITS TRIALS & BLESSINGS.
New Edition, Small 8vo. 3s. 6d.

Also a Cheap Edition, 1s. 6d.; or in paper cover, 1s.

HYMNS AND POEMS FOR THE SICK AND SUFFERING;
In connection with the Service for the Visitation of the Sick. Selected from various Authors.

Edited by **T. V. Fosbery**, M.A., Vicar of St. Giles's, Reading.

New Edition. Small 8vo. 3s. 6d.

LONDON, OXFORD, & CAMBRIDGE.

MESSRS. RIVINGTON'S NEW PUBLICATIONS.

SOI-MÊME; a Story of a Wilful Life.
Small 8vo. 3s. 6d.

THE HAPPINESS OF THE BLESSED,
Considered as to the Particulars of their State: their Recognition of each other in that State: and its Differences of Degrees.

To which are added, Musings on the Church and her Services.

By **Richard Mant**, D.D., sometime Lord Bishop of Down & Connor.

New Edition. Small 8vo. 3s. 6d.

THE HOLY BIBLE.
With Notes and Introductions.

By **Chr. Wordsworth**, D.D., Bishop of Lincoln.

Second Edition. Imperial 8vo.

  Vol. I. Genesis to Deuteronomy. 38s.
  Vol. II. Joshua to Samuel. 21s.
  Vol. III. Kings to Esther. 21s.
  Vol. IV. Job to Song of Solomon. 34s.
  Vol. V. Isaiah to Ezekiel. 32s. 6d.
  Vol. VI. Daniel. 6s.
    The Minor Prophets. 12s.

THE MACCABEES AND THE CHURCH;
Or the History of the Maccabees Considered with Reference to the Present Condition and Prospects of the Church.

Two Sermons preached before the University of Cambridge.

By **Chr. Wordsworth**, D.D., Bishop of Lincoln.

Crown 8vo. 2s. 6d.

LONDON, OXFORD, & CAMBRIDGE.

MESSRS. RIVINGTON'S NEW PUBLICATIONS.

MISCELLANEOUS POEMS.
By Henry Francis Lyte, M.A.
New Edition. Small 8vo. 5s.

PERRANZABULOE, THE LOST CHURCH FOUND;
Or, The Church of England not a New Church, but Ancient, Apostolical, and Independent, and a Protesting Church Nine Hundred Years before the Reformation.

By the Rev. C. T. Collins Trelawny, M.A., formerly Rector of Timsbury, Somerset, and late Fellow of Balliol College, Oxford.

With Illustrations. New Edition. Crown 8vo. 3s. 6d.

CATECHESIS; or, CHRISTIAN INSTRUCTION
Preparatory to Confirmation and First Communion.
By Charles Wordsworth, D.C.L., Bishop of St. Andrew's.

New Edition. Small 8vo. 2s.

WARNINGS OF THE HOLY WEEK, etc.;
Being a Course of Parochial Lectures for the Week before Easter and the Easter Festivals.

By the Rev. W. Adams, M.A., late Vicar of St. Peter's-in-the-East, Oxford, and Fellow of Merton College.

Sixth Edition. Small 8vo. 4s. 6d.

CONSOLATIO; or, COMFORT FOR THE AFFLICTED.
Edited by the Rev. C. E. Kennaway. With a Preface by Samuel Wilberforce, D.D., Lord Bishop of Winchester.

New Edition. Small 8vo. 3s. 6d.

LONDON, OXFORD, & CAMBRIDGE.

MESSRS. RIVINGTON'S NEW PUBLICATIONS.

THE HILLFORD CONFIRMATION: a Tale.
By M. C. Phillpotts.
18mo. 1s.

FROM MORNING TO EVENING:
A Book for Invalids.
From the French of M. L'Abbé Henri Perreyve.
Translated and adapted by an Associate of the Sisterhood of
S. John Baptist, Clewer.
Crown 8vo. 5s.

FAMILY PRAYERS;
Compiled from Various Sources (chiefly from Bishop Hamilton's Manual), and arranged on the Liturgical Principle.
By Edward Meyrick Goulburn, D.D., Dean of Norwich.
New Edition. Crown 8vo, large type, 3s. 6d.
Cheap Edition. 16mo. 1s.

THE ANNUAL REGISTER:
A Review of Public Events at Home and Abroad, for the Year 1870; being the Eighth Volume of an Improved Series.
8vo. 18s.
*** *The Volumes for* 1863 *to* 1869 *may be had, price* 18s. *each.*

A PROSE TRANSLATION OF VIRGIL'S ECLOGUES AND GEORGICS.
By an Oxford Graduate.
Crown 8vo. 2s. 6d.

LONDON, OXFORD, & CAMBRIDGE.

MESSRS. RIVINGTON'S NEW PUBLICATIONS.

THE CAMBRIDGE PARAGRAPH BIBLE
OF THE AUTHORIZED ENGLISH VERSION.

With the Text Revised by a Collation of its Early and other Principal Editions, the Use of the Italic type made Uniform, the Marginal References Re-modelled, and a Critical Introduction prefixed.

By the Rev. **F. H. Scrivener**, M.A., Rector of St. Gerrans; Editor of the Greek Testament, Codex Augiensis, etc. Edited for the Syndics of the University Press.

Crown 4to.

Part I., Genesis to Solomon's Song, 15s.

Part II., Apocrypha and New Testament, 15s.

To be completed in Three Parts.

Part III., Prophetical Books, will be ready during 1871.

⁎ A small number of copies has also been printed, on *good writing paper*, with one column of print and wide margin to each page for MS. notes. *Part I.*, 20s.; *Part II.*, 20s.

QUIET MOMENTS:

A Four Weeks' Course of Thoughts and Meditations, before Evening Prayer and at Sunset.

By **Lady Charlotte Maria Pepys**.

New Edition. Small 8vo. 2s. 6d.

MORNING NOTES OF PRAISE:

A Series of Meditations upon the Morning Psalms.

By **Lady Charlotte Maria Pepys**.

New Edition. Small 8vo. 2s. 6d.

LONDON, OXFORD, & CAMBRIDGE.

MESSRS. RIVINGTON'S NEW PUBLICATIONS.

YESTERDAY, TO-DAY, AND FOR EVER;
A Poem in Twelve Books.
By **Edward Henry Bickersteth**, M.A., Vicar of Christ Church, Hampstead, and Chaplain to the Bishop of Ripon.
Fifth Edition. Small 8vo. 6s.

THE COMMENTARIES OF GAIUS:
Translated, with Notes, by **J. T. Abdy**, LL.D., Regius Professor of Laws in the University of Cambridge, and Barrister-at-Law of the Norfolk Circuit: formerly Fellow of Trinity Hall; and **Bryan Walker**, M.A., M.L.; Fellow and Lecturer of Corpus Christi College, and Law Lecturer of St. John's College, Cambridge; formerly Law Student of Trinity Hall and Chancellor's Legal Medallist.
Crown 8vo. 12s. 6d.

SACRED ALLEGORIES:
The Shadow of the Cross—The Distant Hills—The Old Man's Home—The King's Messengers.
By the Rev. **W. Adams**, M.A., late Fellow of Merton College, Oxford.
Presentation Edition. With Engravings from original designs by Charles W. Cope, R.A., John C. Horsley, A.R.A., Samuel Palmer, Birket Foster, and George Hicks.
Small 4to. 10s. 6d.
The Four Allegories, separately. *Crown 8vo. 2s. 6d. each.*

HERBERT TRESHAM:
A Tale of the Great Rebellion.
By the late Rev. **J. M. Neale**, D.D., sometime Scholar of Trinity College, Cambridge, and late Warden of Sackville College, East Grinsted.
New Edition. Small 8vo. 3s. 6d.

THE MANOR FARM: a Tale.
By **M. C. Phillpotts**, Author of 'The Hillford Confirmation.'
With Four Illustrations. Small 8vo. 3s. 6d.

LONDON, OXFORD, & CAMBRIDGE.

MESSRS. RIVINGTON'S NEW PUBLICATIONS.

LIBER PRECUM PUBLICARUM
ECCLESIÆ ANGLICANÆ.

A Gulielmo Bright, A.M., et Petro Goldsmith Medd, A.M.,
Presbyteris, Collegii Universitatis in Acad. Oxon.
Sociis, Latine redditus.

New Edition, with all the Rubrics in red. Small 8vo. 6s.

BIBLE READINGS FOR FAMILY PRAYER.

By the Rev. W. H. Ridley, M.A., Rector of Hambleden.

Crown 8vo.

Old Testament—Genesis and Exodus. 2s.

New Testament, 3s. 6d. { St. Matthew and St. Mark. 2s.
{ St. Luke and St. John. 2s.

INSTRUCTIONS FOR THE USE OF CANDIDATES FOR HOLY ORDERS,

And of the Parochial Clergy; with Acts of Parliament relating to the same, and Forms proposed to be used.

By Christopher Hodgson, M.A., Secretary to the Governors of Queen Anne's Bounty.

Ninth Edition, Revised and Enlarged, 8vo. 16s.

ENGLAND RENDERED IMPREGNABLE

By the practical Military Organization and efficient Equipment of her National Forces; and her Present Position, Armament, Coast Defences, Administration, and Future Power considered.

By H. A. L., ' The Old Shekarry.'

8vo. With Illustrations. 21s.

LONDON, OXFORD, & CAMBRIDGE.

MESSRS. RIVINGTON'S NEW PUBLICATIONS.

WHO IS RESPONSIBLE FOR THE WAR?

By Scrutator.

With an Appendix, containing Four Letters, reprinted (by permission) from the *Times*.

Crown 8vo. 6s.

AN OUTLINE OF LOGIC.

For the Use of Teachers and Students.

By the Rev. **Francis Garden**, M.A., Trinity College, Cambridge; Sub-Dean of Her Majesty's Chapels Royal, Chaplain to the Household in St. James's Palace, and Professor of Mental and Moral Science, Queen's College, London.

Second Edition. Small 8vo. 4s.

THE LAST THREE BISHOPS.

Appointed by the Crown for the Anglican Church of Canada.

By **Fennings Taylor**, Deputy Clerk of the Senate of Canada.

Second Edition. With Portraits. Small 4to. 10s. 6d.

COMMENTARY on the BOOK OF ISAIAH,

Critical, Historical, and Prophetical;

Including a Revised English Translation, with Introduction and Appendices on the Nature of Scripture Prophecy, the Life and Times of Isaiah, the Genuineness of the later Prophecies, the Structure and History of the whole Book, the Assyrian History in Isaiah's Days, and Various Difficult Passages.

By the Rev. **T. R. Birks**, Vicar of Holy Trinity, Cambridge.

8vo. 12s.

LONDON, OXFORD, & CAMBRIDGE.

MESSRS. RIVINGTON'S NEW PUBLICATIONS.

CATENA CLASSICORUM:
A SERIES OF CLASSICAL AUTHORS,

EDITED BY MEMBERS OF BOTH UNIVERSITIES UNDER THE DIRECTION OF

THE REV. ARTHUR HOLMES, M.A.,

Senior Fellow and Lecturer of Clare College, Cambridge, and Preacher at the Chapel Royal, Whitehall.

AND

THE REV. CHARLES BIGG, M.A.,

Late Senior Student and Tutor of Christ Church, Oxford, Second Classical Master of Cheltenham College.

Crown 8vo.

THE FOLLOWING PARTS HAVE BEEN ALREADY PUBLISHED :—

SOPHOCLIS TRAGOEDIAE.

Edited by R. C. JEBB, M.A., Fellow and Assistant Tutor of Trinity College, Cambridge, and Public Orator of the University.
The Electra, 3s. 6d.   The Ajax, 3s. 6d.

JUVENALIS SATIRAE.

Edited by G. A. SIMCOX, M.A., Fellow and Classical Lecturer of Queen's College, Oxford.
3s. 6d.

THUCYDIDIS HISTORIA.

Edited by CHARLES BIGG, M.A, late Senior Student and Tutor of Christ Church, Oxford.   Second Classical Master of Cheltenham College.
Books I. and II. with Introductions.   6s.

LONDON, OXFORD, & CAMBRIDGE.

MESSRS. RIVINGTON'S NEW PUBLICATIONS.

DEMOSTHENIS ORATIONES PUBLICAE.
Edited by G. H. HESLOP, M.A., Late Fellow and Assistant Tutor of Queen's College, Oxford. Head Master of St. Bees.
        The Olynthiacs. 3s.
        The Philippics. 2s. 6d.

ARISTOPHANIS COMOEDIAE.
Edited by W. C. GREEN, M.A., late Fellow of King's College, Cambridge; Assistant Master at Rugby School.
        The Acharnians and the Knights. 4s.
        The Clouds. 3s. 6d.
        The Wasps. 3s. 6d.

An Edition of the Acharnians and the Knights, Revised and especially adapted for Use in Schools. 4s.

ISOCRATIS ORATIONES.
Edited by JOHN EDWIN SANDYS, M.A., Fellow and Tutor of St. John's College, and Classical Lecturer at Jesus College, Cambridge.
        Ad Demonicum et Panegyricus. 4s. 6d.

PERSII SATIRAE.
Edited by A. PRETOR, M.A., of Trinity College, Cambridge, Classical Lecturer of Trinity Hall. 3s. 6d.

HOMERI ILIAS.
Edited by S. H. REYNOLDS, M.A., Fellow and Tutor of Brasenose College, Oxford.
        Books I. to XII. 6s.

TERENTI COMOEDIAE.
Edited by T. L. PAPILLON, M.A., Fellow of New College, Oxford, and late Fellow of Merton.
        Andria et Eunuchus. 4s. 6d.

LONDON, OXFORD, & CAMBRIDGE.

MESSRS. RIVINGTON'S NEW PUBLICATIONS.

RIVINGTON'S DEVOTIONAL SERIES.
Elegantly printed with red borders. 16mo. 2s. 6d.

THOMAS À KEMPIS, OF THE IMITATION OF CHRIST.
Also a cheap Edition, without the red borders, 1s., or in Cover, 6d.

THE RULE AND EXERCISES OF HOLY LIVING.
By **Jeremy Taylor**, D.D., Bishop of Down, and Connor, and Dromore.
Also a cheap Edition, without the red borders, 1s.

THE RULE AND EXERCISES OF HOLY DYING.
By **Jeremy Taylor**, D.D., Bishop of Down, and Connor, and Dromore.
Also a cheap Edition, without the red borders, 1s.
*** The 'Holy Living' and the 'Holy Dying' may be had bound together in One Volume, 5s., or without the red borders, 2s. 6d.

A SHORT AND PLAIN INSTRUCTION
For the better Understanding of the Lord's Supper; to which is annexed, the Office of the Holy Communion, with proper Helps and Directions.
By **Thomas Wilson**, D.D., late Lord Bishop of Sodor and Man.
Complete Edition, in large type.
Also a cheap Edition, without the red borders, 1s., or in Cover, 6d.

INTRODUCTION TO THE DEVOUT LIFE.
From the French of St. Francis of Sales, Bishop and Prince of Geneva.
A New Translation.

A PRACTICAL TREATISE CONCERNING EVIL THOUGHTS.
By **William Chilcot**, M.A.

ENGLISH POEMS AND PROVERBS.
By **George Herbert**.

LONDON, OXFORD, & CAMBRIDGE.

MESSRS. RIVINGTON'S NEW PUBLICATIONS.

NEW PAMPHLETS.

BY THE RIGHT HON. SIR ROBERT PHILLIMORE, D.C.L.
JUDGMENT,
Delivered by The Right Hon. Sir Robert Phillimore, D.C.L., Official Principal of the Arches Court of Canterbury, in the case of the Office of the Judge promoted by Sheppard *v.* Bennett.
Edited by WALTER G. F. PHILLIMORE, B.C.L., of the Middle Temple, Barrister-at-Law; Fellow of All Souls' College, and Vinerian Scholar, Oxford.
8vo. 2s. 6d.

BY THE REV. H. J. BURFIELD.
THE PEACE OF JERUSALEM:
A Sermon, preached at St. Mary's, before the University of Oxford, on the Fourth Sunday in Advent, December 18, 1870.
8vo. 6d.

BY CANON LIDDON.
ST. PAUL'S AND LONDON:
A Sermon, preached at St. Paul's Cathedral, on the Fourth Sunday after Epiphany, 1871.
8vo. 6d.

BY THE REV. C. F. TARVER.
"THE MEMORY OF THE JUST:"
A Sermon, preached in the Parish Church, St. Peter's, Thanet, on the Third Sunday in Advent, December 11, 1870, after the Funeral of the Rev. John Hodgson, M.A., formerly Vicar of St. Peter's, Thanet.
8vo. 1s.

BY THE REV. E. H. BICKERSTETH.
"THE TIME IS SHORT."
A Farewell Sermon, preached on Sunday, November 13, 1870, by the late Rev. John Henry Holford, M.A., Incumbent of Trinity Church, Gough-square, on resigning the Curacy of Christ Church, Hampstead. To which is appended a Funeral Sermon, preached upon the Death of his Friend and Fellow-labourer, on Sunday, December 18, 1870, by the Rev. E. H. BICKERSTETH, M.A., Vicar of Christ Church.
8vo. 1s.

LONDON, OXFORD, & CAMBRIDGE.

MESSRS. RIVINGTON'S NEW PUBLICATIONS.

Eight Volumes, Crown 8vo, 5s. each.
A New and Uniform Edition of
A DEVOTIONAL COMMENTARY
ON THE
GOSPEL NARRATIVE.

BY THE
REV. ISAAC WILLIAMS, B.D.
FORMERLY FELLOW OF TRINITY COLLEGE, OXFORD.

—oo—

THOUGHTS ON THE STUDY OF THE HOLY GOSPELS.
Characteristic Differences in the Four Gospels—Our Lord's Manifestations of Himself—The Rule of Scriptural Interpretation Furnished by Our Lord—Analogies of the Gospel—Mention of Angels in the Gospels—Places of Our Lord's Abode and Ministry—Our Lord's Mode of Dealing with His Apostles—Conclusion.

A HARMONY OF THE FOUR EVANGELISTS.
Our Lord's Nativity—Our Lord's Ministry (Second Year)—Our Lord's Ministry (Third Year)—The Holy Week—Our Lord's Passion—Our Lord's Resurrection.

OUR LORD'S NATIVITY.
The Birth at Bethlehem—The Baptism in Jordan—The First Passover.

OUR LORD'S MINISTRY. SECOND YEAR.
The Second Passover—Christ with the Twelve—The Twelve sent Forth.

OUR LORD'S MINISTRY. THIRD YEAR.
Teaching in Galilee—Teaching at Jerusalem—Last Journey from Galilee to Jerusalem.

THE HOLY WEEK.
The Approach to Jerusalem—The Teaching in the Temple—The Discourse on the Mount of Olives—The Last Supper.

OUR LORD'S PASSION.
The Hour of Darkness—The Agony—The Apprehension—The Condemnation—The Day of Sorrows—The Hall of Judgment—The Crucifixion—The Sepulture.

OUR LORD'S RESURRECTION.
The Day of Days—The Grave Visited—Christ Appearing—The Going to Emmaus—The Forty Days—The Apostles Assembled—The Lake in Galilee—The Mountain in Galilee—The Return from Galilee.

LONDON, OXFORD, & CAMBRIDGE.

www.ingramcontent.com/pod-product-compliance
Lightning Source LLC
Chambersburg PA
CBHW030807230426
43667CB00008B/1103